IMAGES
of America

PENFIELD

IMAGES
of America

PENFIELD

Martin M. Wamp

ARCADIA
PUBLISHING

ISBN 978-0-7385-3525-8

Published by Arcadia Publishing
Charleston, South Carolina

Printed in the United States of America

Library of Congress Catalog Card Number: 2003117079

For all general information contact Arcadia Publishing at:
Telephone 843-853-2070
Fax 843-853-0044
E-mail sales@arcadiapublishing.com
For customer service and orders:
Toll-Free 1-888-313-2665

Visit us on the Internet at www.arcadiapublishing.com

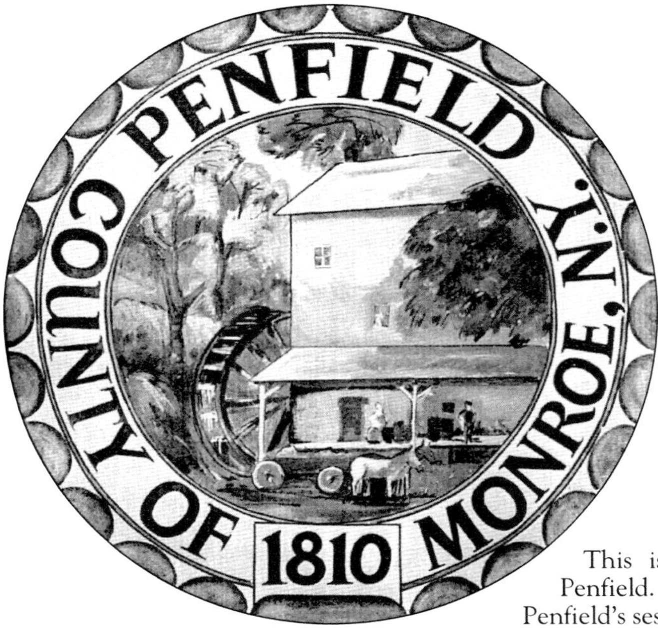

This is the insignia for the town of Penfield. It was created by Claude Lewis for Penfield's sesquicentennial in 1960.

Contents

Acknowledgments

Very special thanks go to Kathy Kanauer, Penfield assistant historian and Penfield Local History Room coordinator, who gave me unending support from the time I started this book until the last page was complete.

Additional thanks go to the following people for their donation of time and resources: Maude Frank, Penfield historian; Chan Philbrick, Penfield town supervisor (1993–2003); Larry Naukam, director of the Rochester Public Library Local History Division; Wally Ashnault; Jan Braman; Zack Buckley; Tom Feigel; Tom Taber; and Jay Thompson. Thanks also go to my mother, Marilynn Wamp, and sister, Marcy Wamp.

The majority of resources and images for this book were courtesy of the Penfield Local History Room, Penfield, New York. Some image reproductions were made at Pro Imaging in Rochester, New York.

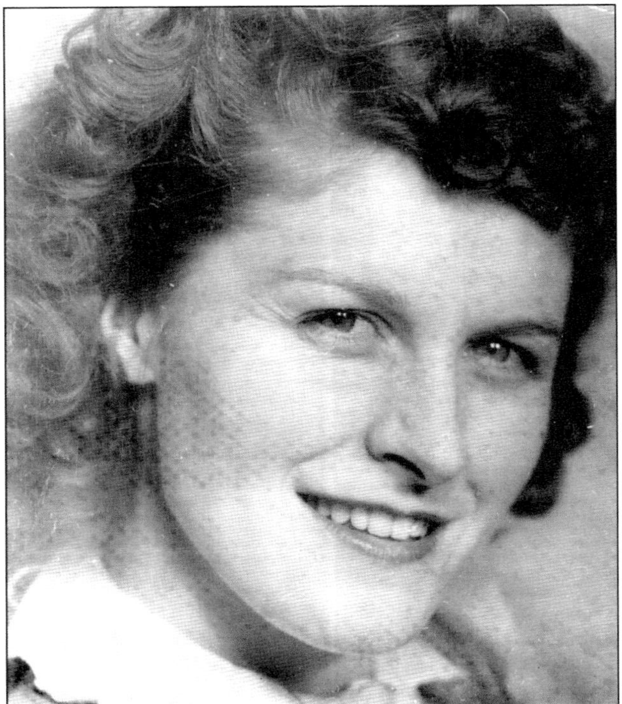

I dedicate this book to Penfield's pioneers, early settlers, and lifelong residents, and to the memory of Frances Feigel Schnarr, a lifelong resident of Penfield and my grandmother.

INTRODUCTION

Three events in history would lead Daniel Penfield to move to an uninhabited wilderness to build a life for himself and his family. Upon visiting this area in western New York in the late 18th century, Penfield saw a very unique opportunity along a creek that was the perfect size and demeanor to successfully create a milling industry and build a town out of a swampland. The area was referred to by Cornelius Treat, an early resident of the town of Mendon, on a tour he made of the area in 1795 with James Wadsworth, a land surveyor. He remarked, "We spent four days exploring the land. . . . After our examination was finished, Mr. Wadsworth was so disgusted with the land that he said he would not take it as a gift, for it was worth nothing, and we made our way home."

The first historic event that would involve Daniel Penfield was Shay's Rebellion. After the American Revolution ended in 1783, a severe economic depression followed, especially to the farmers of western Massachusetts and eastern New York. With farmers unable to pay debts and with the high taxes now being charged by the newly established government, the farmers revolted. The rebellion was led by Capt. Daniel Shay, a veteran of the Revolution and a farmer. The rebellion started at the end of 1786 and continued into the early part of 1787. During that time, Penfield ran a dry goods store in Hillsdale. During the rebellion, his store was burned by an angry mob of farmers. After the rebellion ended, Penfield gave up his interests in dry goods and moved to New York City, where he became a merchant and landowner.

The second historic event, the Phelps and Gorham Purchase of 1790, introduced Daniel Penfield to the lands of western New York. This purchase opened up expansion into the western part of the state. During the American Revolution, Penfield served under Oliver Phelps (first judge of Ontario County). When Phelps and Nathaniel Gorham (president of the Continental Congress) made their purchase of all of western New York lands, Penfield was one of the witnesses on the deed of sale. In 1795, he made the trip to the western part of the state to survey for land. In recognizing the potential of the Irondequoit Creek, he quickly purchased Township 13, Range 4, from Jonathan Fassett, who originally purchased it from Phelps and Gorham in the early 1790s. Later, *c.* 1801, Penfield hired John Strowger to build and run the first flour mill on the creek.

The third historic event to lead Penfield to the town that would one day take his name was the Jeffersonian Embargo of 1807. This embargo ceased all exports from New York City on all goods shipped overseas and into Canada. Penfield was in the merchant trade, and this severely affected his business. For the next few years, he struggled in the midst of the embargo and finally decided to give up his interests in New York City as a merchant and landowner in the Hudson Valley. He gathered up his family and moved *c.* 1810–1811 to western New York, where a burgeoning township was being developed. The opportunity along the creek would no doubt make Penfield one of the largest and most successful milling towns in western New York during the first half of the 19th century.

One

Four Corners

I remember Penfield the way it used to be,
Rolling hills and open fields along the Genesee.
My father and grandpa grew up in this town,
And I believe a better place they never could have found.

—Lorrie M. Neuman,
Penfield's Past,
by Katherine W. Thompson, 1960, 1990

PENFIELD is Township 13 of 4th. Range of The Phelps and Gorham Purchase. It was set off from the Town of Boyle March 30th. 1810, including at that time the Town of Webster, the first election of officers took place April 2nd. 1811.

This note on the history of Penfield is from the 1902 *Plat Book of Monroe County, N.Y.*, by J. M. Lathrop and Company.

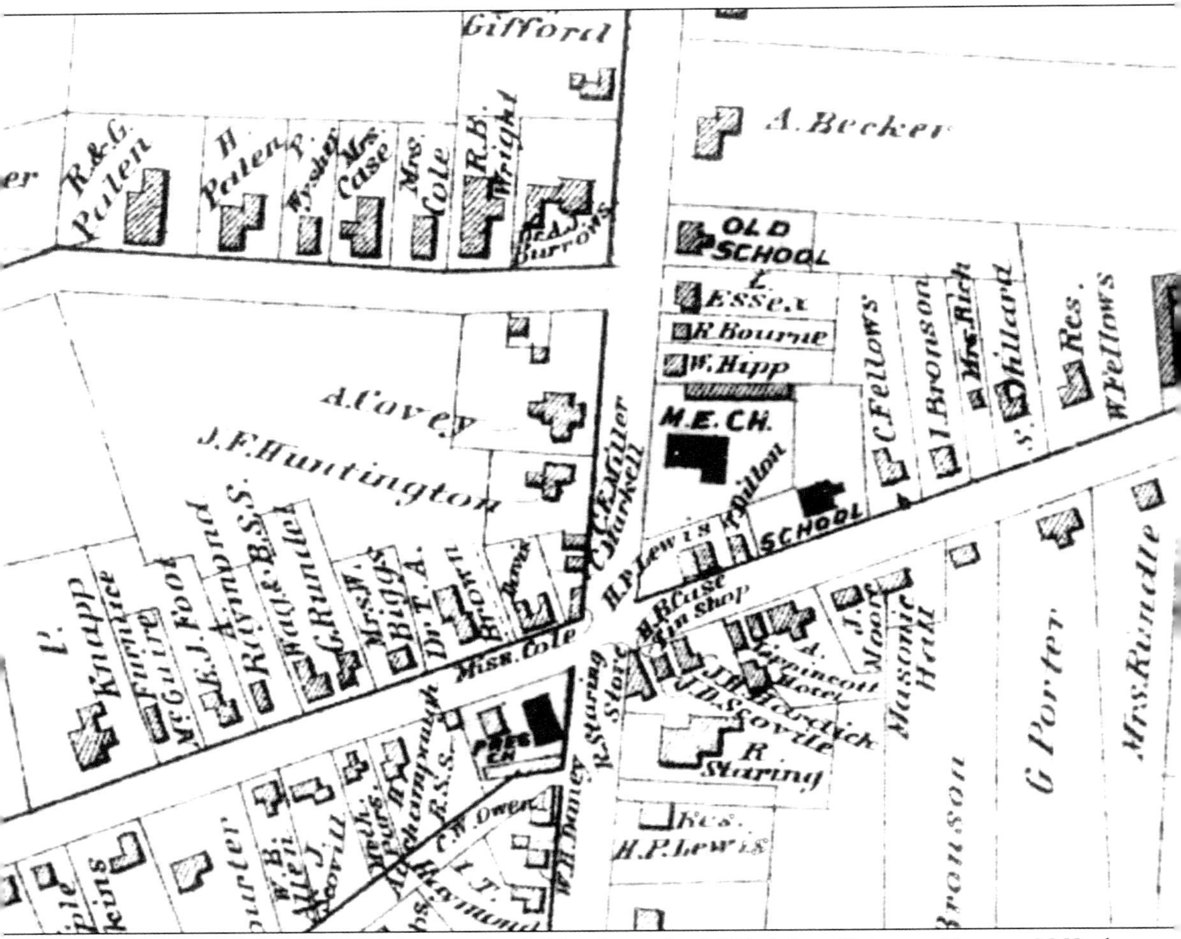

This map of the Four Corners in Penfield is from the 1872 *Atlas of Monroe County*, N.Y., by F. W. Beers and Company.

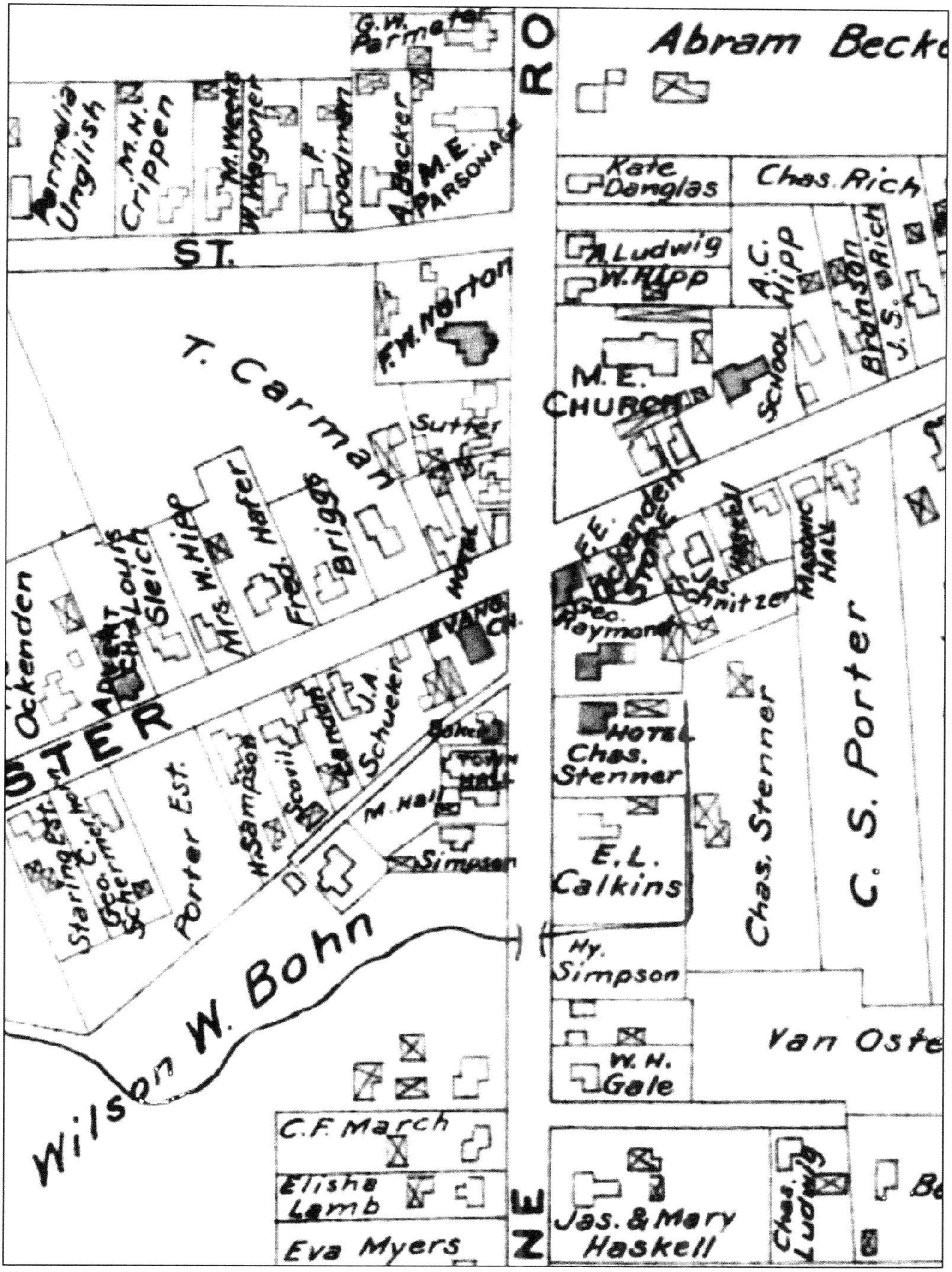

This map of the Four Corners is from the 1902 *Plat Book of Monroe County, N.Y.*, by J. M. Lathrop and Company.

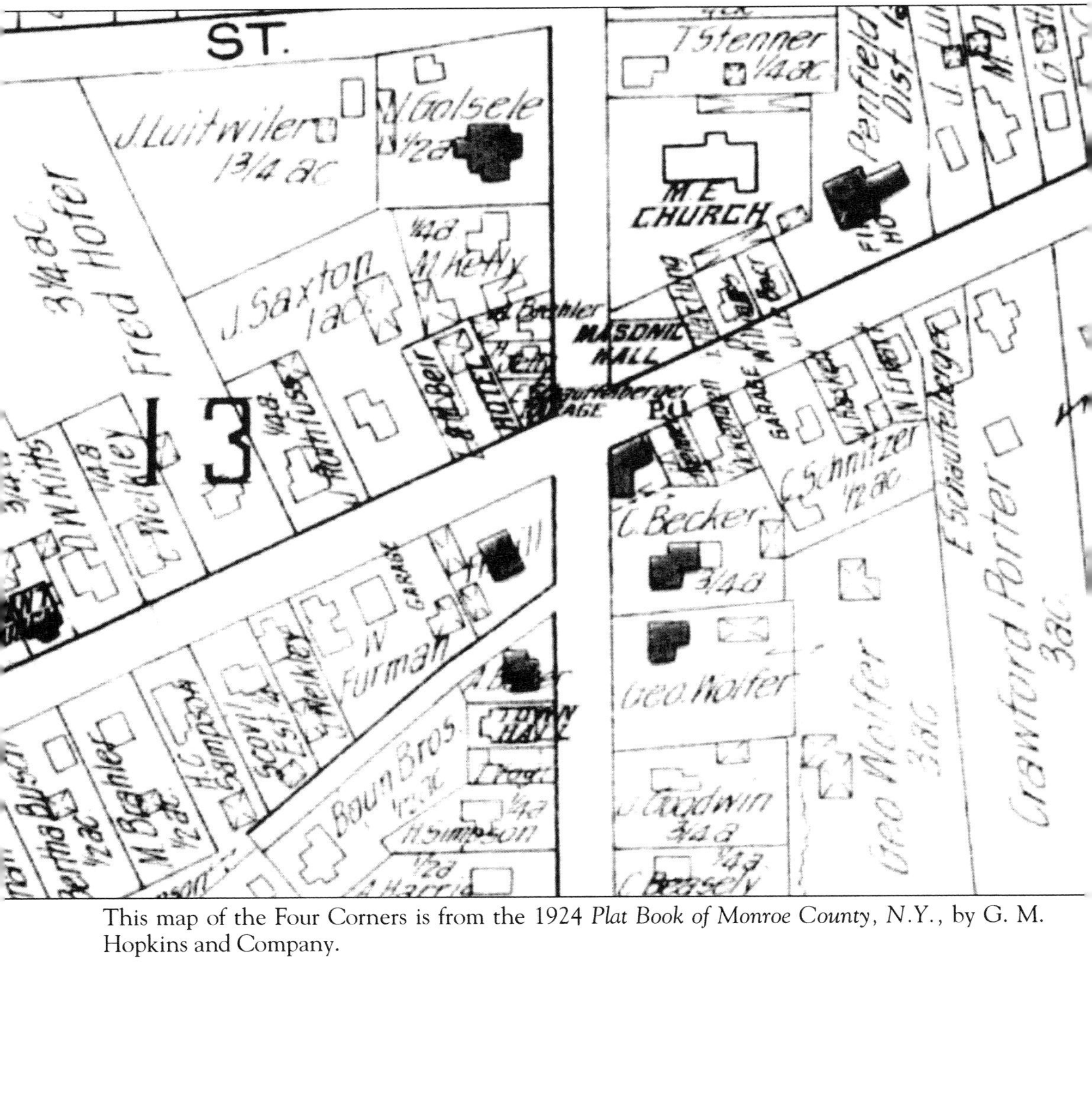

This map of the Four Corners is from the 1924 *Plat Book of Monroe County, N.Y.*, by G. M. Hopkins and Company.

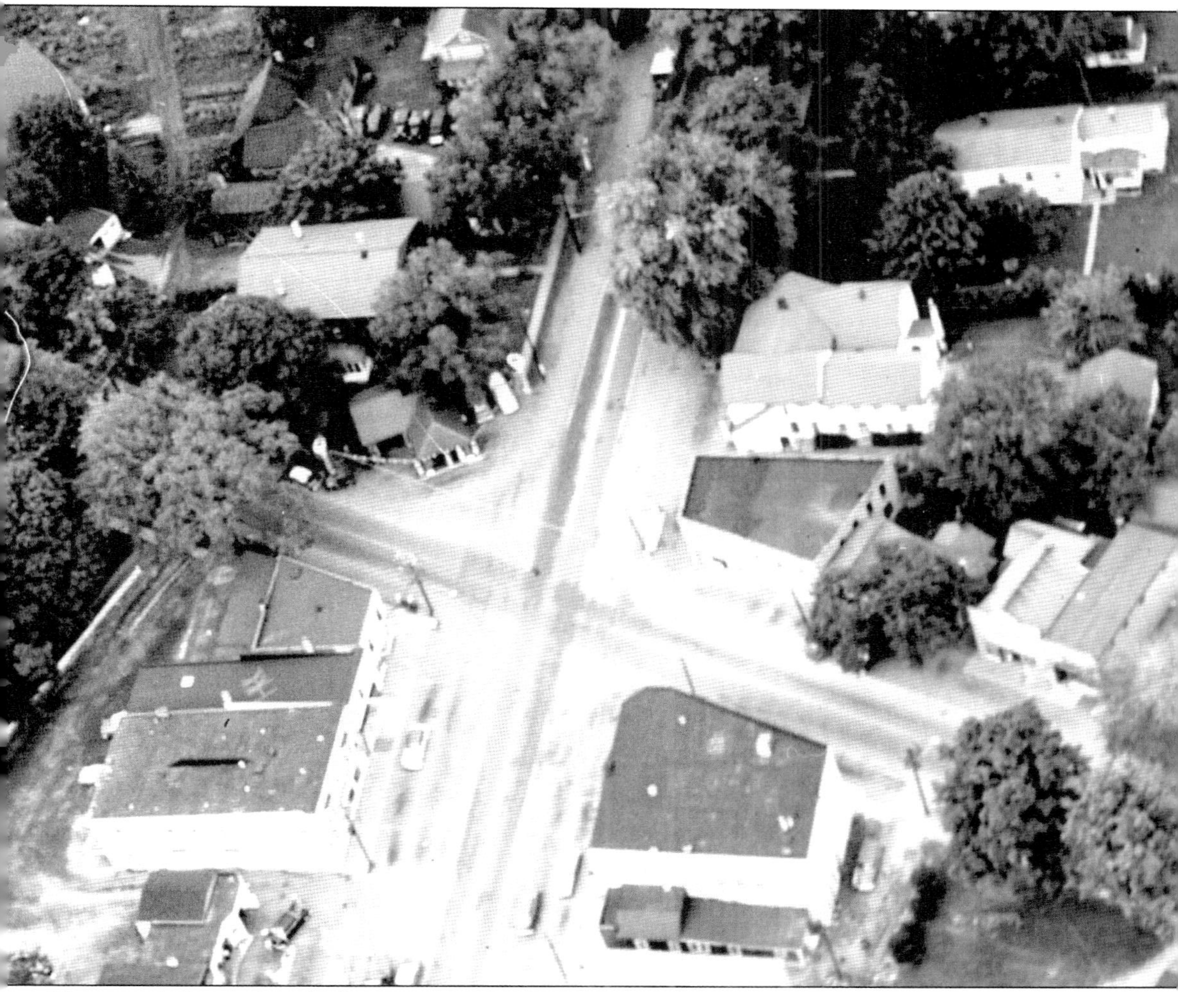

This aerial shot, taken looking west more than 60 years ago, shows Penfield's Four Corners. In the days past, Penfield Road was named Rochester Road. Heading west on this road was the main route from the small community of Penfield to the bustling city of Rochester. The townsfolk in Penfield referred to Rochester Road as West Main and East Main. Five Mile Line Road led from the north to the Four Corners. South Road continued south. Originally, Four Corners was referred to as Main Corners.

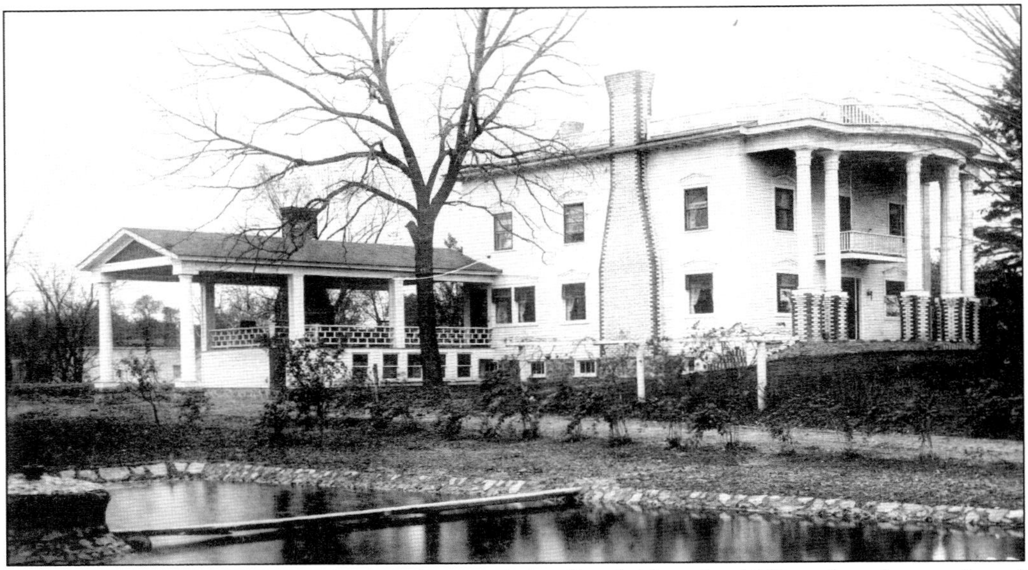

Originally from Ireland, David T. Lawless settled in Penfield in the 1880s, where he purchased a paper mill on the Irondequoit Creek. In 1914, construction ended on this house, at 1745 Penfield Road. The columns on the front of the house were said to be built by Lawless himself. Will Church, an early resident of Penfield, once wrote, "[D. T. Lawless] wanted the house colored Irish Green. His wife and family overruled him for once, and had it painted white." The earliest log cabin in Penfield was located on this lot, built by Jonathan Fassett in 1791–1792. Today, MGM Associates Insurance occupies the house.

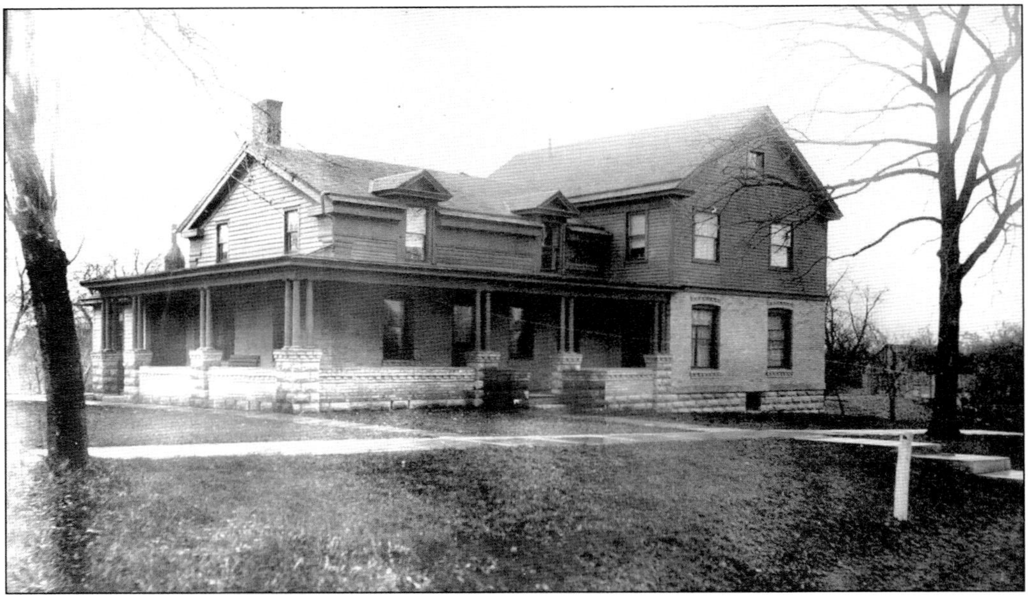

Rev. Jesse Humphrey, a Methodist Episcopal minister, once owned the house at 1783 Penfield Road. By the 1890s, Humphrey's son, Dr. Nathan Matson Humphrey, ran a doctor's office out of the house and would graciously make house calls around the town. He was the town's doctor for over 50 years until his death in 1946. Originally, the east portion of this house had been a wing on the Daniel Penfield House. Today, the house is a restaurant called the Humphrey House.

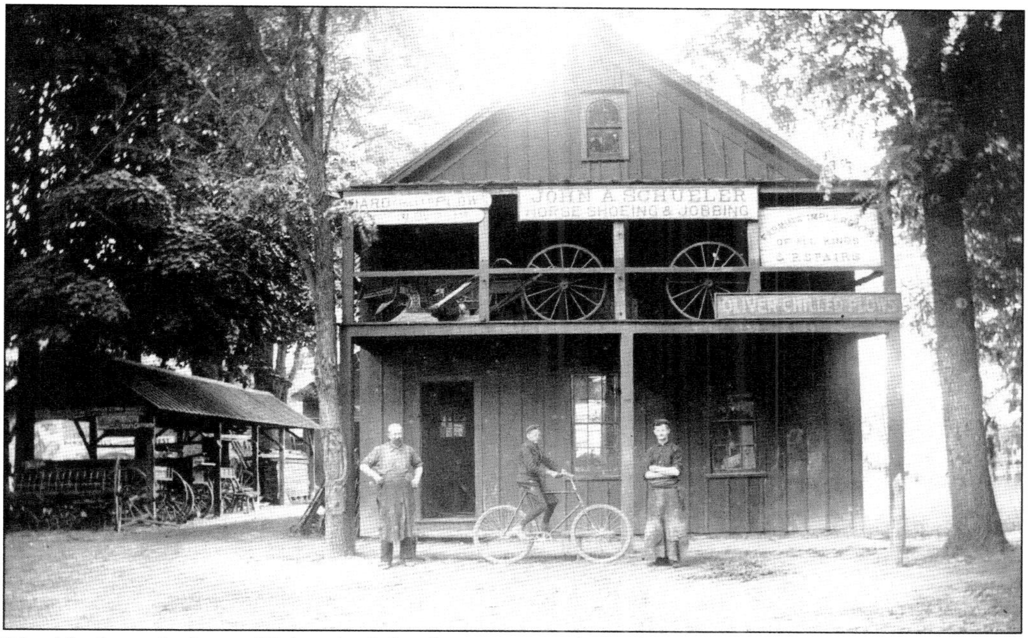

The blacksmith shop of John A. Schueler once stood on the south side of Penfield Road, just west of the Four Corners, as this 1894 photograph shows. Perhaps Schueler is shown standing near the doorway to the shop. He operated this "smithy" during the late 19th century and early 20th century until his death in 1902. (Image courtesy of the Rochester Public Library Local History Division.)

John Schueler

Has moved into the shop formerly occupied by Hiram Auchampaugh where he will carry on a general

Blacksmithing

Wagon making and repairing business. He will have on sale

Syracuse Chilled Plow

Cultivators, harrows and extras. He is also agent for the

CORTLAND WAGONS

And Cariages, Adriance, Platt & Co Mower and Binders and Champion Horse Rake.

This advertisement for John A. Schueler's blacksmith shop appeared in the April 15, 1893, issue of the *Penfield Press*.

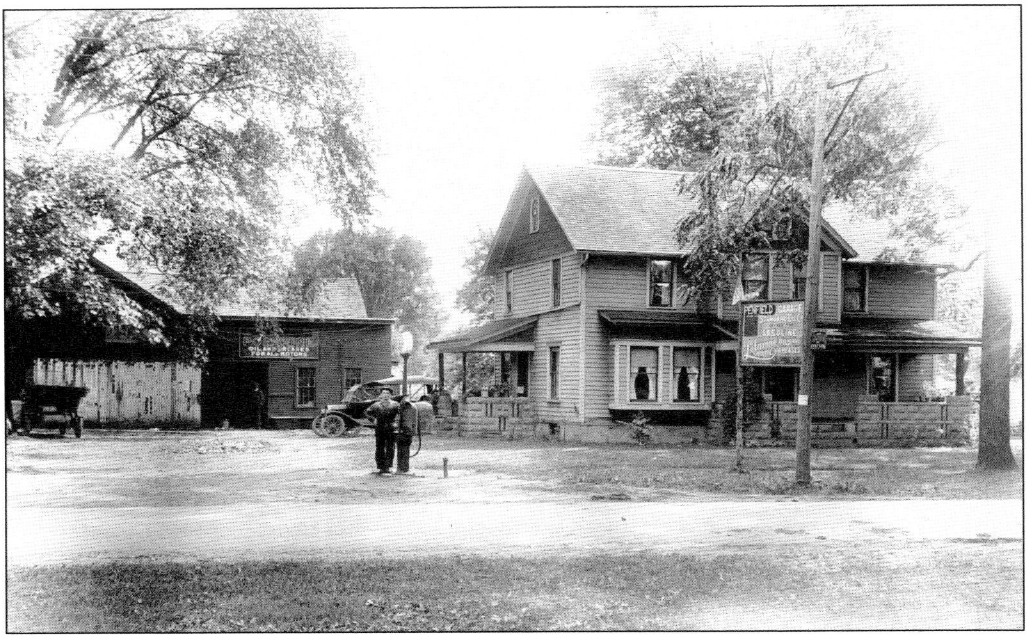

By the 1920s, the Penfield Garage occupied the land at 1815 Penfield Road, where the Schueler blacksmith shop once stood. The repair shop was owned by Winfield Furman, perhaps pictured here by the gasoline pump. Automotive repair shops progressively replaced the blacksmith. Today, coincidence would have it that close to where this building stood is an automotive service shop.

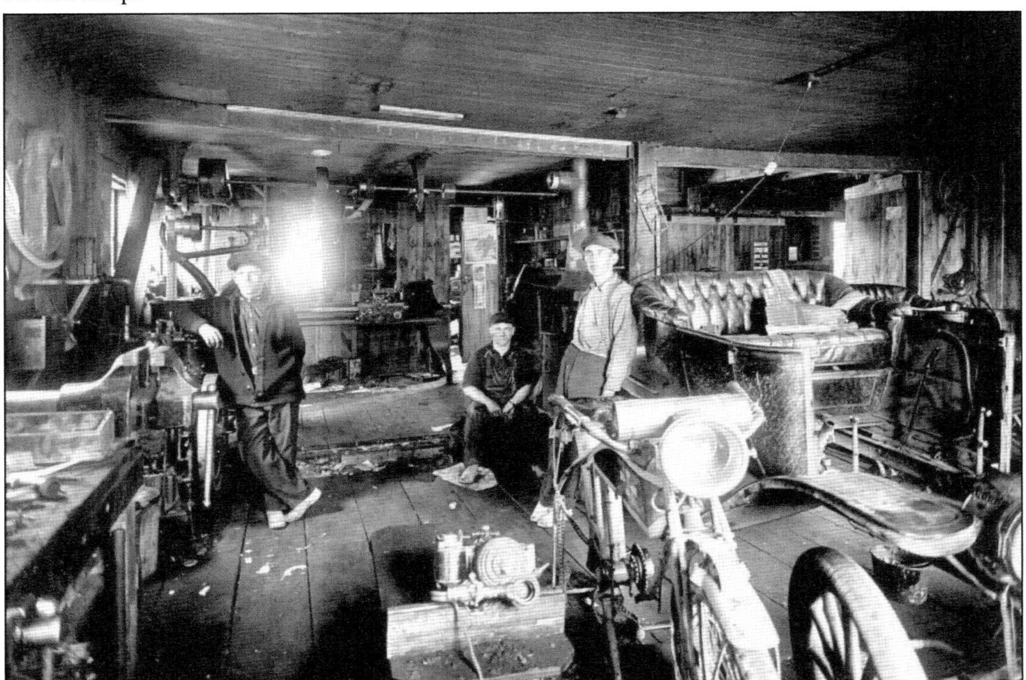

The inside of the Penfield Garage is pictured c. 1925.

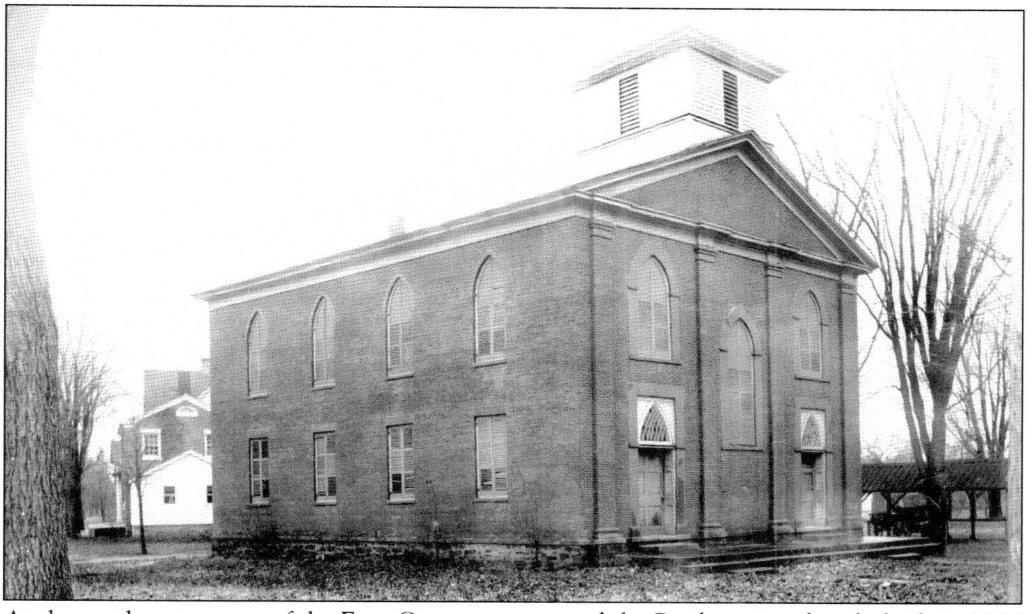

At the southwest corner of the Four Corners once stood the Presbyterian church, built in 1826 on land donated by Daniel Penfield. The bricks of the church were from Samuel Rich's brickyard on Thomas Creek in Perinton (then spelled Perrinton). The doors of the church were built wide enough to fit Mary Penfield's wheelchair. In 1878, church services began for the German Evangelical congregation. The services continued until 1914. The building was razed in 1962 after being used for many years as an apartment building.

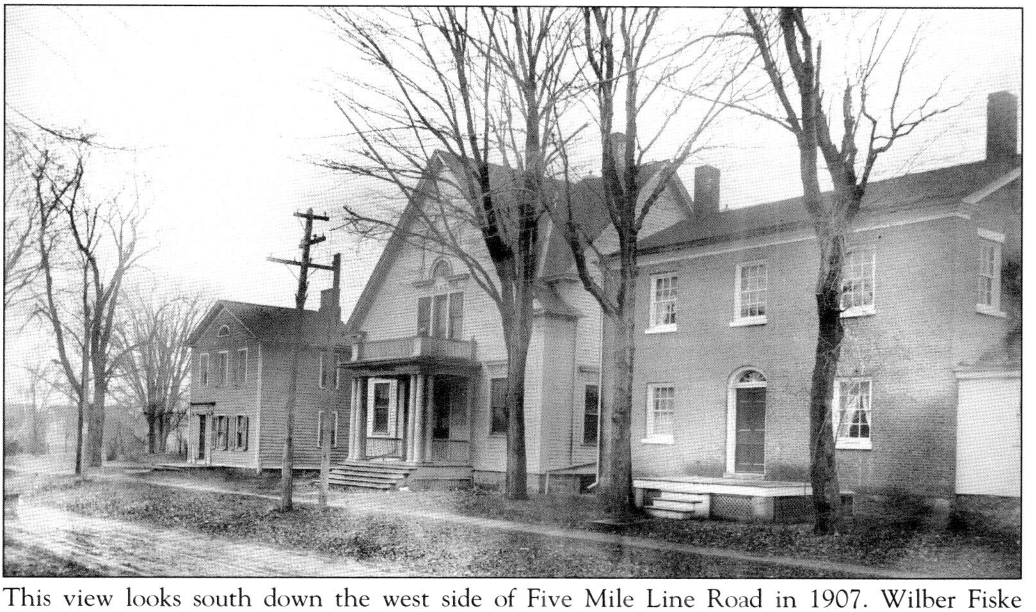

This view looks south down the west side of Five Mile Line Road in 1907. Wilber Fiske Owen Jr., grandson of Calvin Owen, an early resident of Penfield, remarked in *I Remember When . . . Penfield*, by Verna K. Brahler, "South Road was ankle deep in dust when dry and ankle deep in mud when wet. There were no street lights then and few houses." In 1913, streetlights were erected in Penfield.

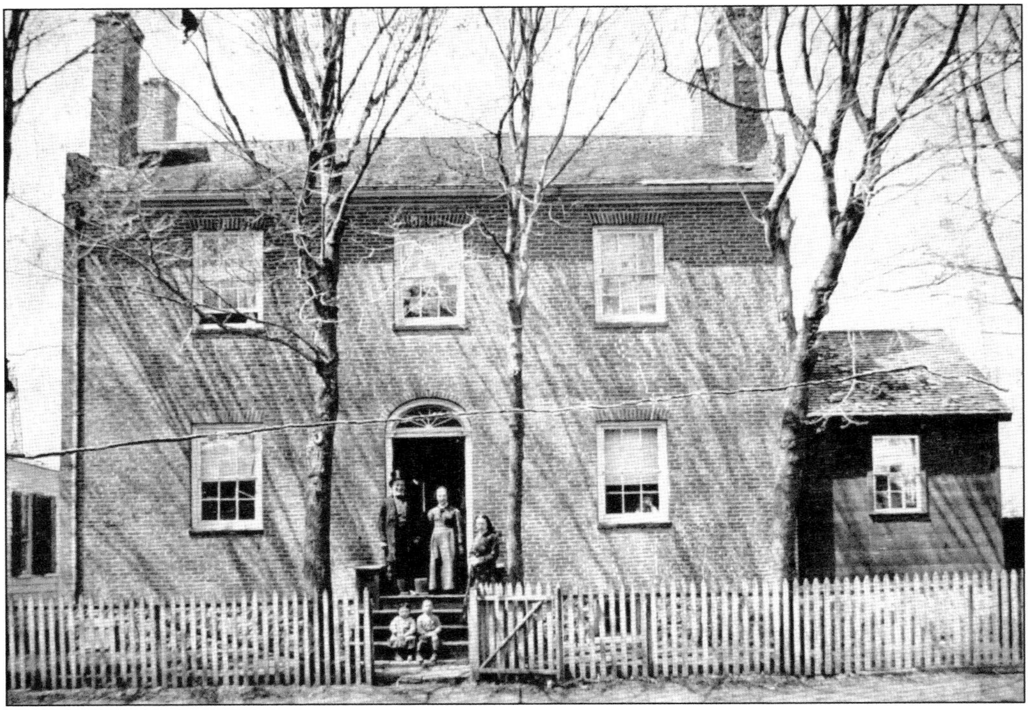

In 1828, Ira Mann, an early pioneer of Penfield, built the house at 2129 Five Mile Line Road. Calvin Owen and his wife can be seen standing on the front stoop. Owen owned this house for many years and kept a library, perhaps for town use. This house was designated as a Penfield landmark in 1975. Today, business offices occupy the house.

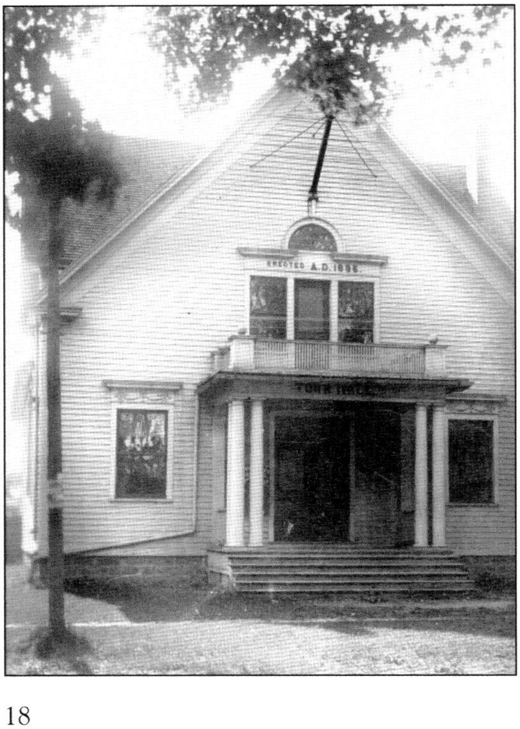

The Penfield Town Hall was built in 1895. In 1966, the town hall was moved to a new building on Atlantic Avenue. In the 1950s, the town's library was located in the downstairs of this building, and when the town hall was moved, the library took over the use of the whole building until it was moved to the Baird Road Community Center in 1985. This building, at 2131 Five Mile Line Road, was designated as a Penfield landmark in 1981. Today, it is occupied by a maternity clothing shop.

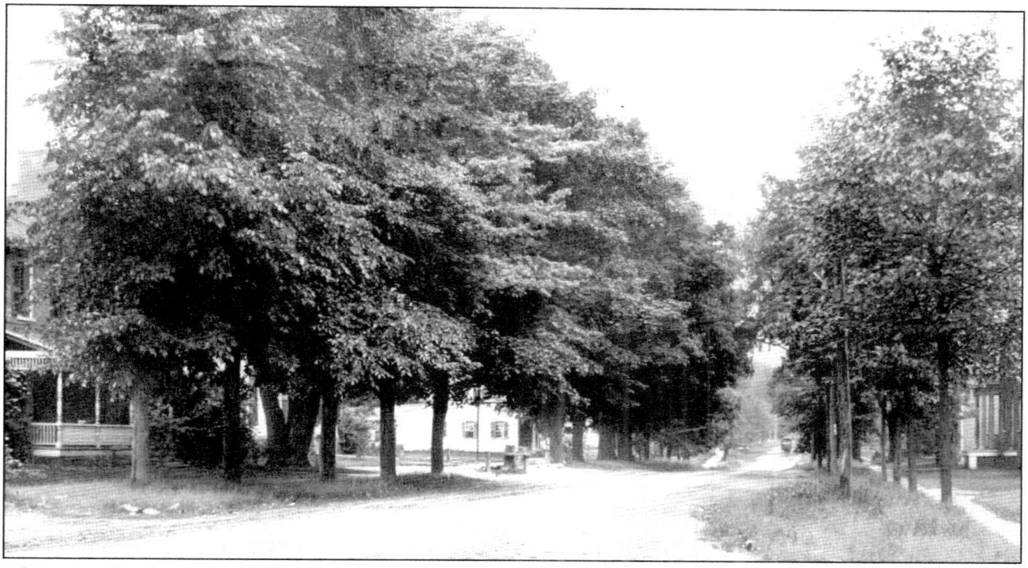

This view looks south down Five Mile Line Road away from the Four Corners *c*. 1900.

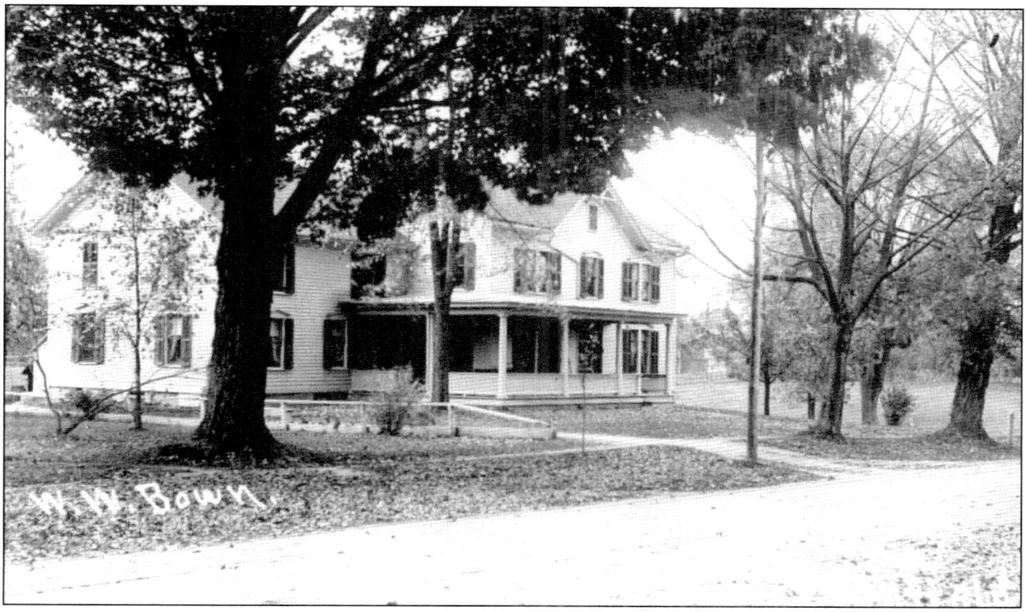

At 2149 Five Mile Line Road (west side) stands the house built in 1878 for Wilson W. Bown, a nurseryman in Penfield. The old Bown house on the property was burned in a town celebration. A. F. Church recalled, "That evening there was a big celebration; Penfield band and Fairport band, bonfire, speeches, anvil firing, and the burning down of the old house on the Bown Estate—June 15, 1896."

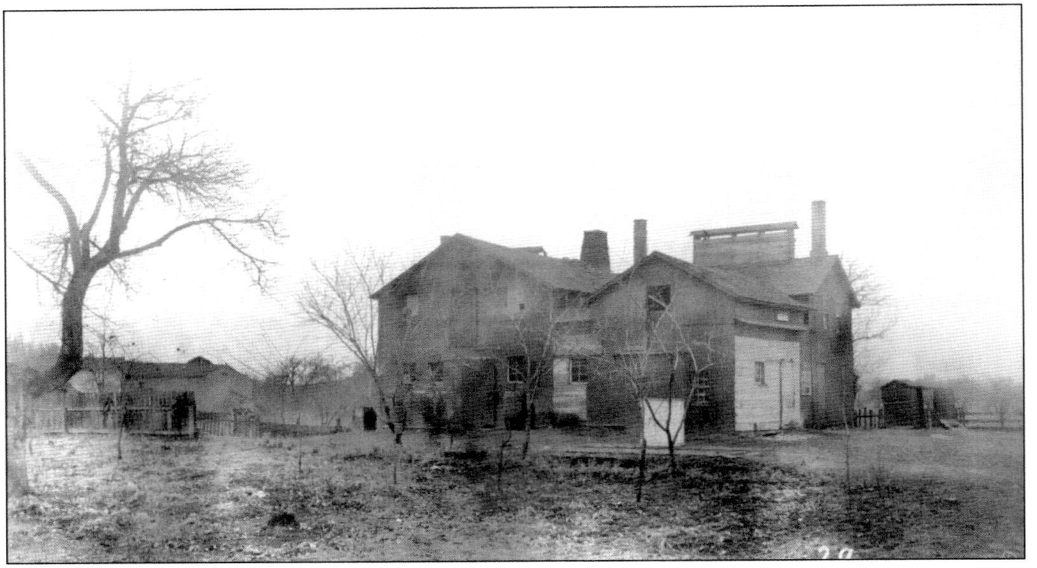

These barns stood on W. W. Bown's property and were used for fruit evaporation. This photograph was taken in 1907.

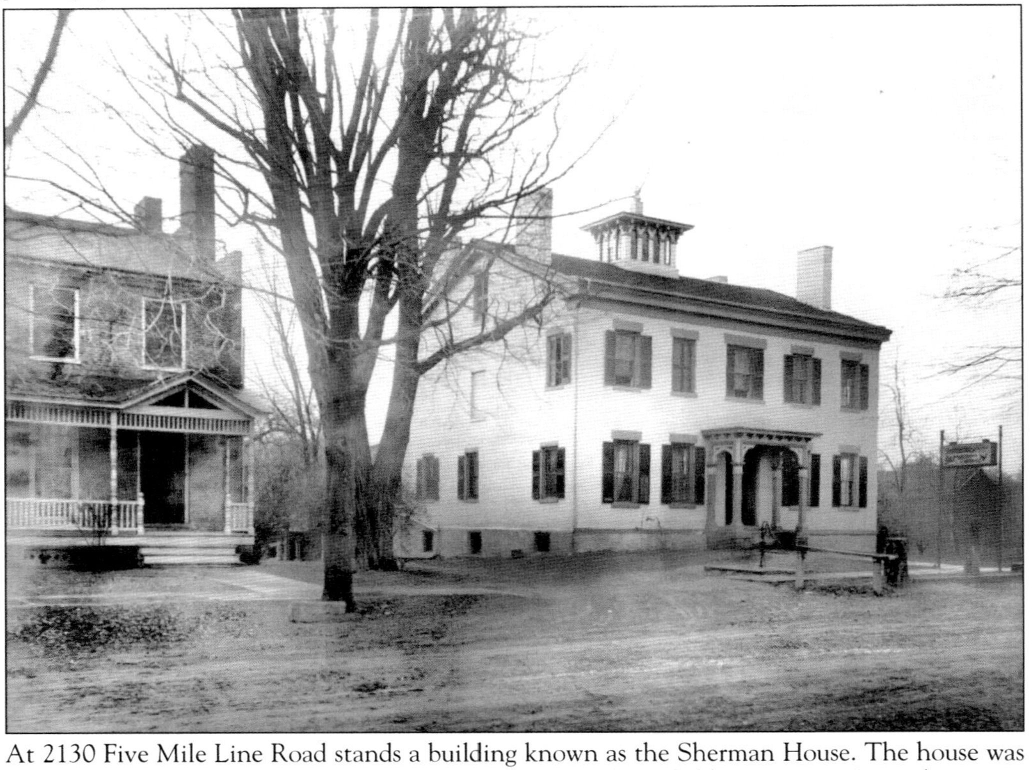

At 2130 Five Mile Line Road stands a building known as the Sherman House. The house was built sometime before 1840 for George Penfield, Daniel Penfield's son. By 1870, it became a hotel owned by Jared Sherman. Today, the Sherman House is used as an office building. The house on the left, at 2126 Five Mile Line Road, was built in 1825 for Leonard Adams, a lawyer in Penfield. Today, the house is the Chinese restaurant Kam Wah.

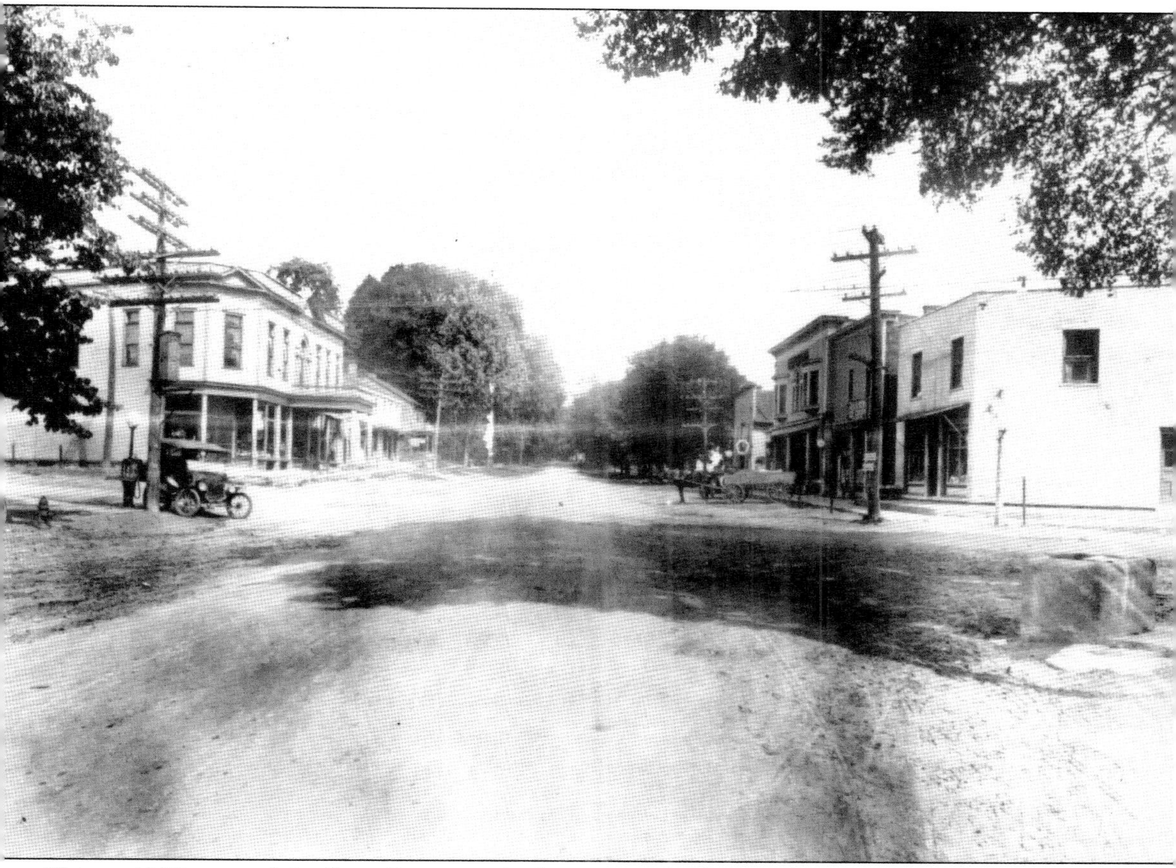

This *c.* 1900 view of the Four Corners is looking east. The lot on the right, in the southeast corner, was once a general store owned by Robert Staring in the 1860s. The September 24, 1863, issue of the *Penfield Extra* noted, "We understand that Mr. R. Staring has purchased the Brick Block, of Mr. J. Lewis, in this village, and intends fitting it up for a country store, success to the enterprise." This block burned to the ground on June 24, 1899, while owned by George A. Raymond and was later rebuilt. Today, Tuxedo Park occupies the old Staring Store.

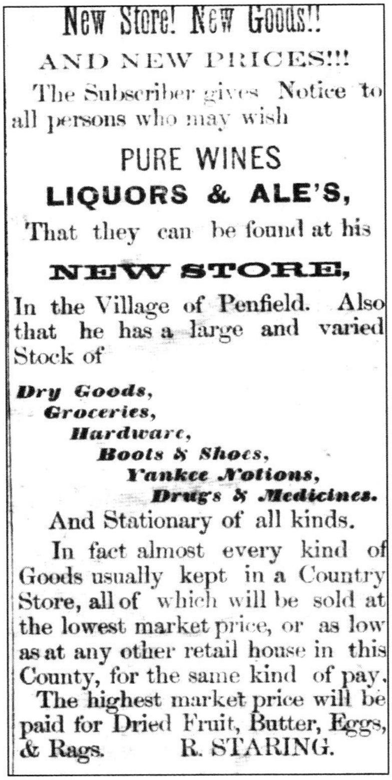

New Store! New Goods!!
AND NEW PRICES!!!
The Subscriber gives Notice to all persons who may wish
PURE WINES
LIQUORS & ALE'S,
That they can be found at his
NEW STORE,
In the Village of Penfield. Also that he has a large and varied Stock of
Dry Goods,
Groceries,
Hardware,
Boots & Shoes,
Yankee Notions,
Drugs & Medicines.
And Stationary of all kinds.
In fact almost every kind of Goods usually kept in a Country Store, all of which will be sold at the lowest market price, or as low as at any other retail house in this County, for the same kind of pay.
The highest market price will be paid for Dried Fruit, Butter, Eggs, & Rags. R. STARING.

This advertisement was featured in the February 5, 1866, issue of the *Penfield Extra*.

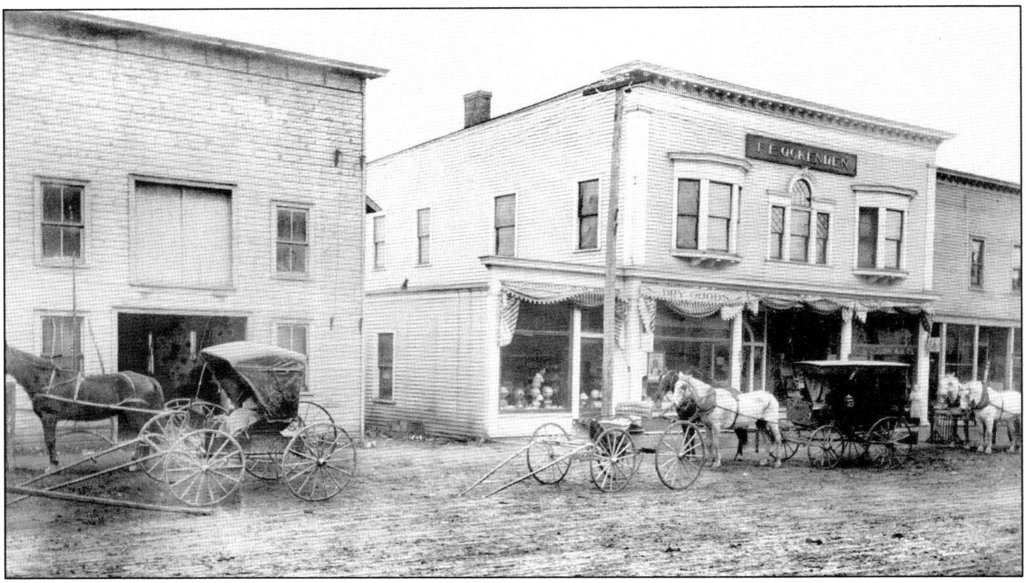

F. E. Ockenden operated the dry goods store on the south side at 1825 Penfield Road. The Ockenden family was in business at the Four Corners for more than 55 years. The building to the left was a blacksmith shop owned by Joseph Schnitzer. Much like cars would be parked outside stores today, horse-drawn buggies can be seen lining the street. Donna B's Hair Design and the Cambridge Company, a mortgage company, now occupy the old Ockenden building.

This advertisement of the Penfield, Brighton, and Rochester Stage was featured in the February 5, 1866, issue of the *Penfield Extra*. O. Van Ostrand was the proprietor of the Union Hotel, and Robert Starting was the owner. The hotel was located on the south side of Penfield Road east. Today, Al's Automotive occupies the lot where the hotel stood.

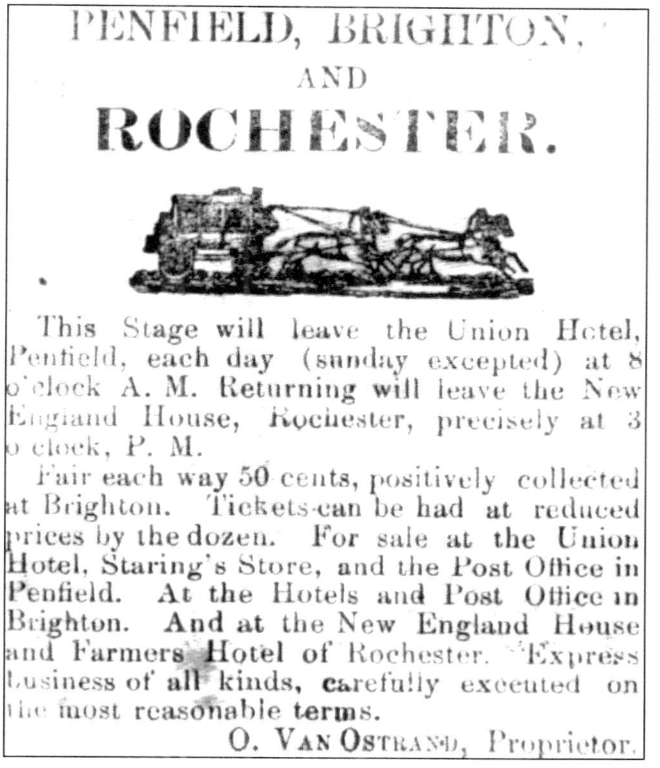

PENFIELD, BRIGHTON,

AND

ROCHESTER.

This Stage will leave the Union Hotel, Penfield, each day (sunday excepted) at 8 o'clock A. M. Returning will leave the New England House, Rochester, precisely at 3 o clock, P. M.

Fair each way 50 cents, positively collected at Brighton. Tickets can be had at reduced prices by the dozen. For sale at the Union Hotel, Staring's Store, and the Post Office in Penfield. At the Hotels and Post Office in Brighton. And at the New England House and Farmers Hotel of Rochester. Express business of all kinds, carefully executed on the most reasonable terms.

O. VAN OSTRAND, Proprietor.

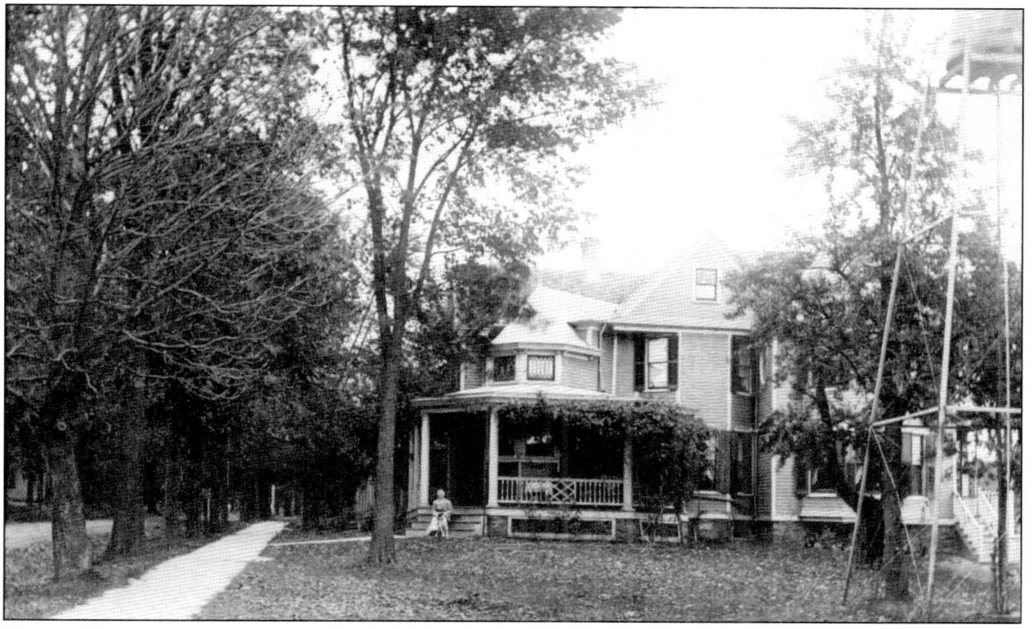

George Porter, a carpenter in Penfield, built this Queen Anne–style house c. 1870. Located at 1853 Penfield Road, the house was remodeled over the years and was eventually converted to a day-care center. Today, Tots University Child Care Campus occupies the house.

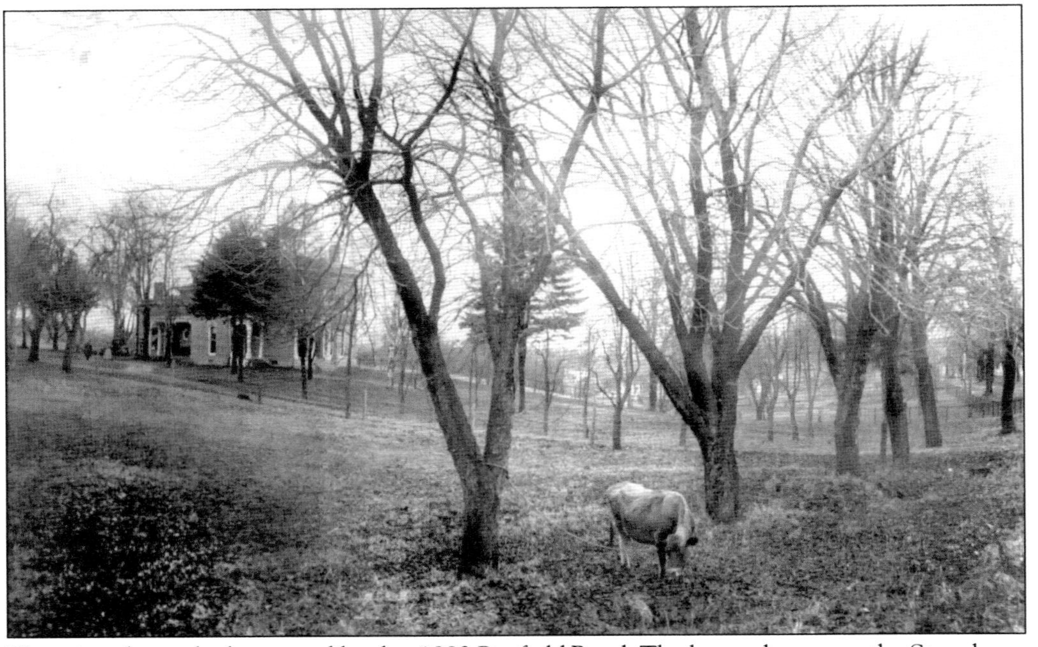

This view shows the house and land at 1883 Penfield Road. The house, known as the Strawberry Castle, took four years to build and was finished in 1878 for George and Catherine Southworth. George Southworth worked as a Penfield nurseryman specializing in growing strawberries until his death in 1898. Catherine Southworth died in 1902, and the property was purchased by August Schaufelberger, also a nurseryman and landowner around Penfield.

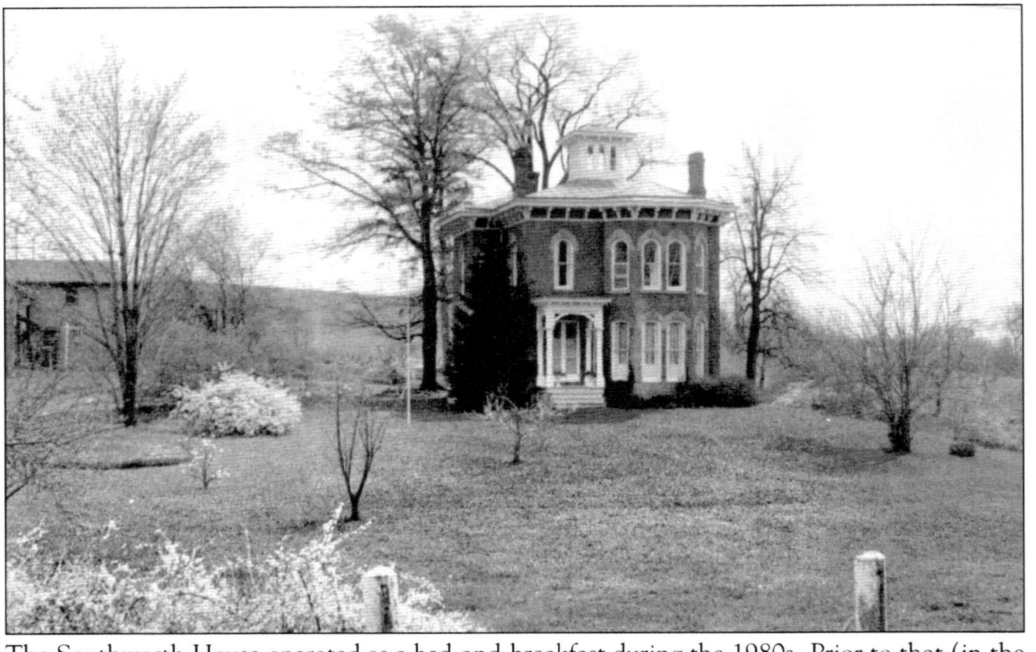

The Southworth House operated as a bed-and-breakfast during the 1980s. Prior to that (in the mid-1900s), the house was named Hill and Hollow and was owned by Edwin Porter and family. It was designated as a Penfield landmark in 1977. Today, it is privately owned.

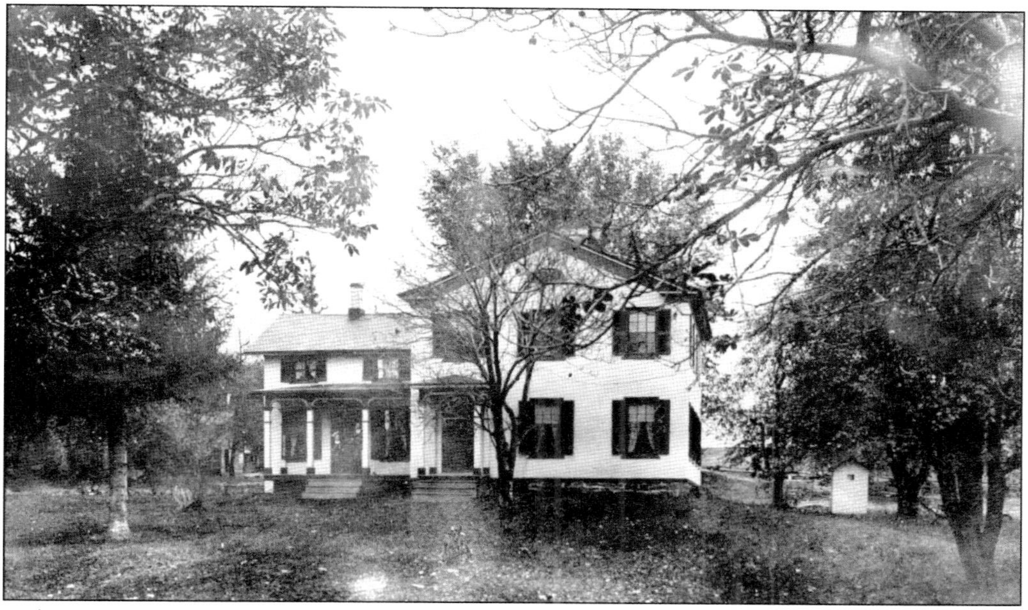

Nelson Fullam, a Penfield farmer, built this house at 1895 Penfield Road in 1835. His father, Elisha Fullam, was a veteran of the Revolutionary War and was one of the first settlers of Penfield in 1801. Elisa became a miller, working for Daniel Penfield. John Fahrer and family also owned the house during the early to mid-20th century. By 1924, Fahrer owned more than 75 acres of farmland behind his house and a large set of woods on the back of his property, which became known locally as Fahrer Woods. The Fullam-Fahrer House was designated as a Penfield landmark in 1977.

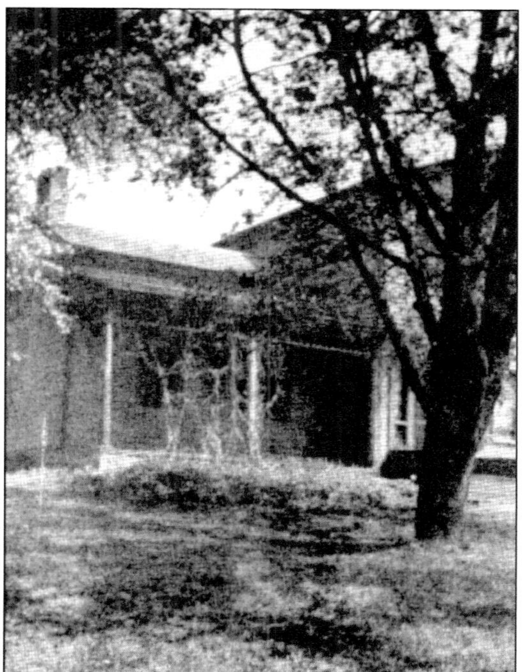

John Weaver built the house at 1884 Penfield Road in 1832. Originally a one-story structure, the house has been expanded over the years. A farmer by trade, John Weaver also operated a tannery on his property beside Honey Creek. Honey Creek still flows to the Four Corners and down to the Irondequoit Creek. In 1876, the house became a parsonage for the Penfield Baptist Church. In 1977, the John Weaver House became listed as a Penfield landmark.

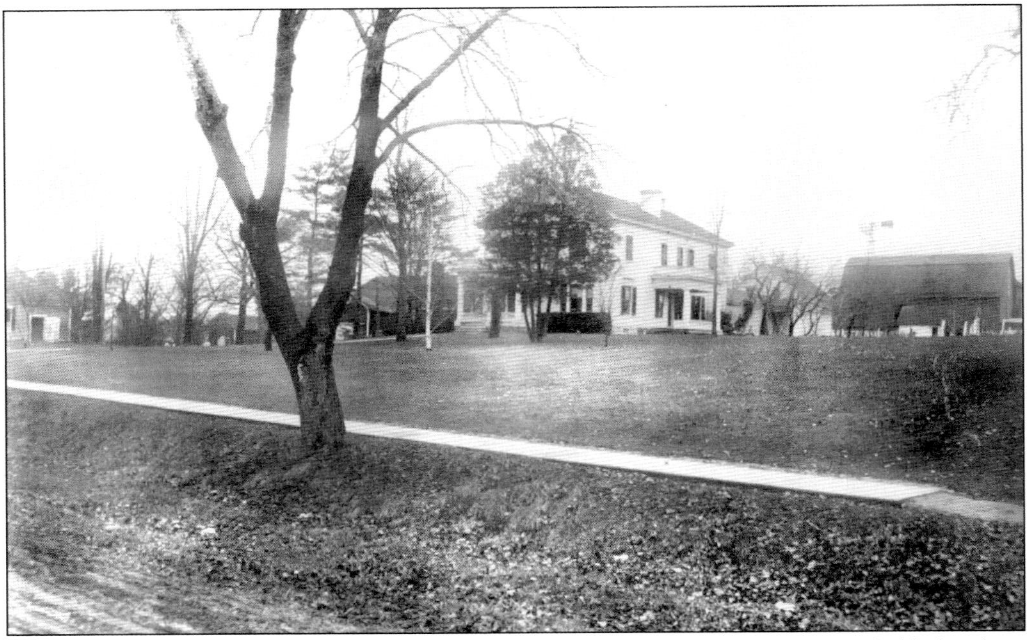

At 1880 Penfield Road stands a house built in 1816 for Henry Fellows, Daniel Penfield's brother-in-law. Fellows worked as a farmer in Penfield. His father, Gen. Jonathan Fellows, served under George Washington during the Revolutionary War. The Henry Fellows House was designated as a Penfield landmark in 1977.

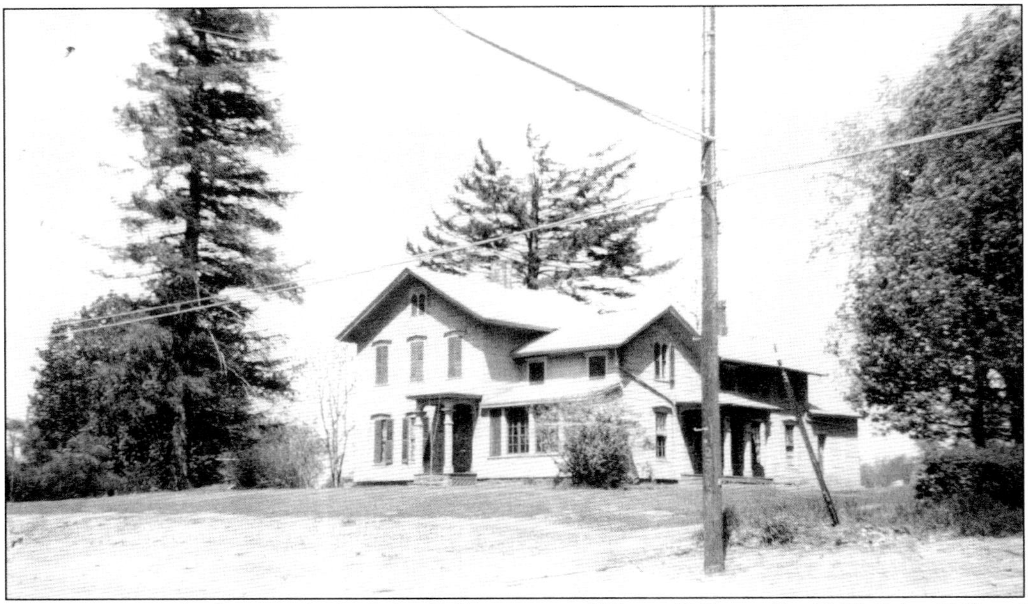

This house was built in 1868 for John Fellows, son of Henry Fellows. By 1900, John Fellows' son-in-law and daughter, Catherine Fellows Ryan, took ownership of the house. In the early 1960s, the 46-acre farmland behind the house was sold to the town of Penfield for an athletic field. The John Fellows House, located at 1876 Penfield Road, was designated as a Penfield landmark in 1977.

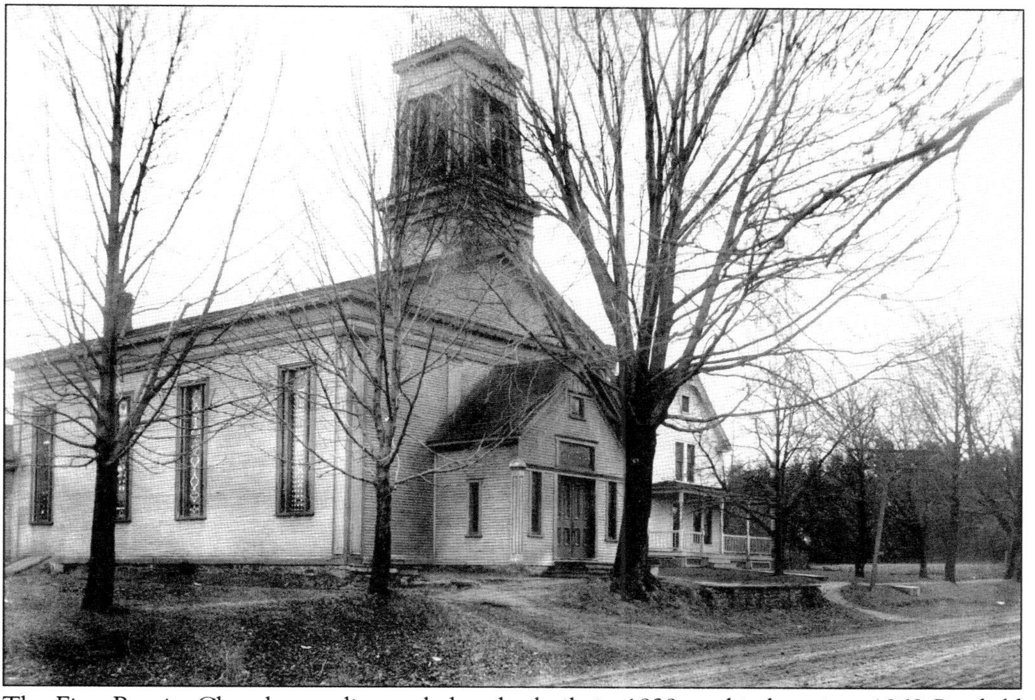

The First Baptist Church was dismantled and rebuilt in 1839 at this location, 1862 Penfield Road. The congregation originally occupied this structure at the northwest corner of Penfield and Baird Roads. In 1862, the church was remodeled, and in 1940, a school was added. In the July 16, 1863, issue of the *Penfield Extra,* it was reported, "Lightning struck our Baptist Church last week, paying no regard to the lightning rod; it tore siding and plastering considerable, but did not set the building on fire." The church was designated as a Penfield landmark in 1977.

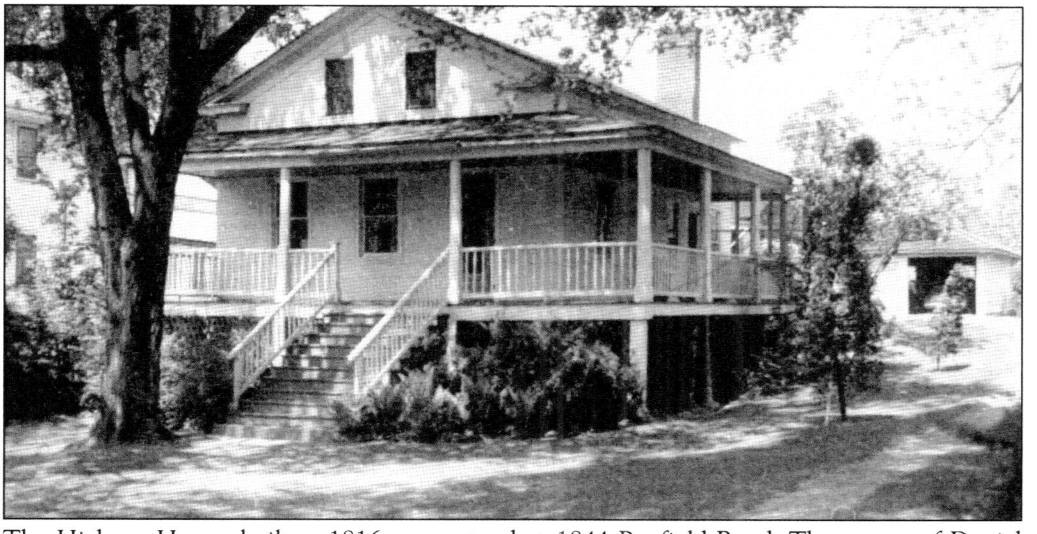

The High-up House, built *c.* 1816, once stood at 1844 Penfield Road. The names of Daniel Penfield, Elisha Fullam, and Henry Fellows all appear on deeds as owners of the house in the 1800s. The house was built up off the ground using wooden beams, which was a very unique style of building, especially in 1816.

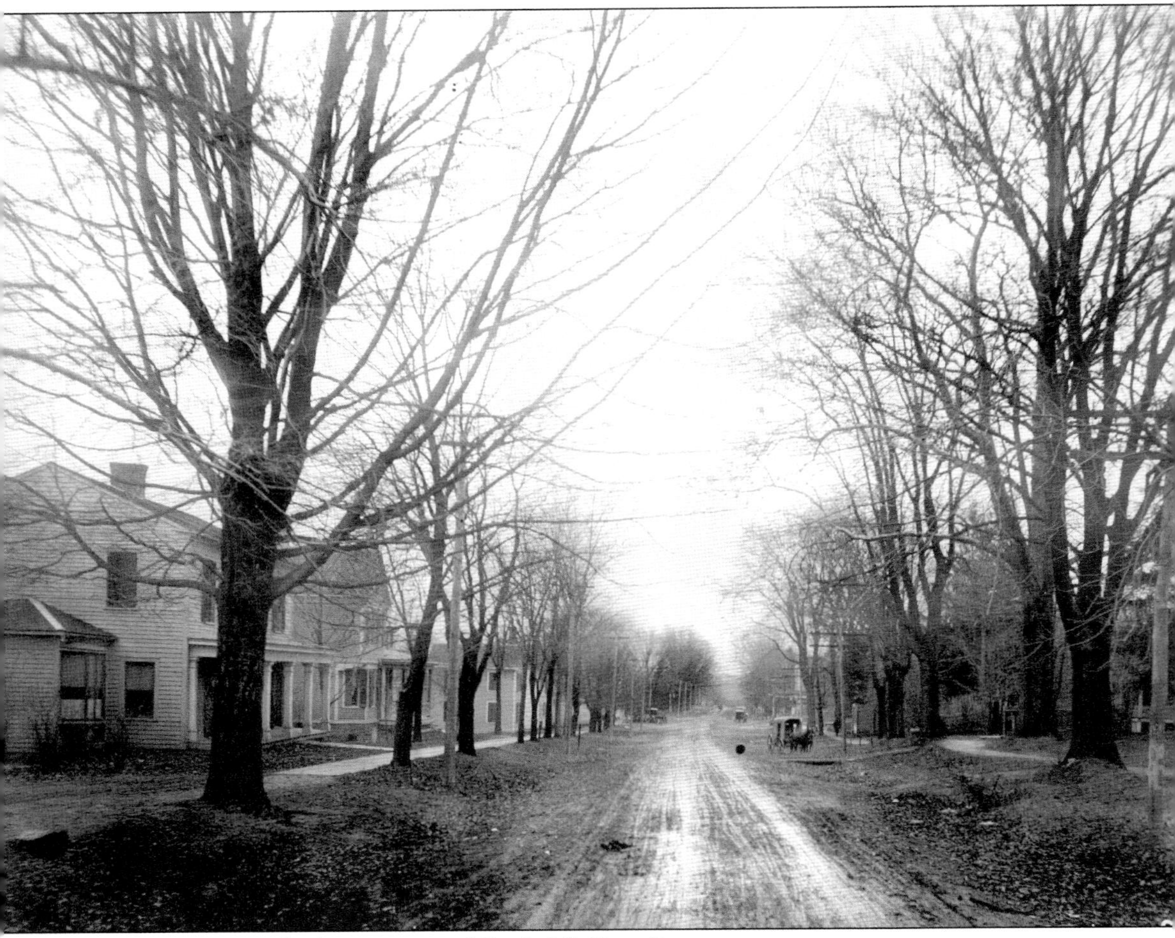

This 1907 view looks west toward Penfield's Four Corners.

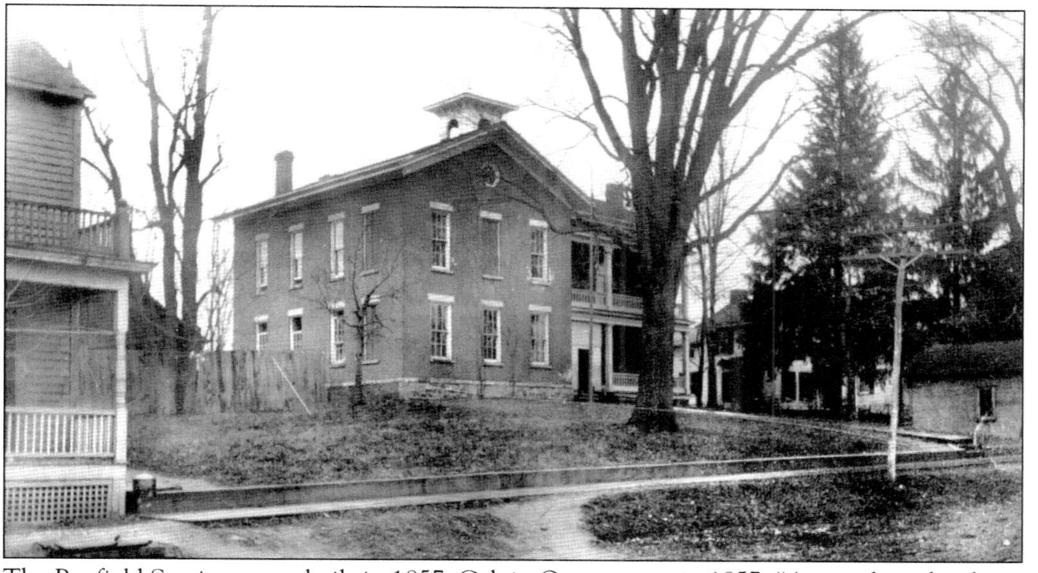

The Penfield Seminary was built in 1857. Calvin Owen wrote in 1857, "An academy has been built in our village this past summer and a well built brick building and capable of accommodating a hundred and fifty students. Builders were S. and W. Beilbys carpenters, and E. Hazen the mason." The building was purchased in 1907 by the newly formed Penfield Hose Company No. 1. In 1910, a total of 28 fire hydrants were installed around the town.

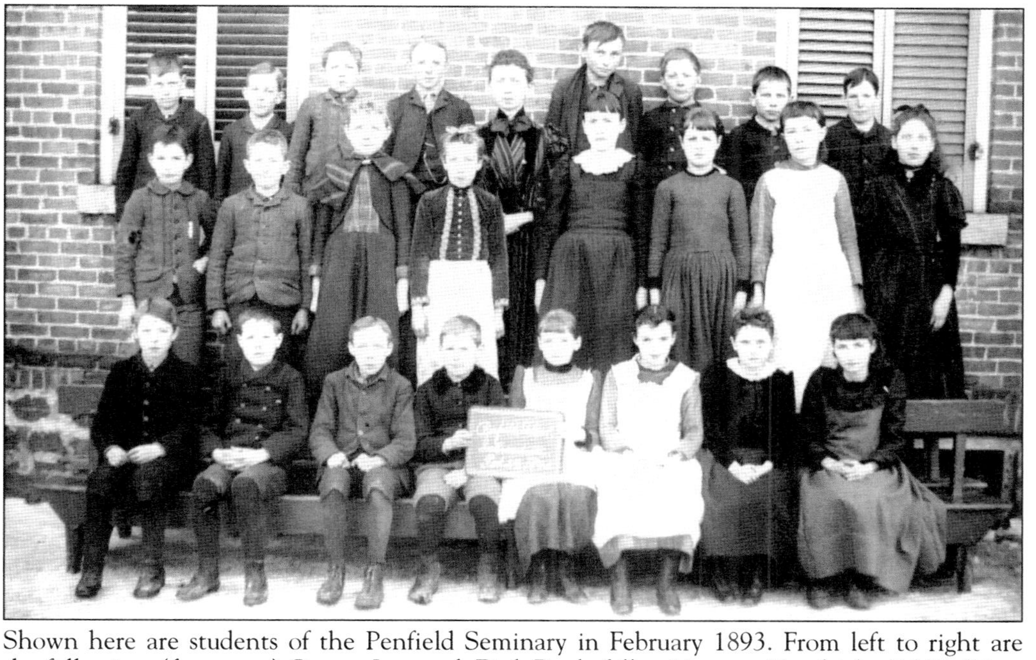

Shown here are students of the Penfield Seminary in February 1893. From left to right are the following: (front row) George Leonard, Dick Rockefeller, Herman Hendricks, Ed Welkley, Katie Jacobs, Retta Gale, Lulu Covey, and Nellie Lawless; (middle row) Lewis Bronson, George Hartung, Alice Dake, Emma Hendricks, May Jetty, Rose March, Rosa Mauerhofer, and Nellie Carmer; (back row) Elmer Hipp, ? Church, Frank Hartung, Ed Jacobs, unidentified, Peter Mort, Fred Buhlman, Arthur Hipp, and Lowell Fox.

PENFIELD SEMINARY!

CIRCULAR. FALL TERM.

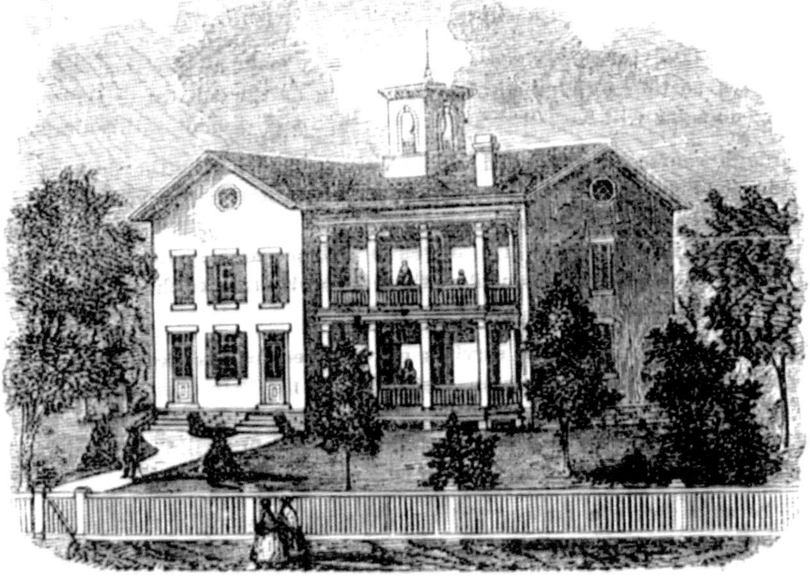

OFFICERS:

JAMES HARRIS, Pres't. **J. W. WILSON**, Sec'y.

A. HIGBY,	A. S. CLARKE,	WM. FELLOWS,
L. ALLYN,	JOHN BURNS,	E. K. WEAVER,
B. HOWE,	CHAS. WEAVER,	A. COVEY,
	W. M. LLOYD.	

A. B. CAMPBELL, A. M., Principal and Teacher of Belle-Lettres.
Mrs. A. E. CAMPBELL, Preceptress in Mathematics and French.
C. G. BEACH, Assistant in Male Department.
A. A. HOPKINS, Professor of Music.
———————— Teacher in Juvenile Department.

This Institution is situated in the pleasant village of Penfield, seven miles by stage from Rochester, and three from Fairport, or Pittsford Station, on the New York Central Rail Road. This place is sufficiently removed from the baneful influences of a large city, and yet abundant in everything for the comfort and advantage of a student life.

The trustees take pleasure in introducing to the friends and patrons of this Seminary, the large and able corps of Teachers, who have had many years experience in conducting Academies east, with eminent success, and we trust that all will manifest a zeal to enhance the success of this heretofore prosperous Seminary.

The charges for a 14-week term in 1857 ranged from $4.50 to $10 for "common English," plus an additional $2 for a music course. In the August 10, 1865, issue of the *Penfield Extra*, an advertisement reads, "SCHOOL TEACHER WANTED—We have a Splendid Seminary in Penfield, which would do a good business by advertising. Our last teacher was too poor to advertise, consequently became poorer every day."

Two

Four Corners, Continued

We saw many, many pleasant villages on our short journey, but we saw none that looked like home. . . . In fact, Penfield is a beautiful town in a splendid country surrounding it.

—*Penfield Extra*, June 20, 1863

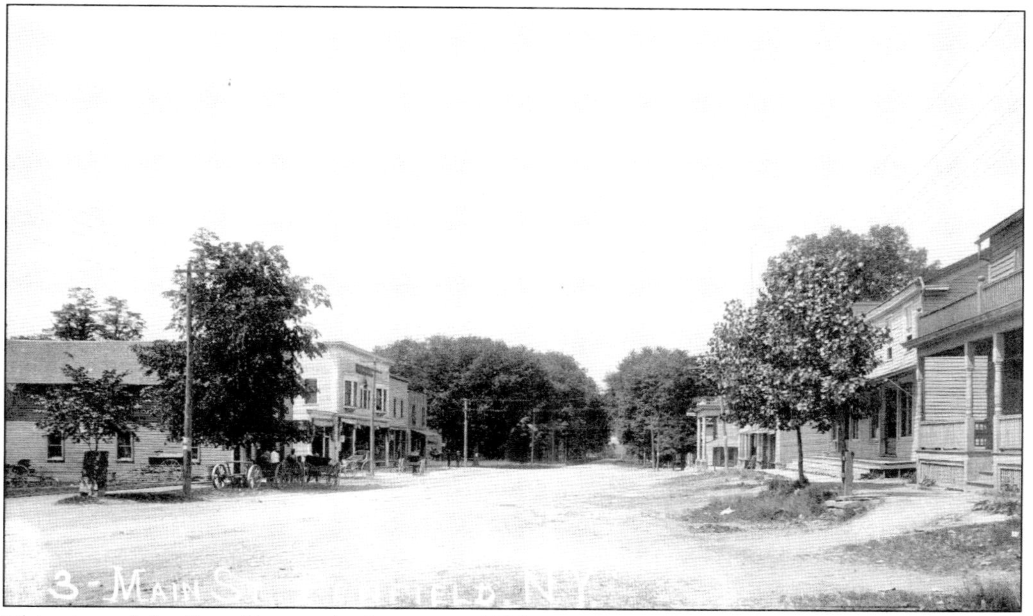

This view of the Four Corners looks west c. 1900.

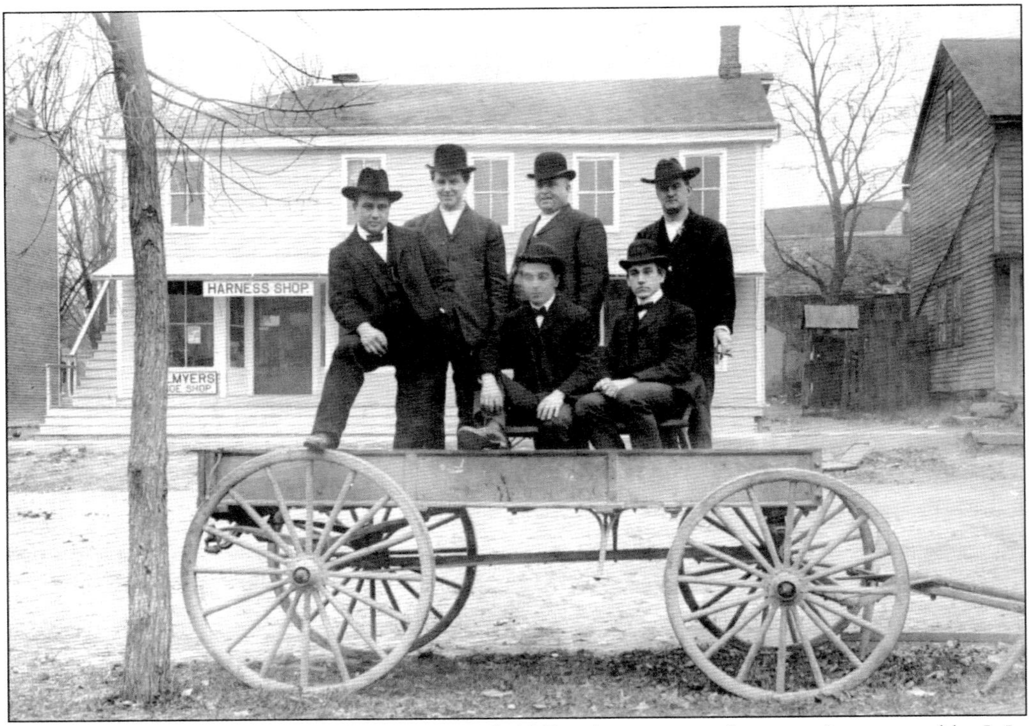

The building in the background at 1830 Penfield Road was once a harness shop owned by J. L. Myers. Before the official town hall was built, town meetings were held on the second floor. In recent years, the building became a restaurant, but nothing occupies it today.

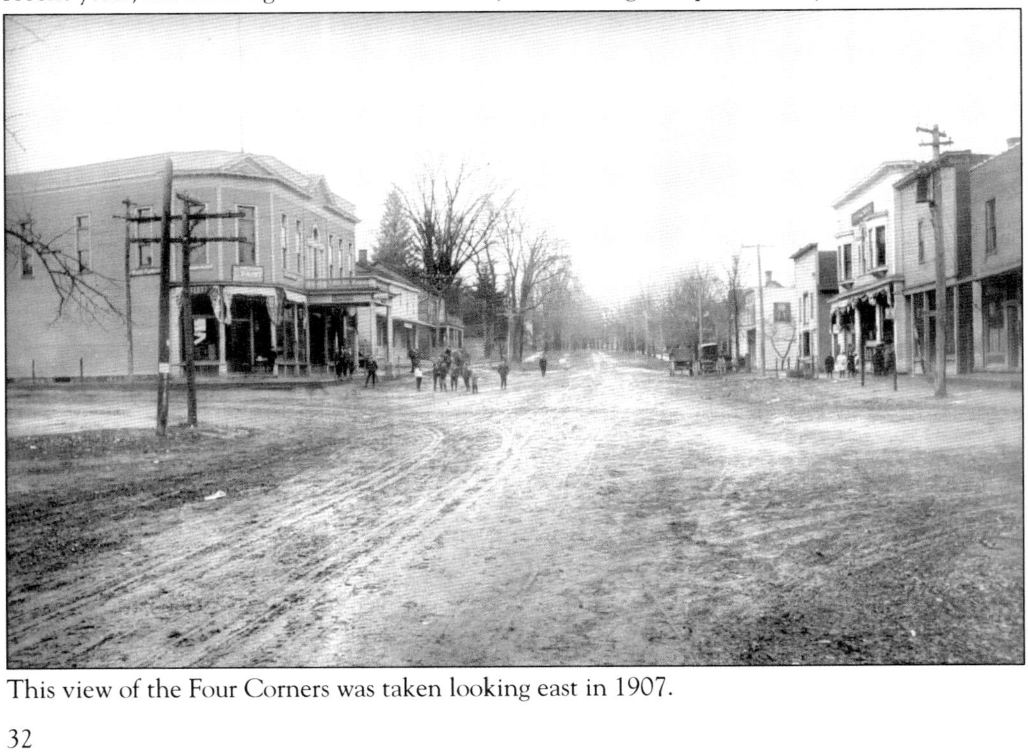

This view of the Four Corners was taken looking east in 1907.

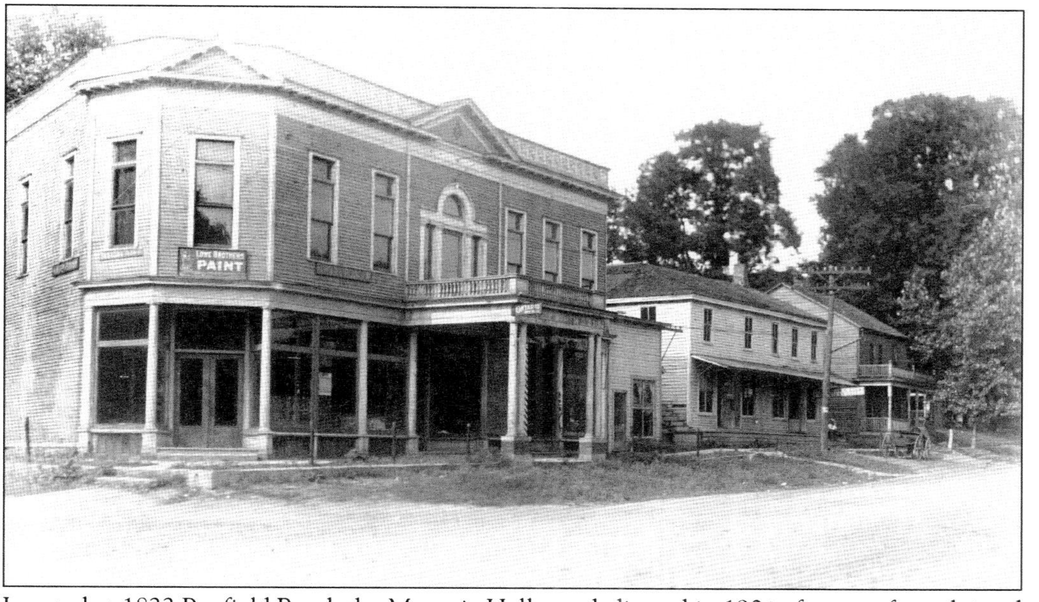

Located at 1822 Penfield Road, the Masonic Hall was dedicated in 1904 after past fires claimed other structures on this lot. Peter Shoecraft owned a building at the corner—the Shoecraft Tavern, which burned in 1854. The lot stood vacant for many years before the Masonic Hall was built and used for town concerts and temperance meetings.

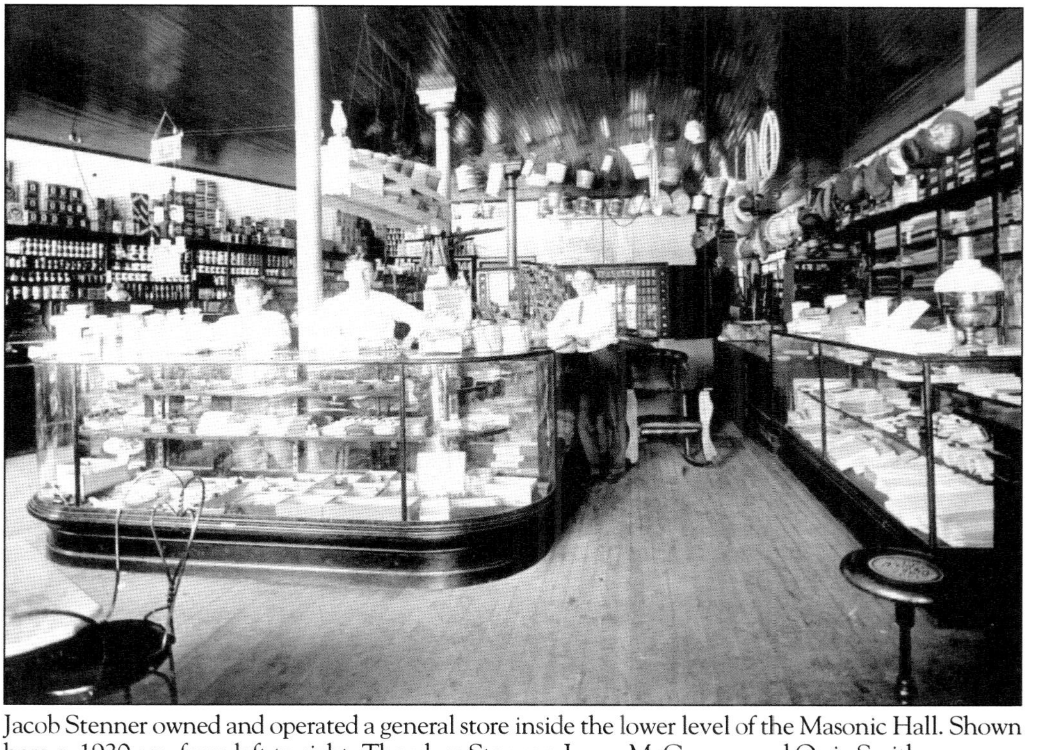

Jacob Stenner owned and operated a general store inside the lower level of the Masonic Hall. Shown here *c.* 1920 are, from left to right, Theodore Stenner, James McGowan, and Orrie Smith.

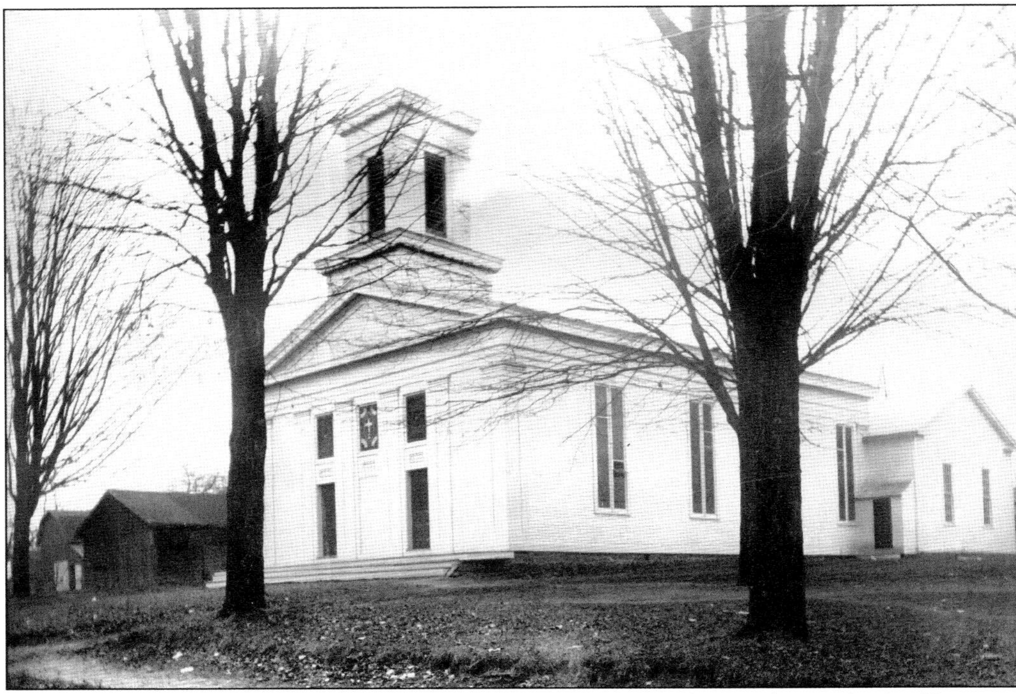

The church at 2106 Five Mile Line Road was built in 1843 to house the Methodist Episcopal congregation. The total cost of the Greek Revival building and lot was $9,000. Today, the church houses services for the New Beginnings Christian congregation. A craft store called the Enchanted Rose Garden also occupies the church.

GEORGE C. SCHERMERHORN'S

Is the place to buy your Dry **Goods, Groceries**, Boots and Shoes, Paints and **Oils. Our** Turnbull Bros. Boots & Shoes **are the best in** the world; every pair warranted. **We also carry a**

Full Line of School Supplies,

Drugs and Patent Medicines,

Try our Vanilla Drip Syrup, the best in the **market. Our** Crown Baking Powder is the best 20 cent **powder made. Give** us a call. Public Telephone. P. O. Building,

PENFIELD, **N. Y.**

This advertisement was taken from the April 15, 1893, issue of the *Penfield Press*.

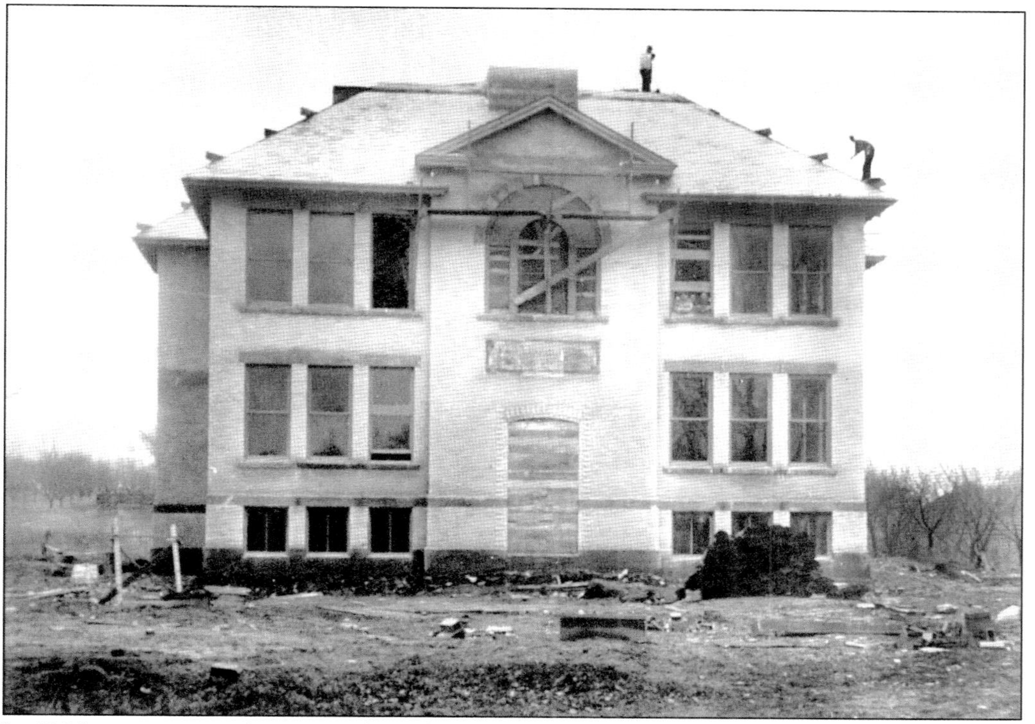

In 1906, construction began on the public school building at 2070 Five Mile Line Road. The grade school classes were held on the first floor, and the high school classes were held on the second floor.

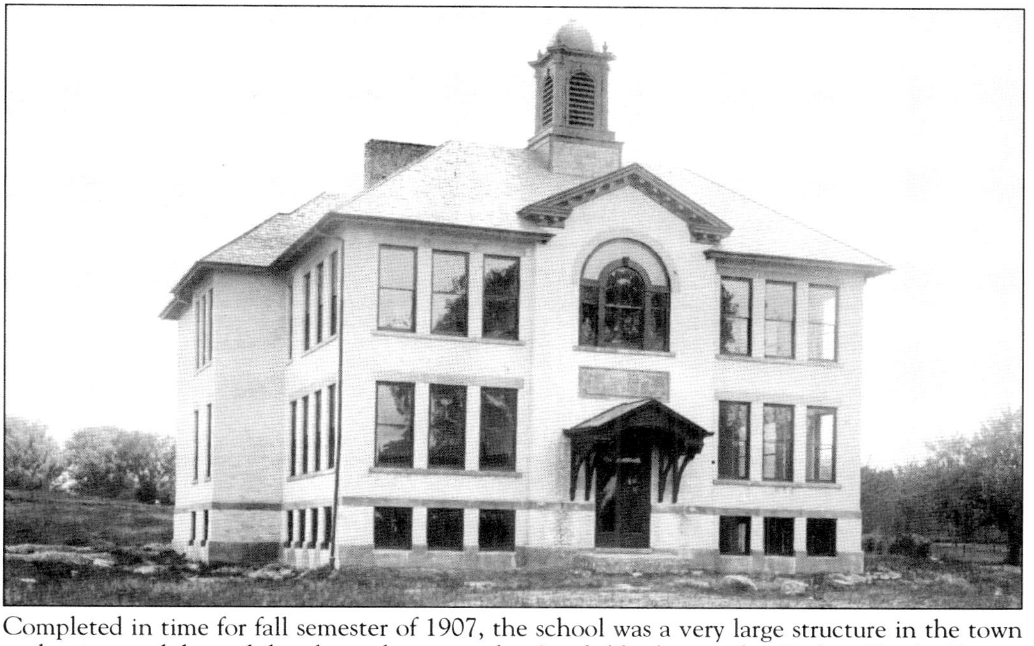

Completed in time for fall semester of 1907, the school was a very large structure in the town at the time and showed the planned progress that Penfield is known for. Today, Charles Finney Corporate School and the New Covenant Fellowship occupy the old high school building.

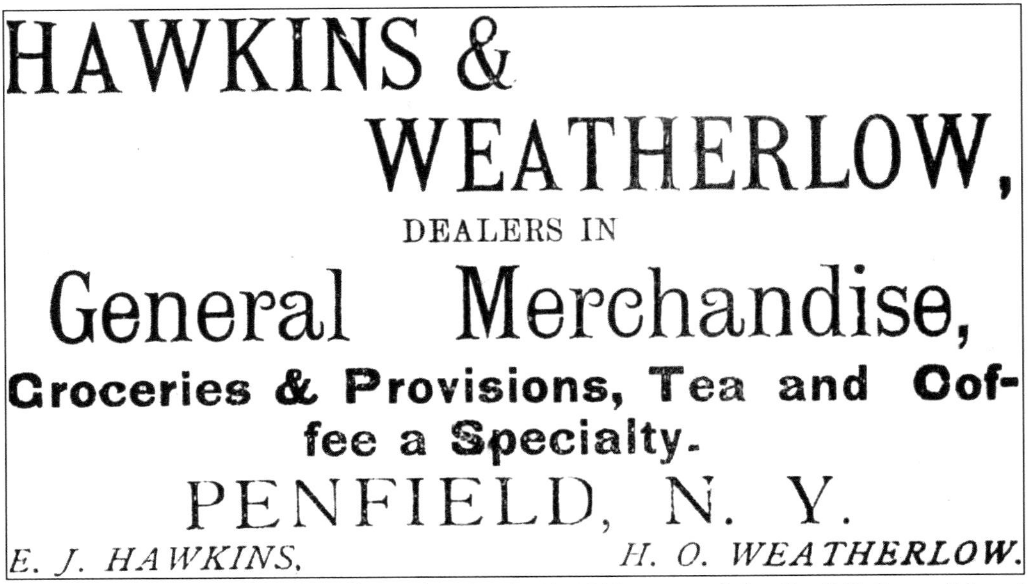

This advertisement was taken from the April 15, 1893, issue of the *Penfield Press*. Edward Hawkins and Hiram Weatherlow operated a general store at the Four Corners. The two men also operated a "general goods wagon," in which they would load up general supplies and deliver them around the Penfield area. After their partnership dissolved, Hawkins moved to New York City to work as a buyer for the company that became Macy's.

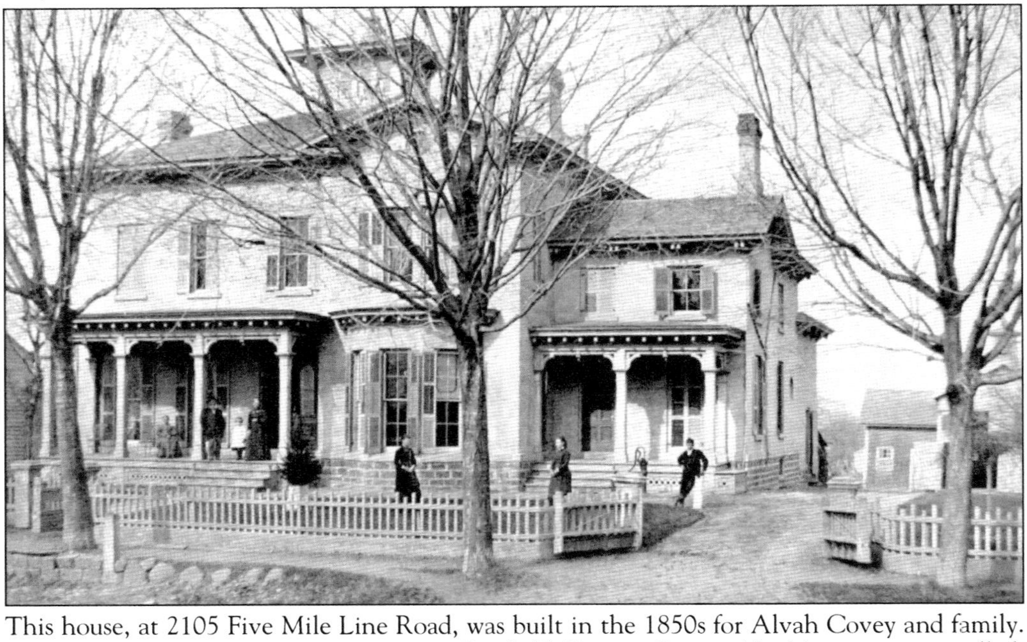

This house, at 2105 Five Mile Line Road, was built in the 1850s for Alvah Covey and family. Born in 1810, Covey was a nurseryman in Penfield. Eugene Covey, Alvah's son, once recalled, "Alvah Covey was a strong Abolitionist and friend of Frederick Douglass. His home was a station on the Underground Railroad, and he often sheltered slaves running away from the south." The road adjacent to the Covey House is aptly named Liberty Street, perhaps since the Covey House was a shelter for newly freed slaves.

The meat market at 2115 Five Mile Line Road was owned by Leo Brahler *c.* 1900. "Little Nellie" Williams operated the *Penfield Extra* in this building in the early to mid-1860s. Samuel Rich and Henry Ward operated a business out of this building in the 1820s. The building was extensively remodeled, and today, Park Side Sports Collectibles and Salon 2111 occupy it.

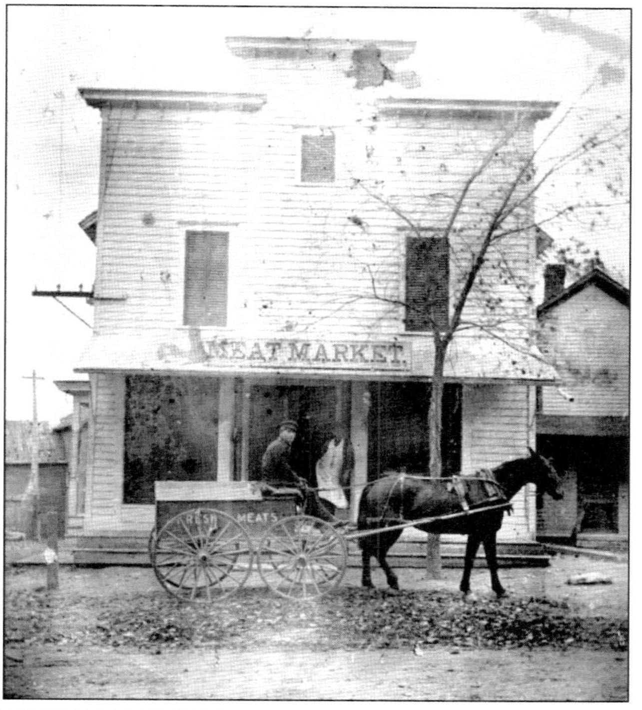

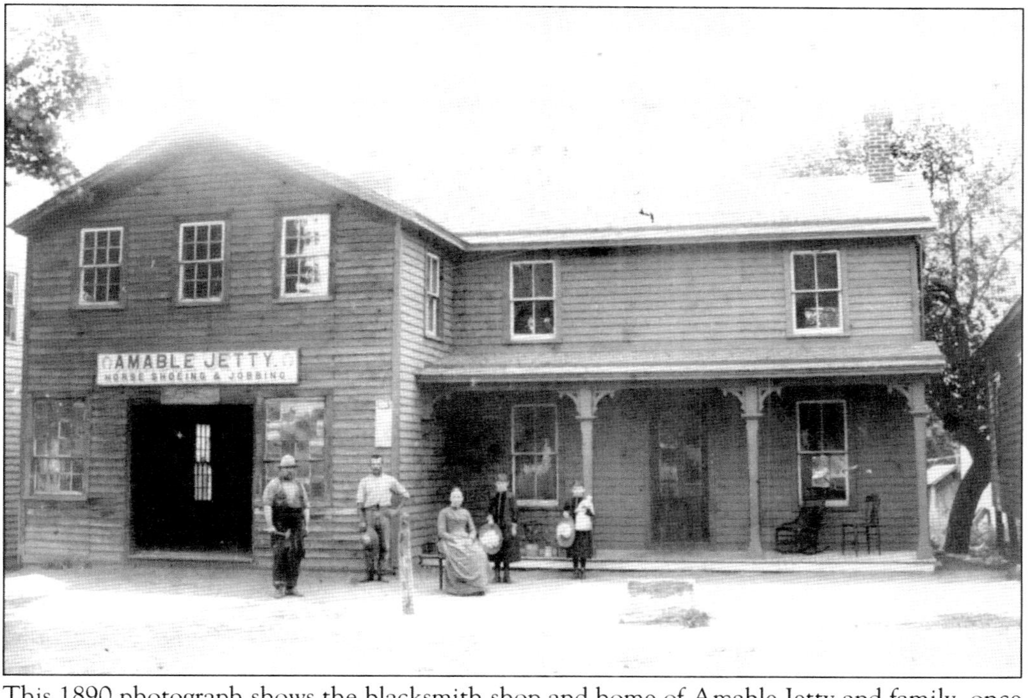

This 1890 photograph shows the blacksmith shop and home of Amable Jetty and family, once located at 2117 Five Mile Line Road, on the west side. Shown here are, from left to right, Amable, Byron, Louise, May, and Delia Jetty. The building remained in the family until 1982 and was razed years later.

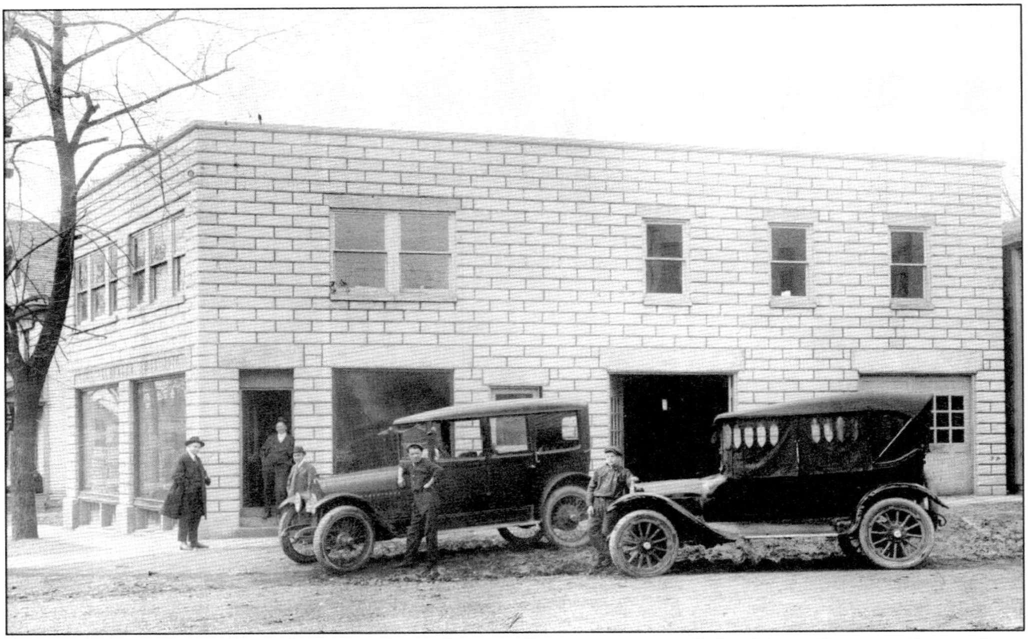

This building, constructed in 1916 on the northwest corner of the Four Corners, housed an Overland car dealership, owned by brothers Ernest and Ameal Schaufelberger. In the early 1800s, the structure that was originally on this lot was called the Globe Building. A. F. Church once wrote, "The old Globe Building—have heard my mother tell about it . . . a rather large building for those times, must have been about 1820, for my mother as a girl attended drawing school taught by Professor Pennyman." The Schaufelberger building was razed in 1992. Today, Schaufelberger Park occupies the lot.

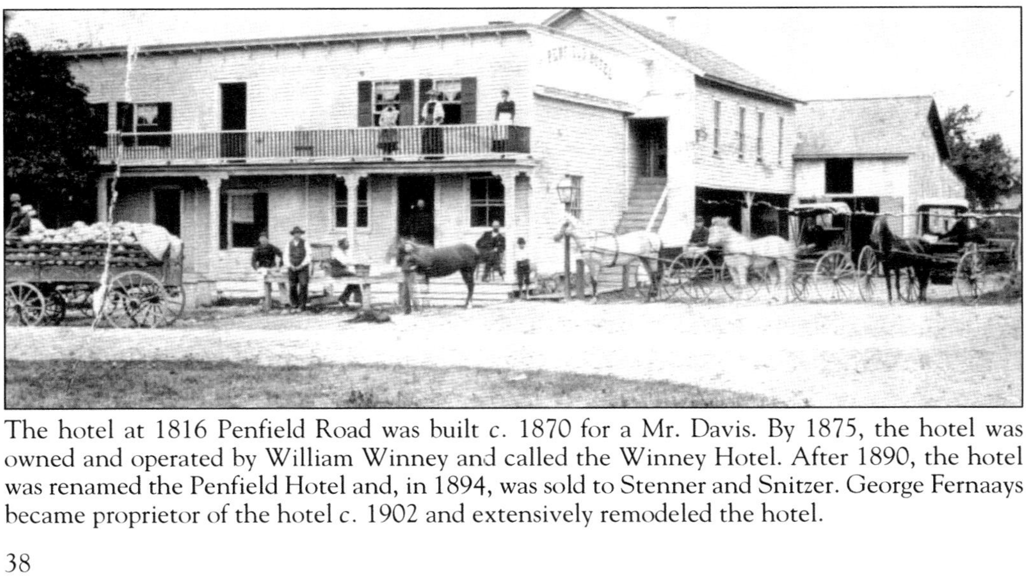

The hotel at 1816 Penfield Road was built *c.* 1870 for a Mr. Davis. By 1875, the hotel was owned and operated by William Winney and called the Winney Hotel. After 1890, the hotel was renamed the Penfield Hotel and, in 1894, was sold to Stenner and Snitzer. George Fernaays became proprietor of the hotel *c.* 1902 and extensively remodeled the hotel.

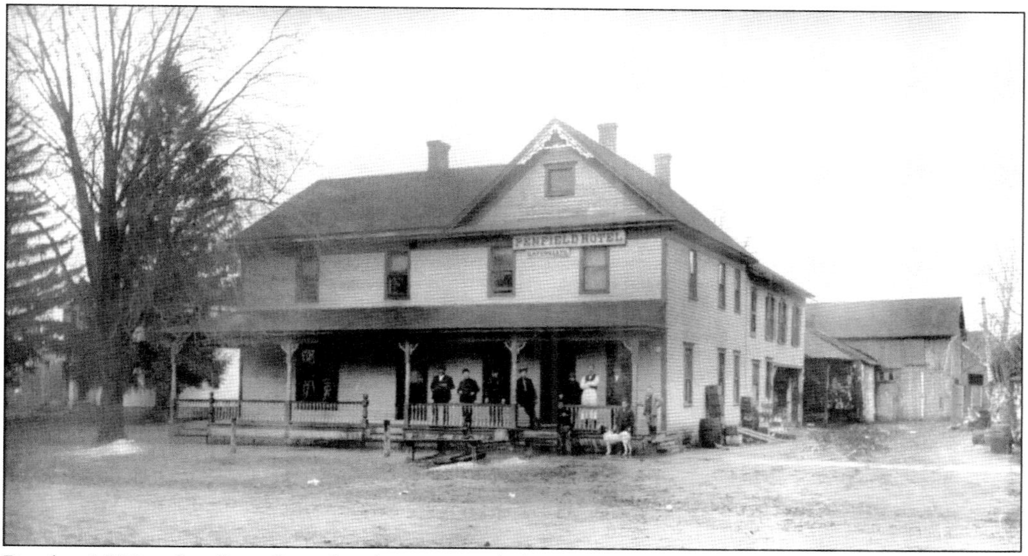

By the 1930s, the Roy Suss family occupied the old hotel and ran a restaurant called the Penfield Tavern. The tavern was torn down in 2003 after being vacant for a couple of years. In 2004, Canandaigua National Bank and Trust built a new structure as it would have looked 100 years earlier.

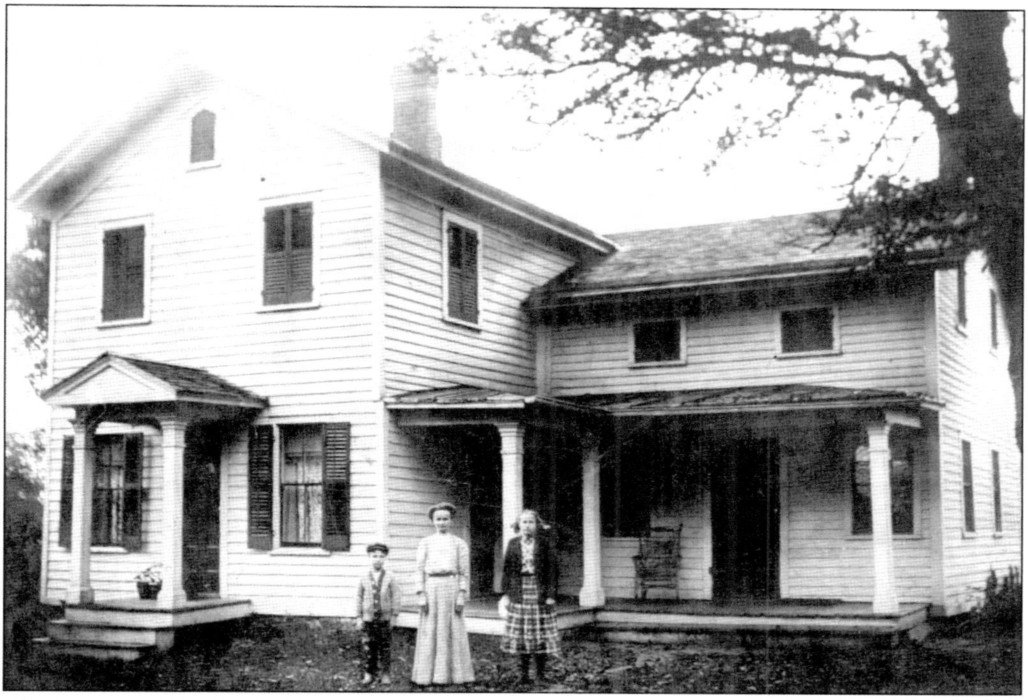

The house at 1802 Penfield Road was owned in the 1870s by George Rundell. There was also a wagon and blacksmith shop on this property during that time. By 1891, Fred Hofer and family owned the house. In 1953, Fred Hofer's son, Harland Hofer, purchased the Overland car dealership from his uncle Ameal Schaufelburger and operated the dealership into the early 1980s.

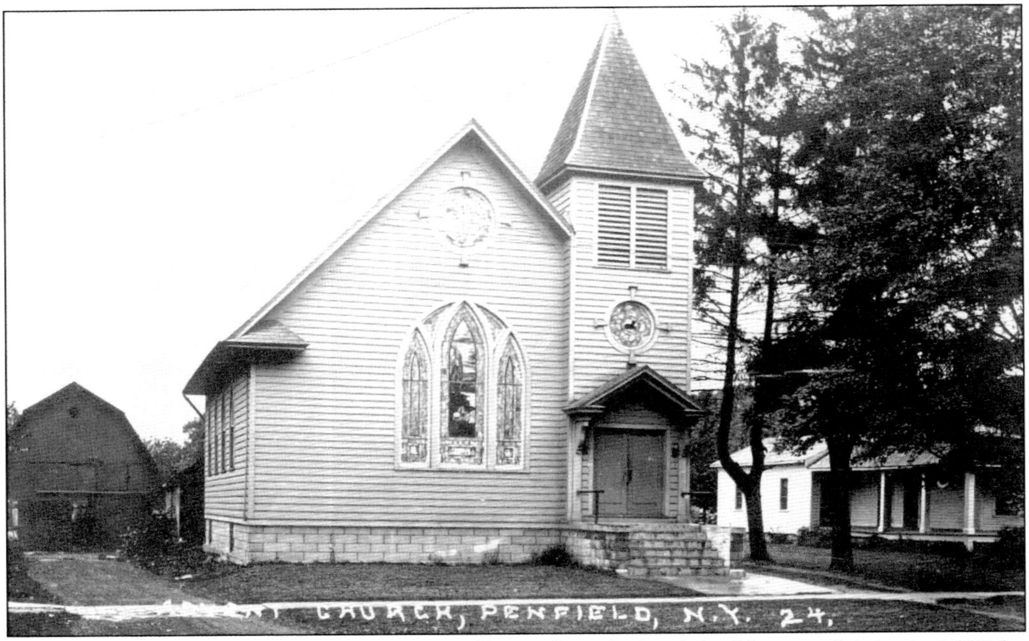

The Advent Christian congregation originally purchased a brick building on this lot in 1895 for church services. The building was once owned by Daniel Penfield, who used the building for his store and office. The church in this photograph was built in 1915 and continued services until 1977. Today, the church structure is used as an office building.

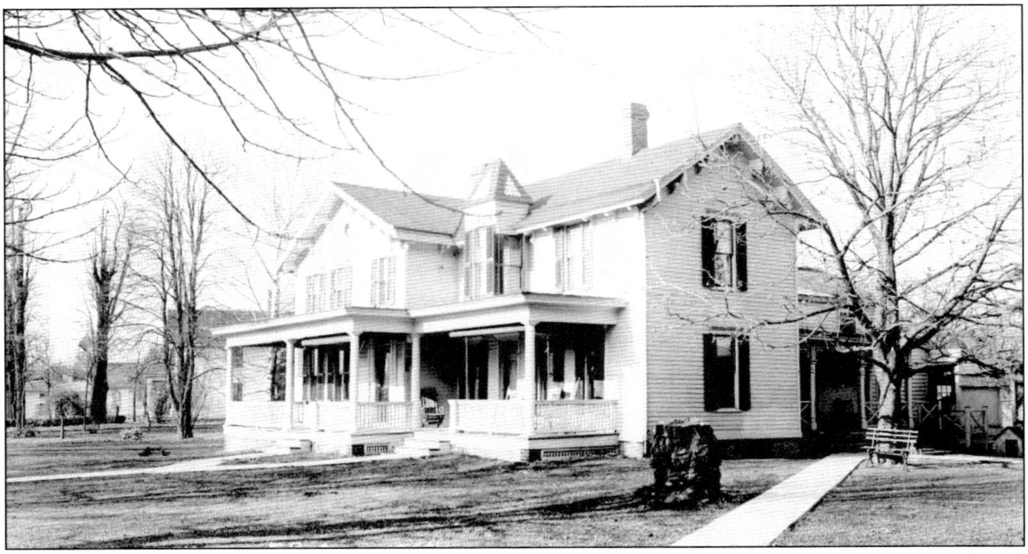

F. E. Ockenden once lived at 1790 Penfield Road. By the late 1940s, Dr. E. S. Deuel and family lived here. The Deuel children—Peter, Geoffrey, and Pamela—gained quite a bit of notoriety. Peter and Geoffrey pursued acting; Pamela, music. Geoffrey was in the 1970 film *Chisum* with John Wayne and continues to act today. Pamela gained success in Christian music. Peter changed his last name to Duel and was in television shows such as *Gidget*, *Love on the Rooftop*, and *Alias Smith and Jones*. Sadly, on New Years Eve 1971, Peter died at the age of 31. He is buried near his parents in Oakwood Cemetery.

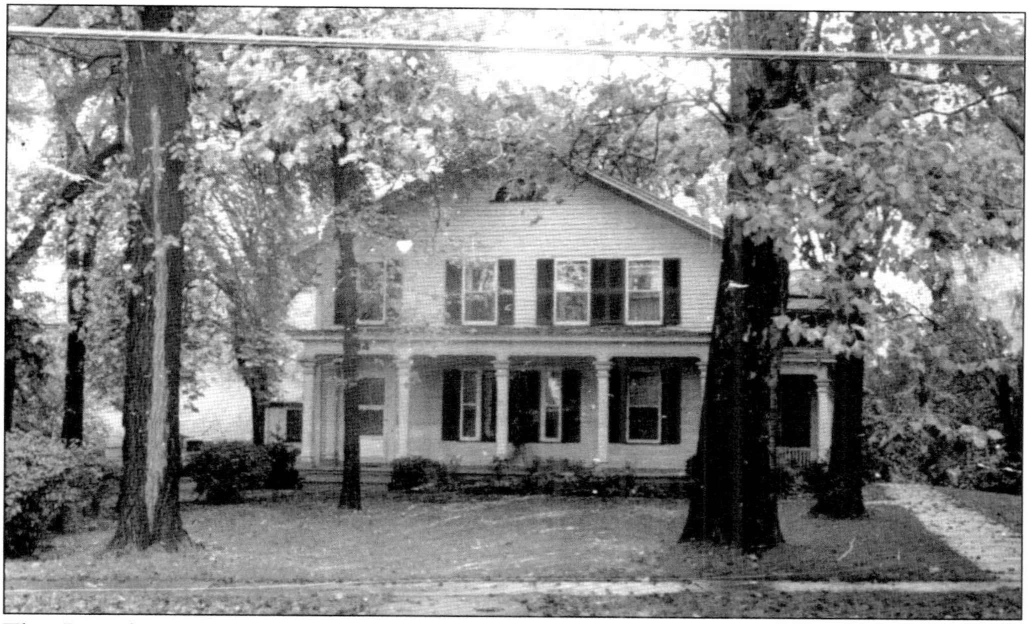

The Daniel Penfield House, located at 1784 Penfield Road, was built *c.* 1811. When it was built, it was considered to be the finest house in all of Monroe County. By 1902, it was purchased by Horace and Mary Ranney. In later years, it became home to a restaurant named the Yellow Rose Café. Today, Salon Enza occupies the house. The Penfield House was designated as a Penfield landmark in 2003.

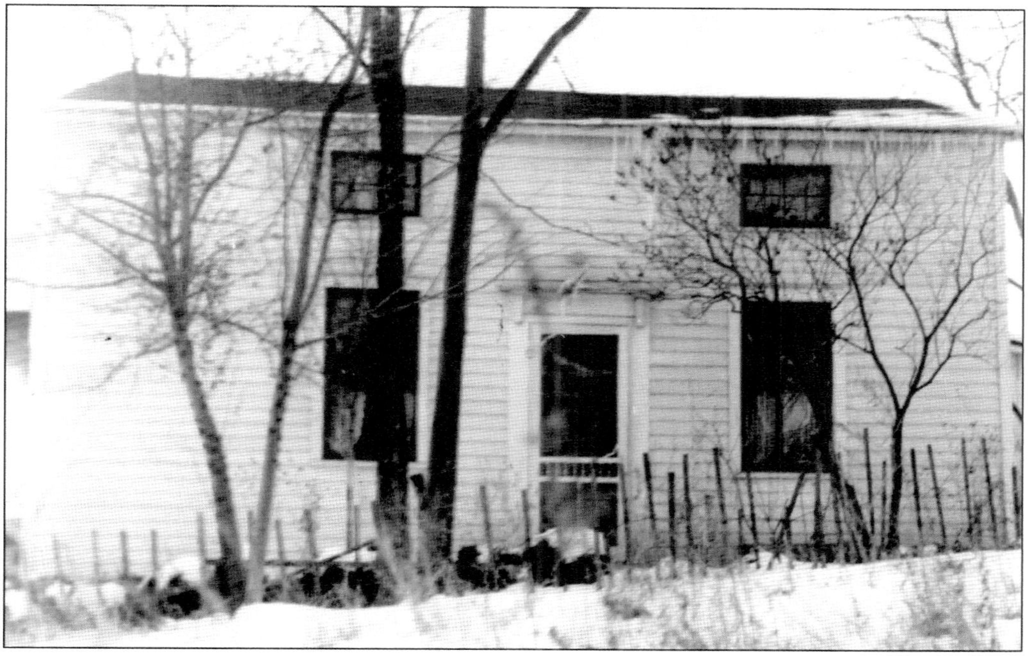

This house once stood at 1775 Penfield Road, across from the St. Joseph's Cemetery. Originally, it was a wing on the Daniel Penfield House. Today, a restaurant named the Legends Grill occupies the lot.

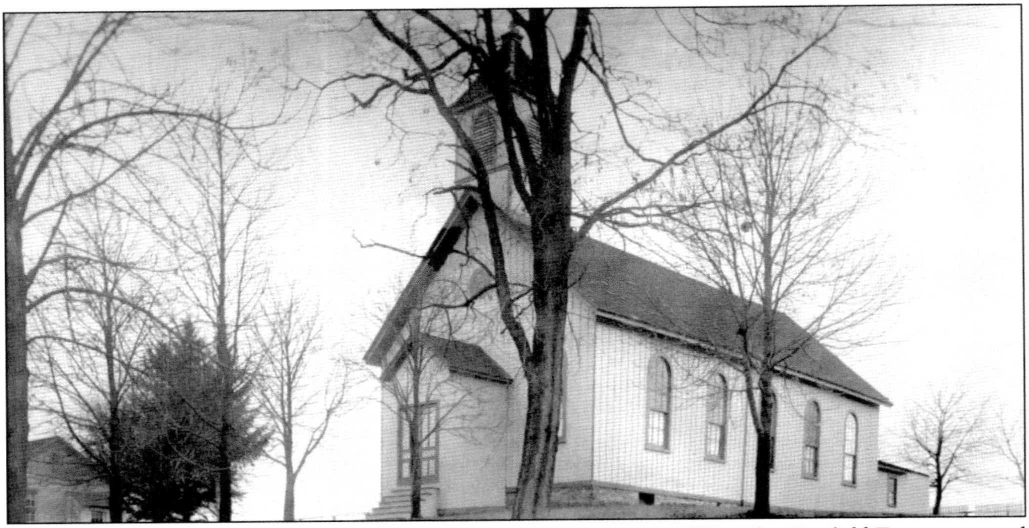

The first St. Joseph's Catholic Church in Penfield was built in 1872. The *Penfield Extra* reported in the August 10, 1865, issue, "CATHOLIC CHURCH—we are soon to have a new Catholic church in town and a German school. The site has been purchased [and] preparations are now being made for building. The site is known as Hunt Hill, about a quarter of a mile west of our main corners, a rather pleasant location."

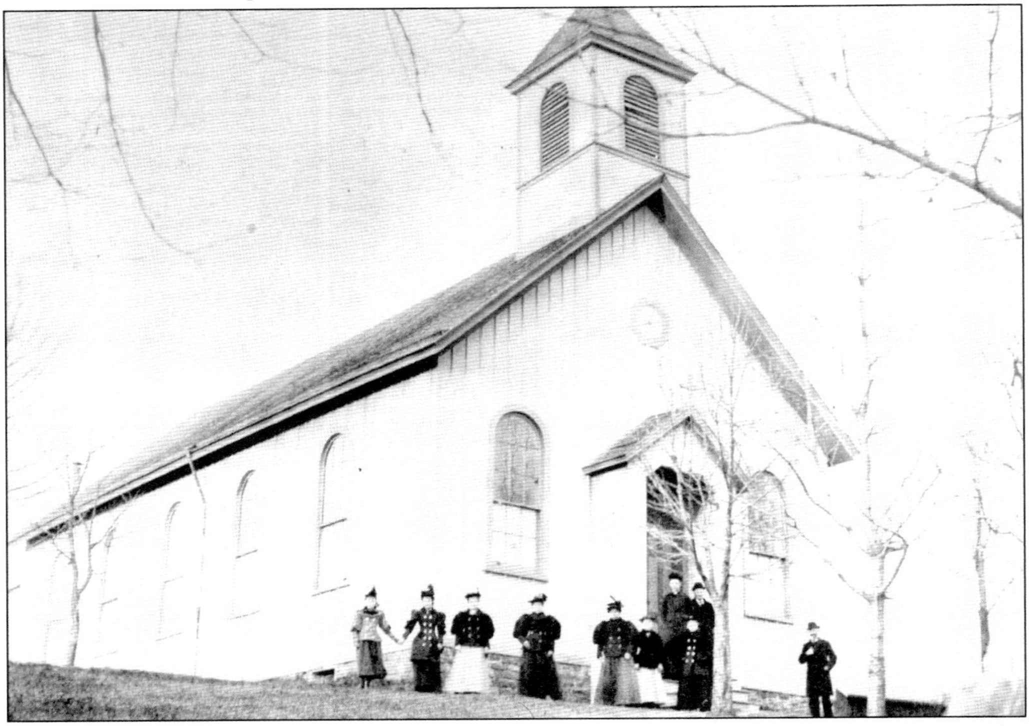

The "little white church on Hunt Hill" stood for 98 years. This image from 1895 shows the Weicher Sisters Choir and Reverend Boppel. The first couple to be married in the church was Jacob Stenner and Sophia Schmitt, on August 14, 1876. The St. Joseph's Catholic Cemetery still occupies the land on Hunt Hill.

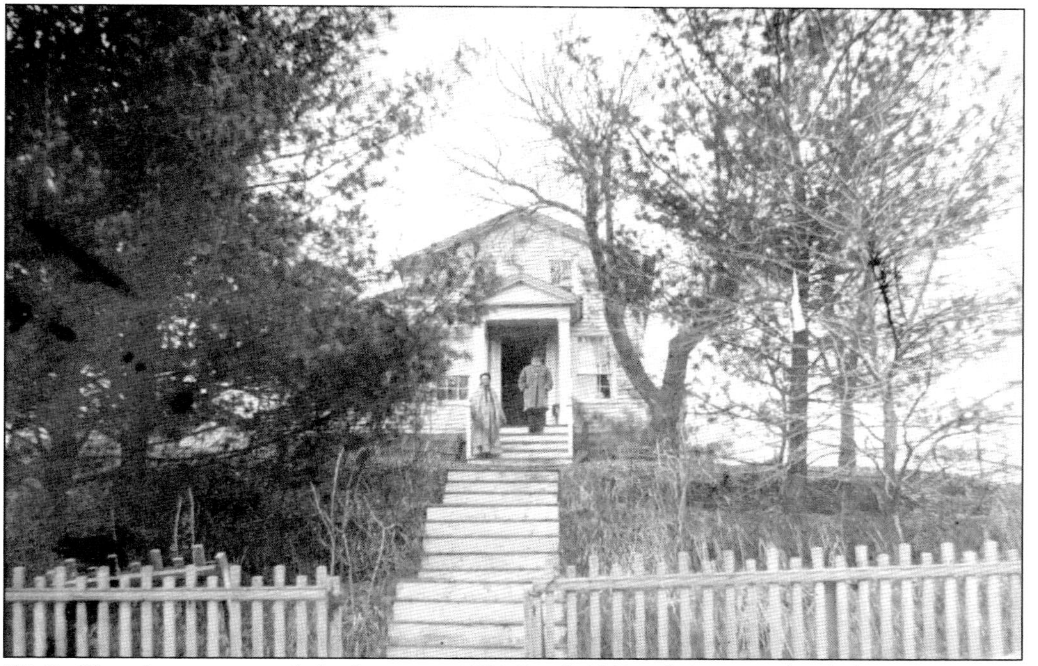

W. F. Church once owned the house at 1770 Penfield Road. He was the father of Aristides Frances "Tide" Church, a carpenter and a diary keeper of daily events around Penfield for more than 40 years. In 1919, A. F. Church was appointed as the first official historian of the town. He died in Penfield in 1937.

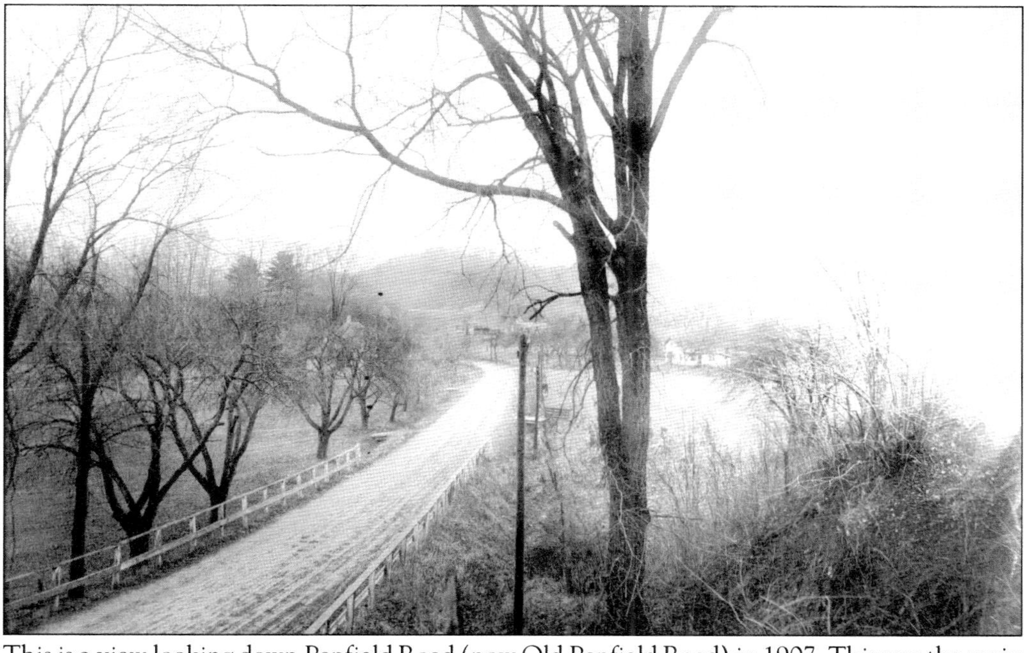

This is a view looking down Penfield Road (now Old Penfield Road) in 1907. This was the main route from Penfield's Four Corners to the city of Rochester.

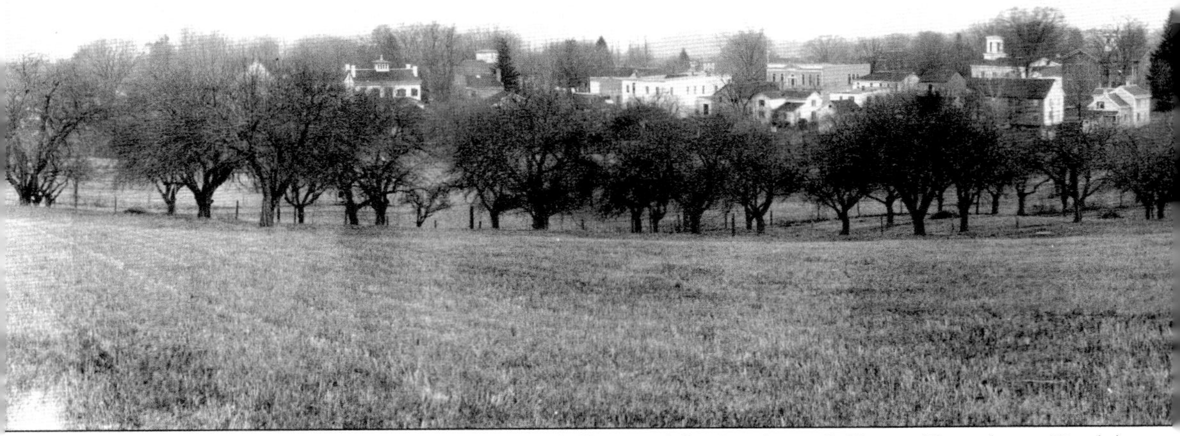

This photograph was taken in 1907 from a hill west of the Southworth House (Strawberry Castle),

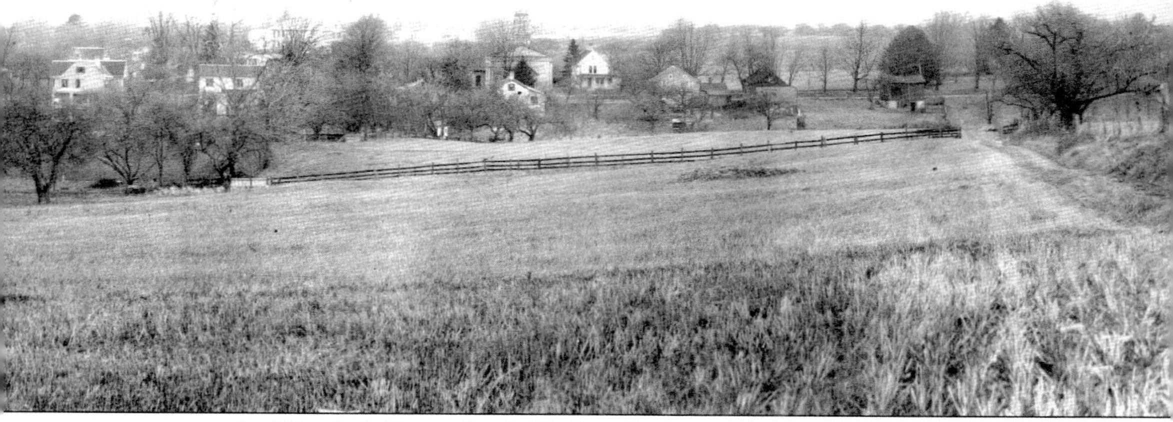
now atop present-day Woodside Drive. Penfield's Four Corners and surroundings are visible.

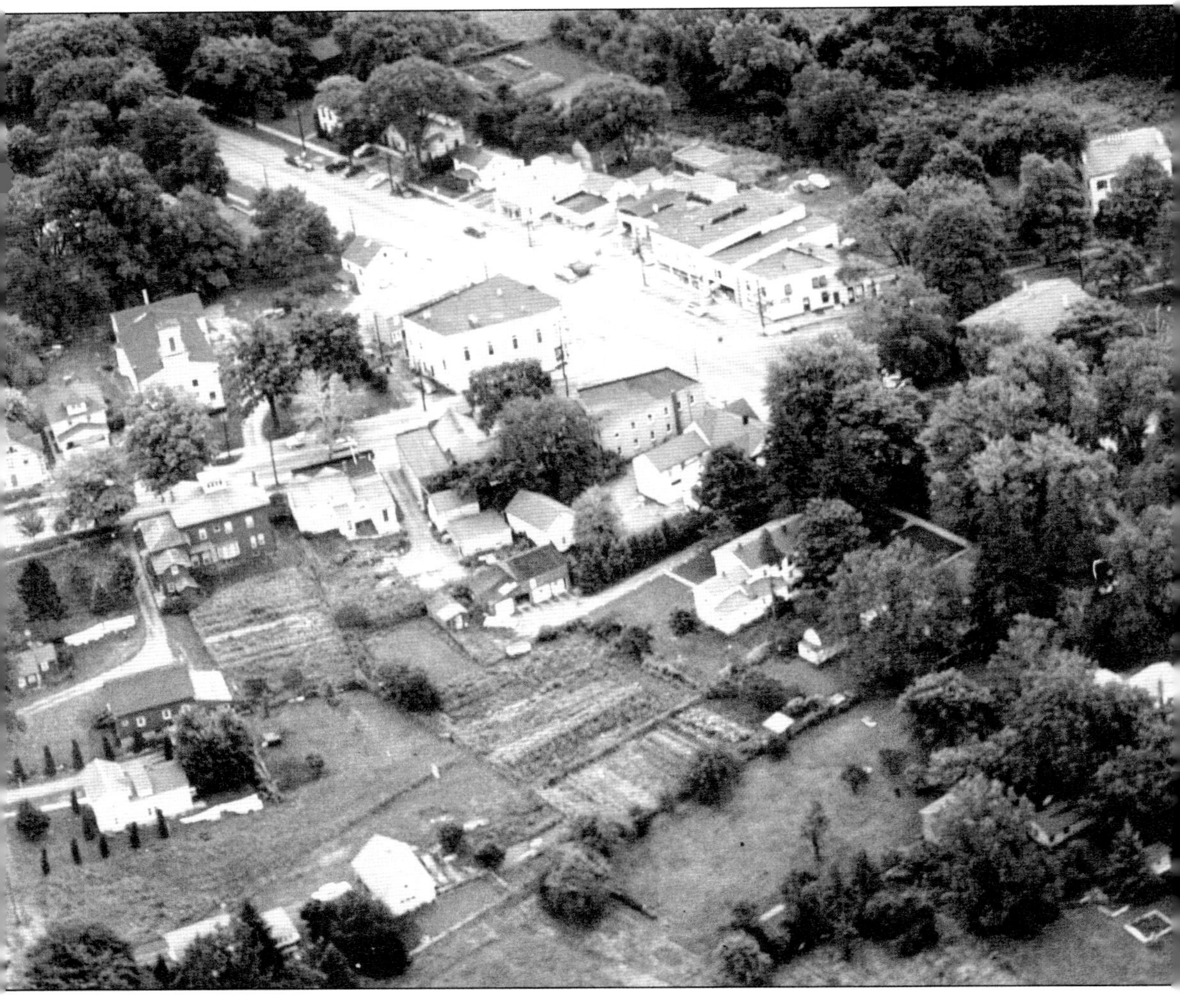

This aerial view of the Four Corners looks southeast more than 60 years ago. Large oak trees once lined the streets at Four Corners. Most of the trees on Penfield Road were removed when the road was widened.

Three

Mills of the Irondequoit

Penfield, in the early days was a busy place; with its mills and factories. The Irondequoit creek was fine water power and its banks were lined with all sorts of industries. Penfield, as a part of the Genesee country was noted for the excellent quality of its wheat and the flour mills did a thriving business.

—A. F. Church, March 28, 1935

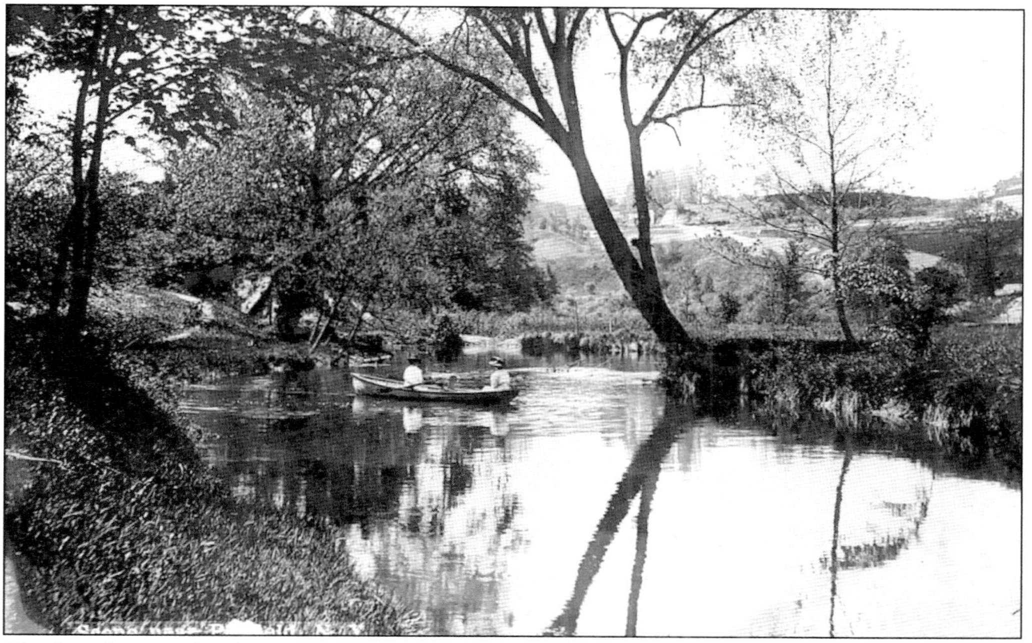

The Irondequoit Creek was primarily used to power the mills, but Penfielders also used the creek for recreation.

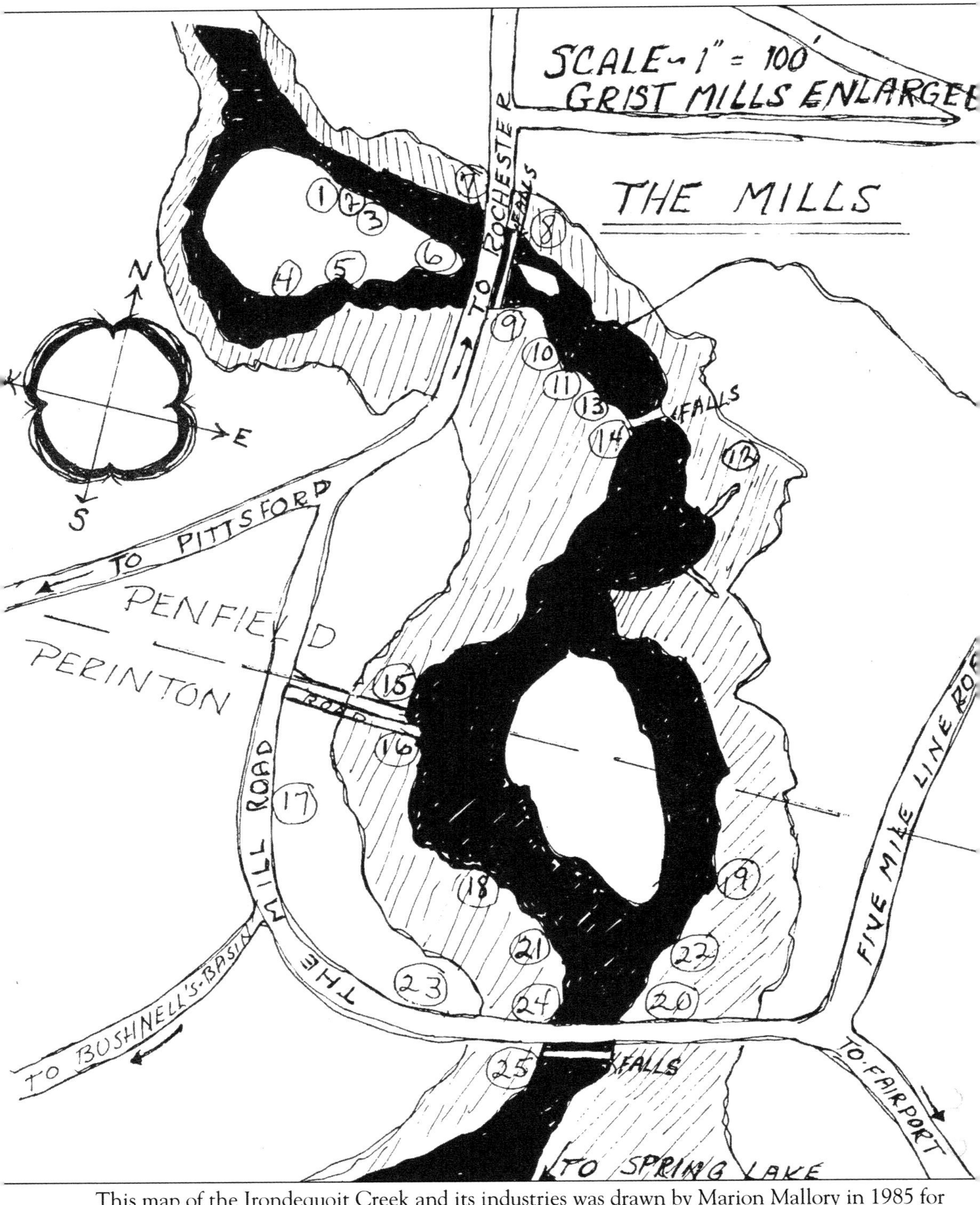

This map of the Irondequoit Creek and its industries was drawn by Marion Mallory in 1985 for the Penfield Local History Room display entitled "The Mills on the Irondequoit."

MILLS AND RELATED INDUSTRIES ALONG
ONE MILE OF IRONDEQUOIT CREEK

Starting at the "Hollow"

1. Triphammer - Abram Bronson - 1800
2. Sawmill - built by Eli Lyon for Daniel Penfield in 1800
3. Sawmill - Jacob Westerman - 1872
4. Ashery - a cash crop for settlers
5. Oil mill and soap factory
6. Distillery - Wm. McKinstry - 1804
7. "Yellow Mill" - flouring mill - 1814 Daniel Penfield's - It burned, was repainted and became the "White Mill"

Old Washington Street

8. Clothing mill - Josiah Kellogg - 1805
9. Grist mill - Daniel Penfield - 1803
10. Distillery
11. Tannery - Fellows & Keyes - 1820
12. Blacksmithy - Peter Auchampaugh
13. Woolen mill - Levi Duncan
14. Livingston Mill - flouring mill in 1836, later became Lawless Paper Mill
15. Slaughter house - S. C. Carpenter

Perinton Town Line

16. Carding mill - S. C. Carpenter
17. Cooperage - Isaac Mott
18. Ironworks - John Coles
19. Forge - John Coles
20. Sawmill and shingle factory
21. Carding mill - 1835
22. Tannery - Lincoln & Arey - 1852
23. Sawmill - Rich, Lincoln & Lathrop
24. Flouring mill - Andrew Lincoln - 1847
25. Grist mill - Rich, Lincoln & Lathrop 1821

Because the course of the creek has been changed in recent years, it is difficult to pinpoint exact locations. Mills also existed in other sections of Penfield. The Daisy Flour Mill on Blossom Road is the only mill structure still standing.

This list of mills and related industries on the Irondequoit Creek corresponds to the map on the previous page.

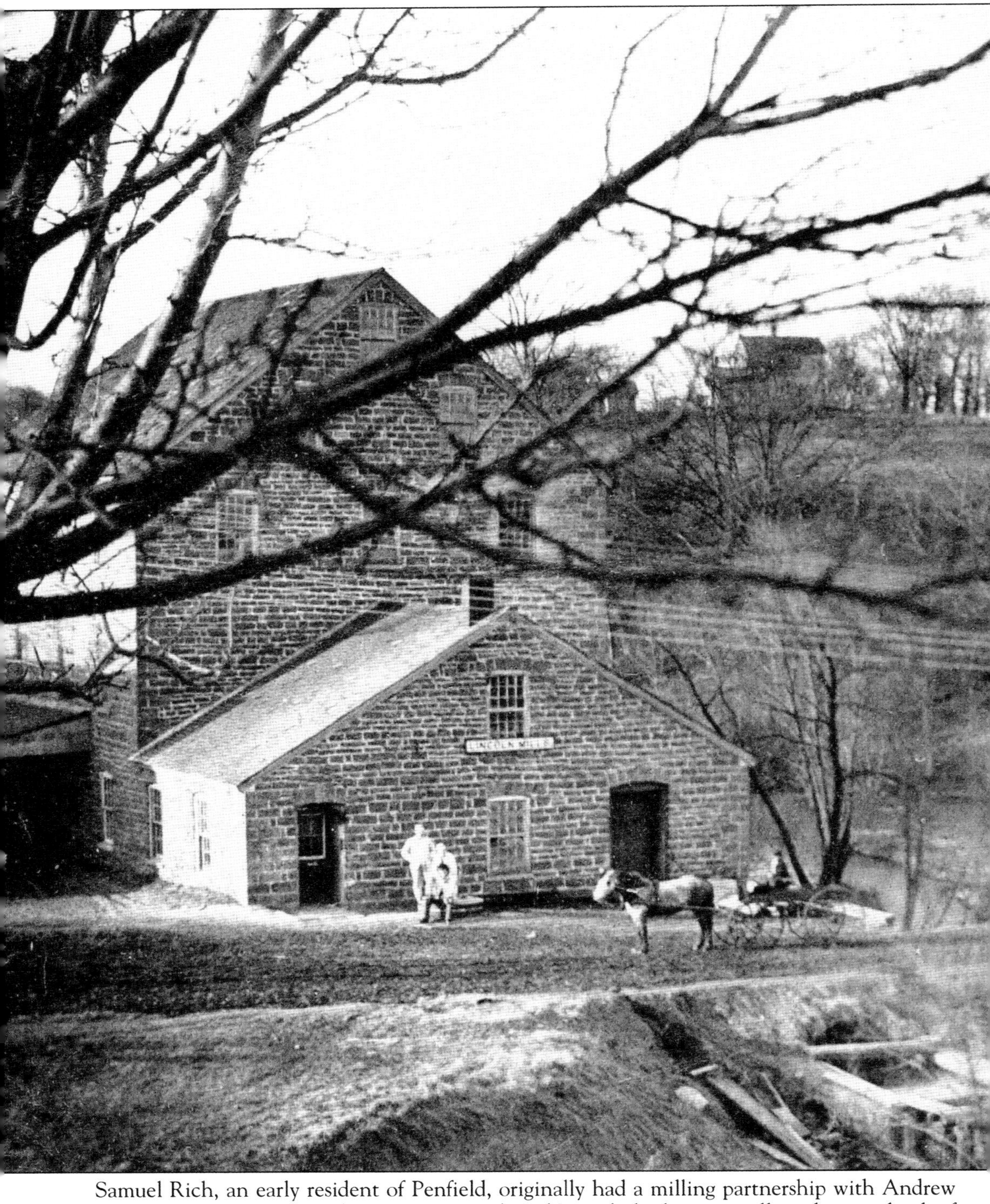

Samuel Rich, an early resident of Penfield, originally had a milling partnership with Andrew Lincoln, another early resident. In 1821, Rich and Lincoln built a gristmill on the west bank of the Irondequoit Creek on the Perinton-Penfield line. Their partnership dissolved by 1847, and the gristmill was subsequently washed away in a flood. Lincoln then built a flour mill, again on

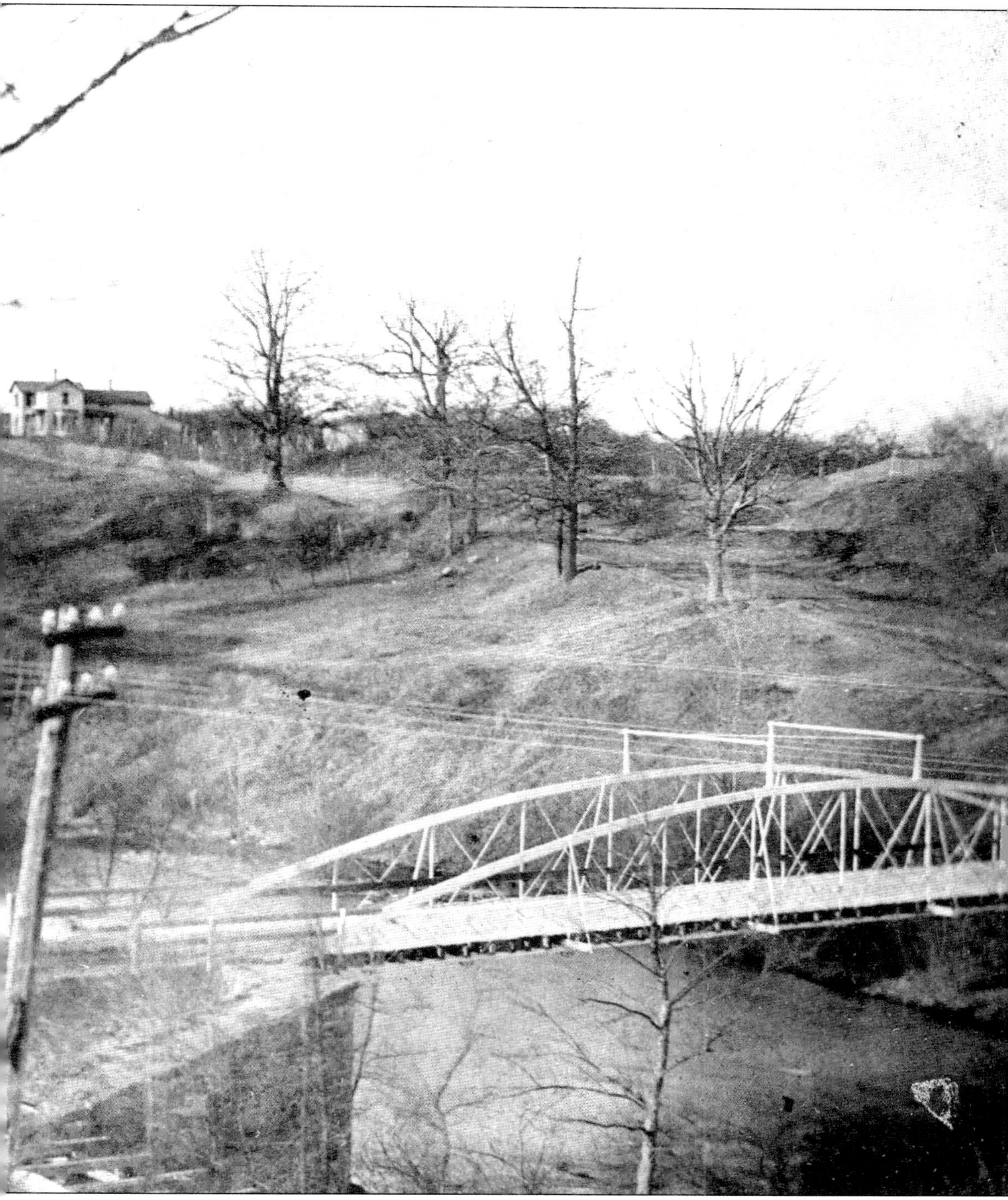

the west bank, shown here. Rich moved downstream and built a set of mills. The old Lincoln Bridge can also be seen, and the homes in the background are on Five Mile Line Road, leading north into Penfield's Four Corners.

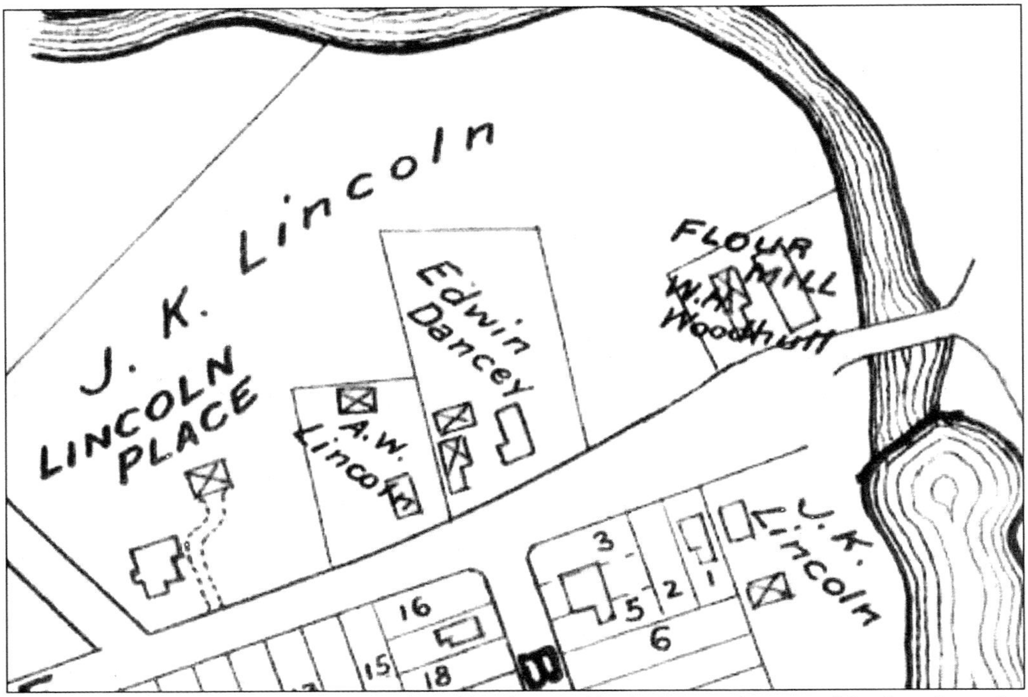

This map shows the Irondequoit Creek and land owned by J. K. Lincoln, son of Andrew Lincoln. The map is from the 1902 *Plat Book of Monroe County, N.Y.*, by J. M. Lathrop and Company. By 1902, the Lincoln Mill was operated by W. H. Woodhull, who continued to run the mill until a fire broke out *c.* 1920 and burned the interior of the mill. In the 1920s, the Rochester Gas and Electric Company took over the building for storage purposes while using the creek for the waterpower.

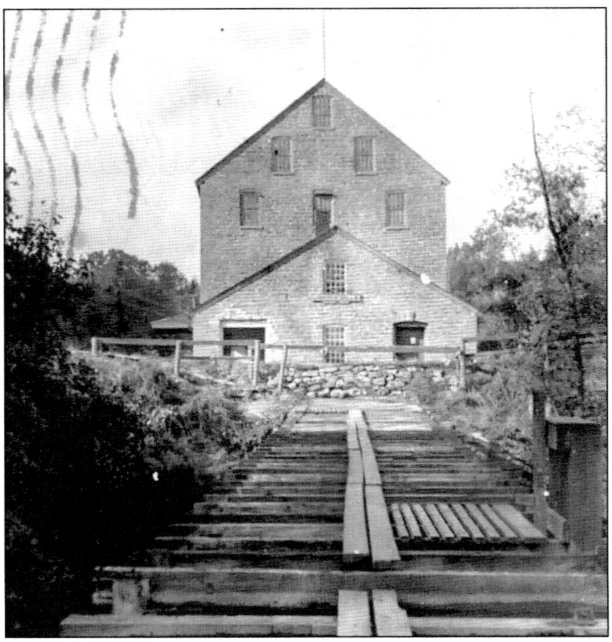

This image shows the Lincoln Mill, along with the millrace flume that ran from Lincoln Pond, under the road, and into the mill. A. F. Church once recalled, "On the left side across the [Five Mile Line] road was the Lincoln Mill and one of the largest mills on the stream. A stone building . . . with sheds and store houses, in those years did a thriving business."

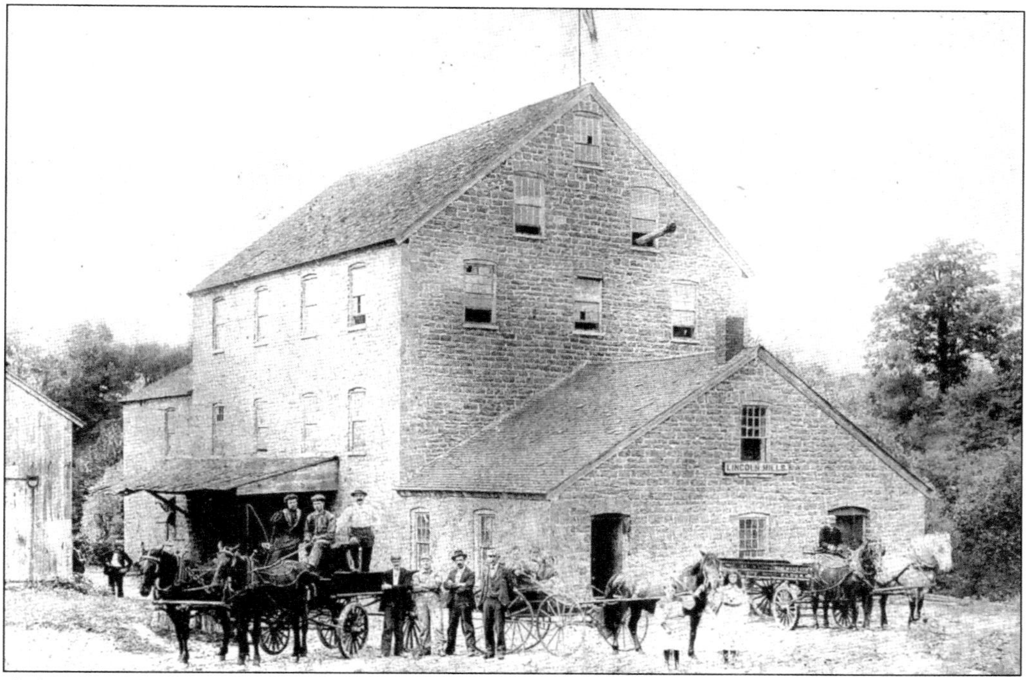

"[The Lincoln Mill employed] two and most of the time three millers, besides bookkeepers, teamsters, and other help. They used to haul their flour to Fairport and shipped it [via the Erie Canal] to New York, Boston, and other places." —A. F. Church, March 1919.

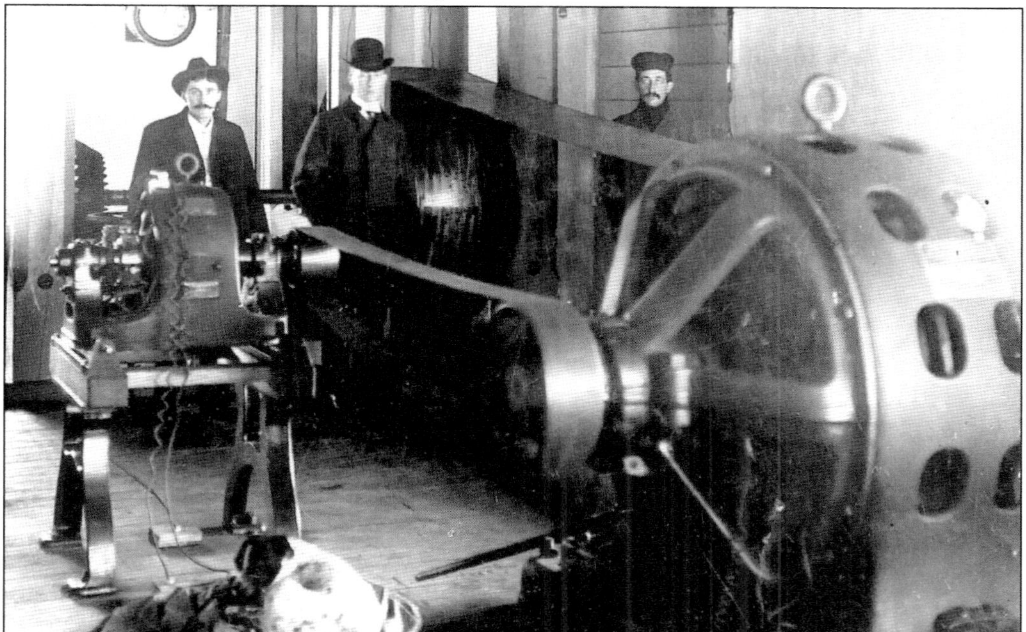

After many years, a dynamo was installed in the Lincoln Mill. Shep, the dog in this picture, once helped save two children from drowning in the Irondequoit Creek. His barking alerted some nearby mill workers, who rescued the children.

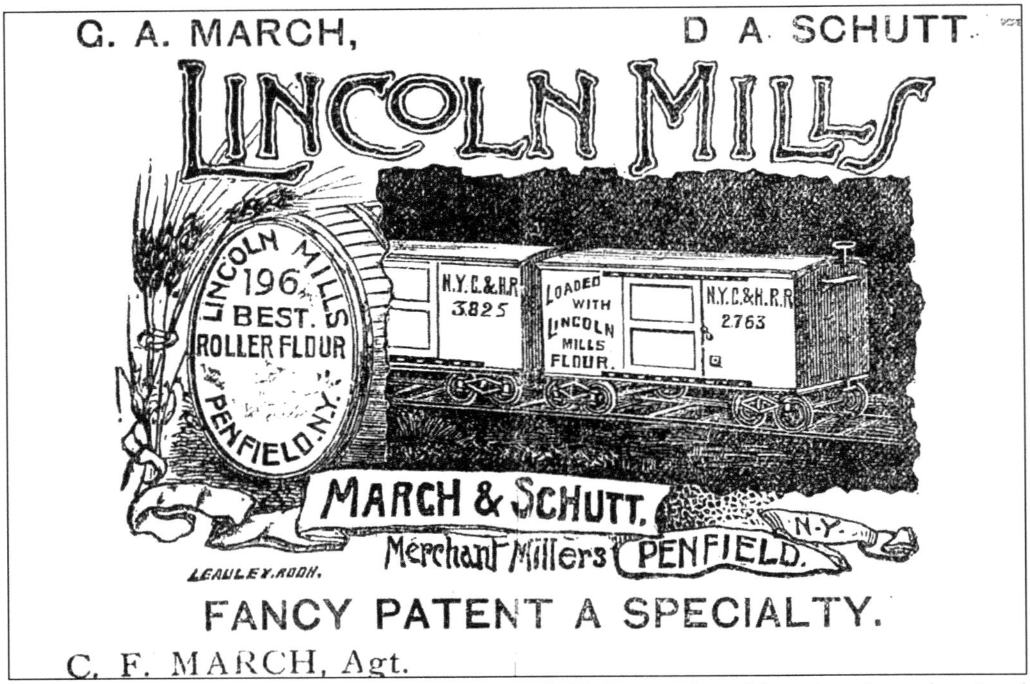

Many considered the Lincoln Mill to be in Penfield (hence the address listed on this April 15, 1893, *Penfield Press* advertisement), but it was not. The flour produced in the mills on the Irondequoit Creek was either taken to Fairport and shipped on the Erie Canal or was taken by railway. The closest railroad station in those days was at Penfield Station (present-day East Rochester). In 1897, the village of Despatch was built and became the new name of the railway station.

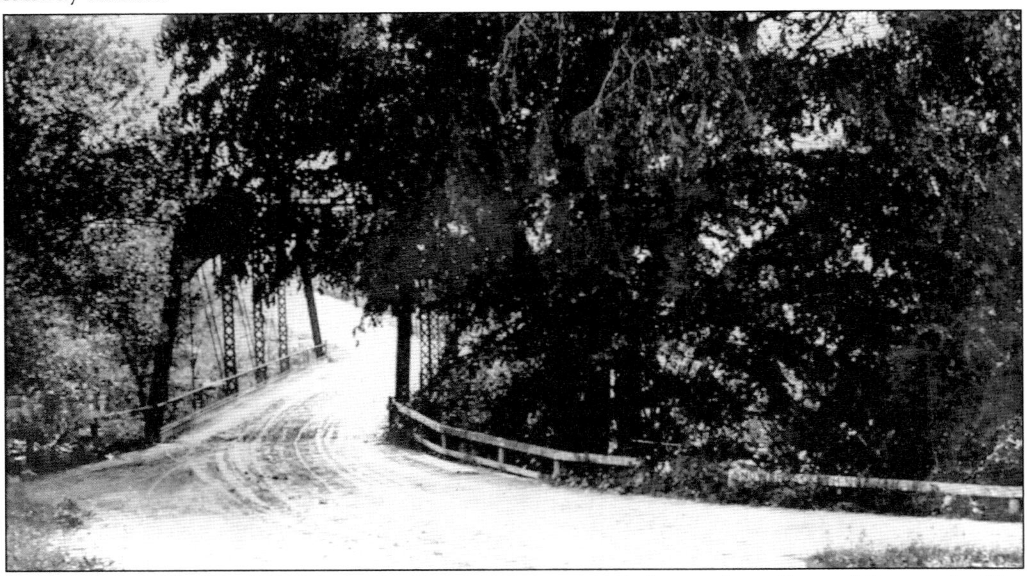

The route across the old Lincoln Bridge, traveling west, led into the village of Despatch. The northeast lane across the bridge led into Penfield's Four Corners, and the southeast lane led into the village of Fairport. The Linden Avenue Bridge now spans this location.

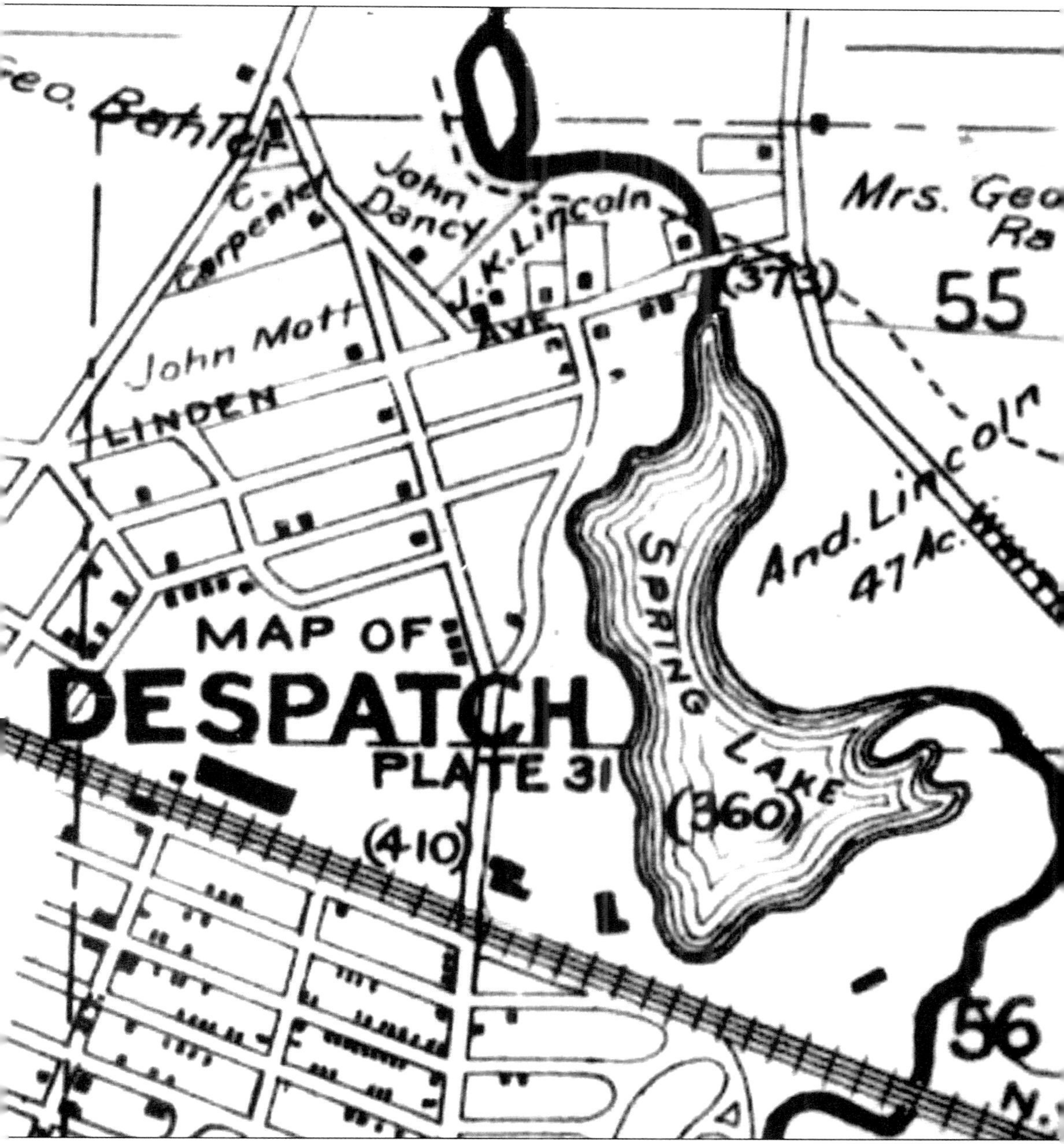

This map of Spring Lake and Despatch is from the 1902 *Plat Book of Monroe County, N.Y.*, by J. M. Lathrop and Company. "The Lincoln Pond, afterwards known as Spring Lake, while not in Penfield, was so near we always called it ours. It was said to cover about 60 acres and furnished, in summer, the finest bathing and swimming pools, boating, and fishing grounds. In the winter, it was noted for miles around as a skating park." —A. F. Church, March 28, 1935.

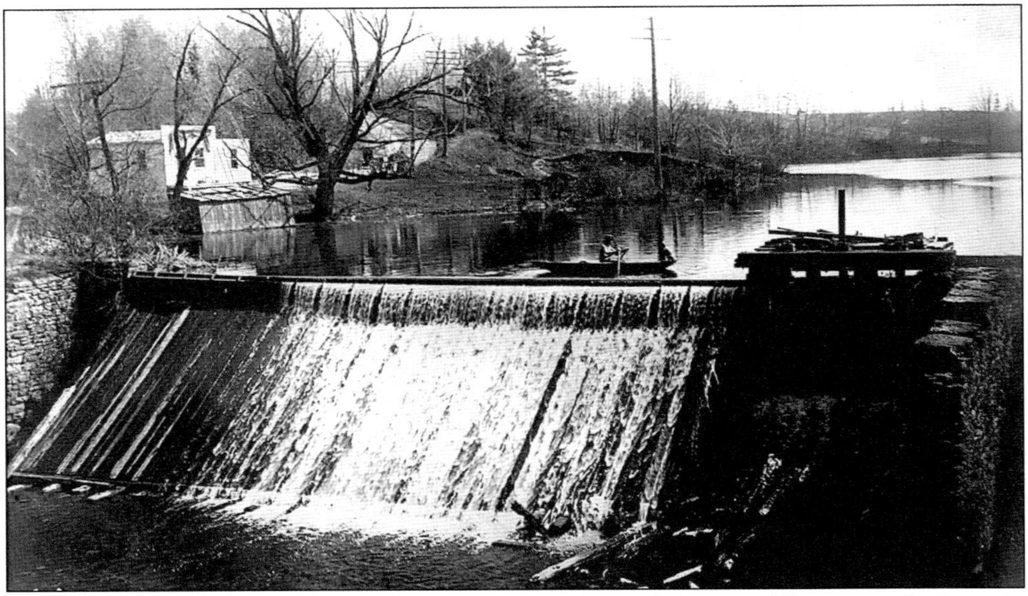

Harry Ludwig, a farmer who lived on Atlantic Avenue, can be seen paddling up to the Lincoln Dam, on Spring Lake. The Pond Lily was the white building on the east bank of the millpond. This building was used for a saloon. The Pond Lily burned on November 11, 1916.

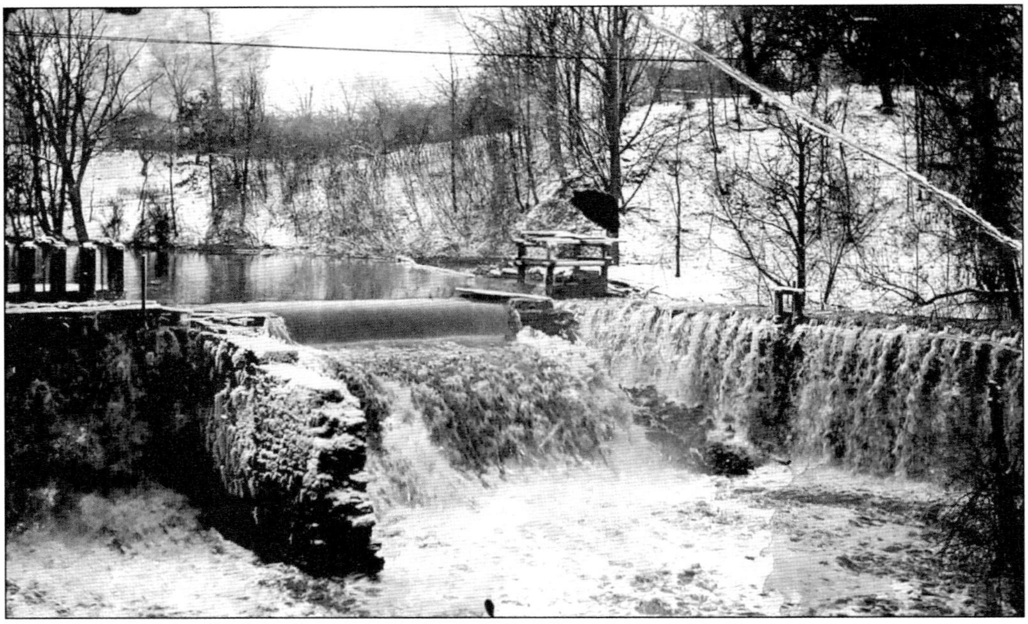

Grace Raymond, who lived on Five Mile Line Road across from the Lincoln Mills, recalled in a 1940 article, "Early one morning in March 1916, we heard an awful roar and knew at once what had taken place. There was an ice jam and a spring flood and the [Lincoln] dam went out. The gates were raised but the pressure was too great and the end had come."

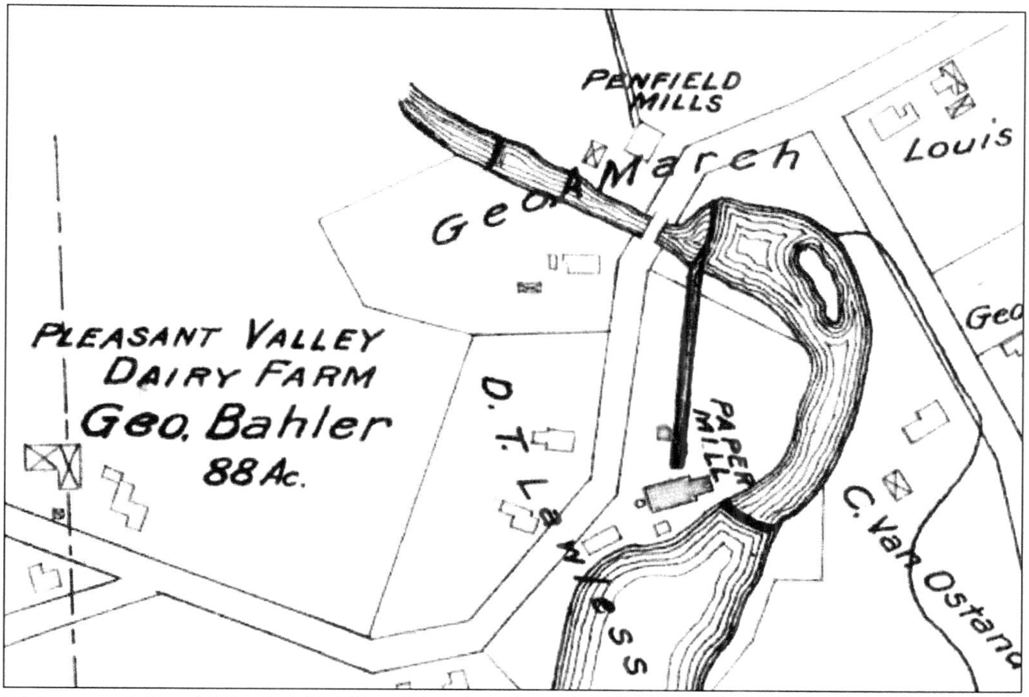

This map of the old Penfield Mill and Lawless Paper Mill is from the 1902 *Plat Book of Monroe County*, N.Y., by J. M. Lathrop and Company.

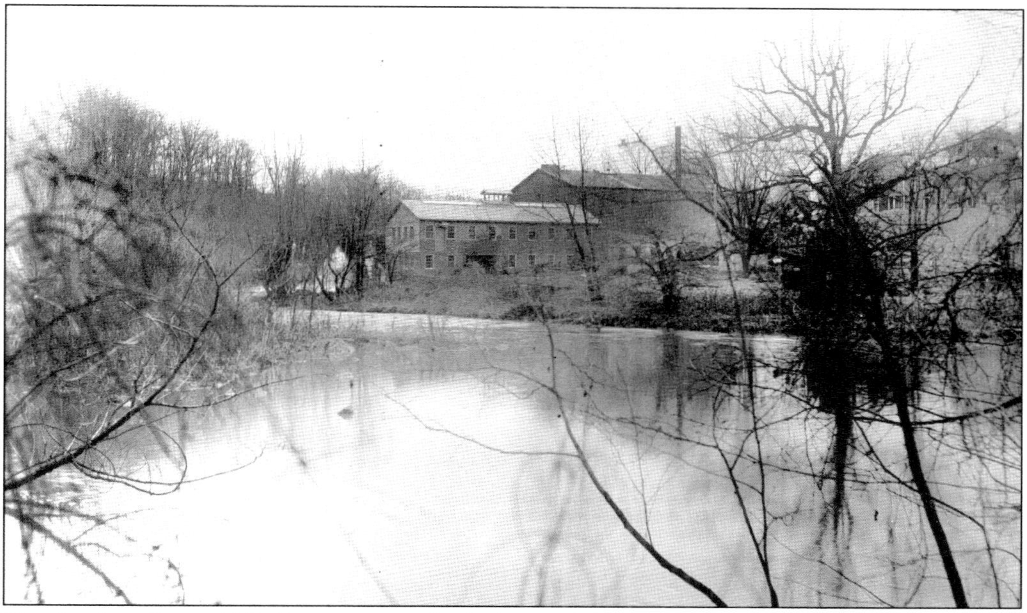

The Lawless Paper Mill Company was built (around 1836) on the site of the old Livingston Mill, once owned by James K. Livingston. At the time the Livingston Mill was built at a cost of $40,000, it was considered to be the finest flouring mill in western New York, outside of Rochester. Three fires destroyed the mill, and it was rebuilt by new owners between 1868 and 1880. After the third fire, David T. Lawless acquired the mill site.

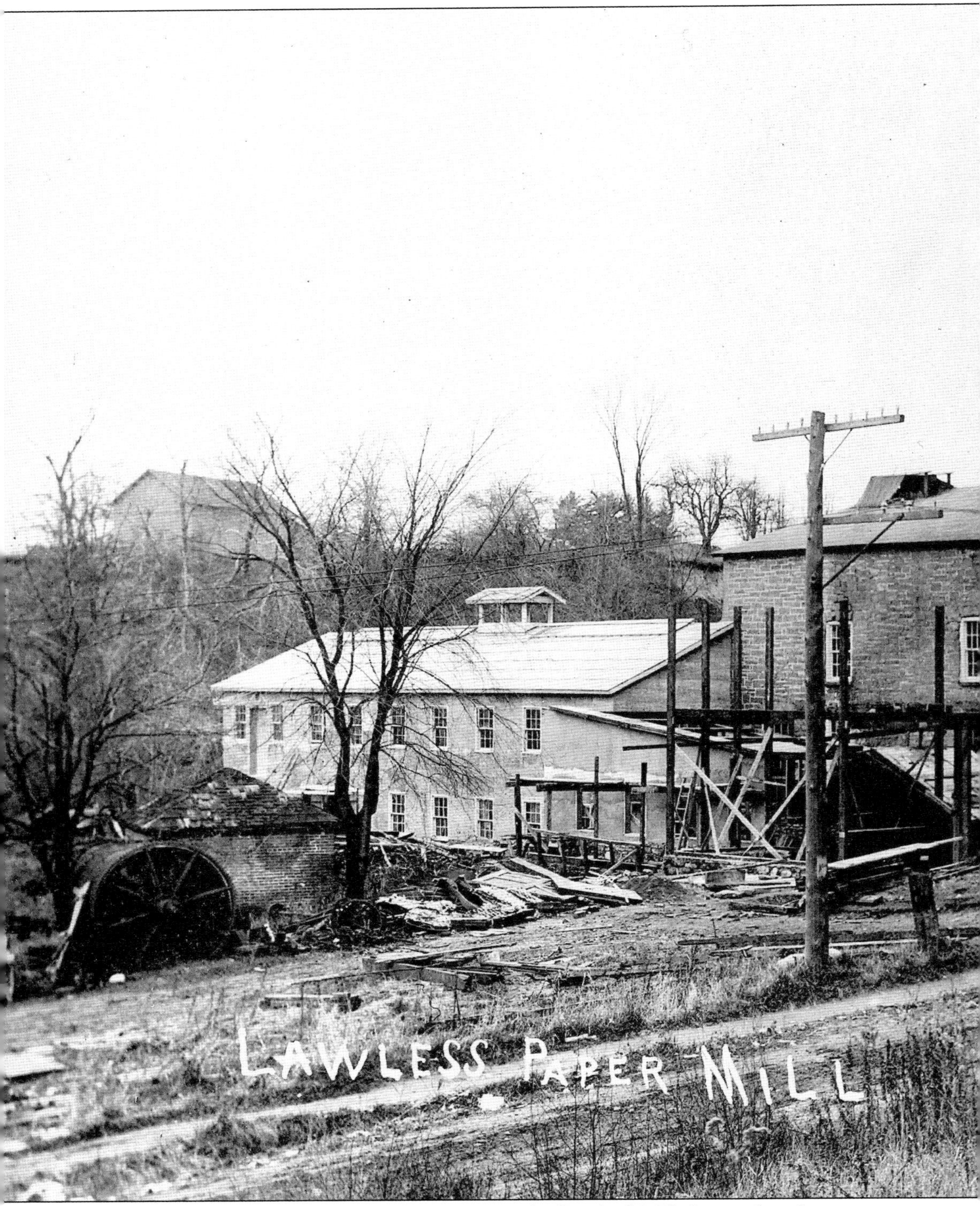

Will Church once recalled, "One day in passing the [Lawless] Mill, I saw a big chimney going up

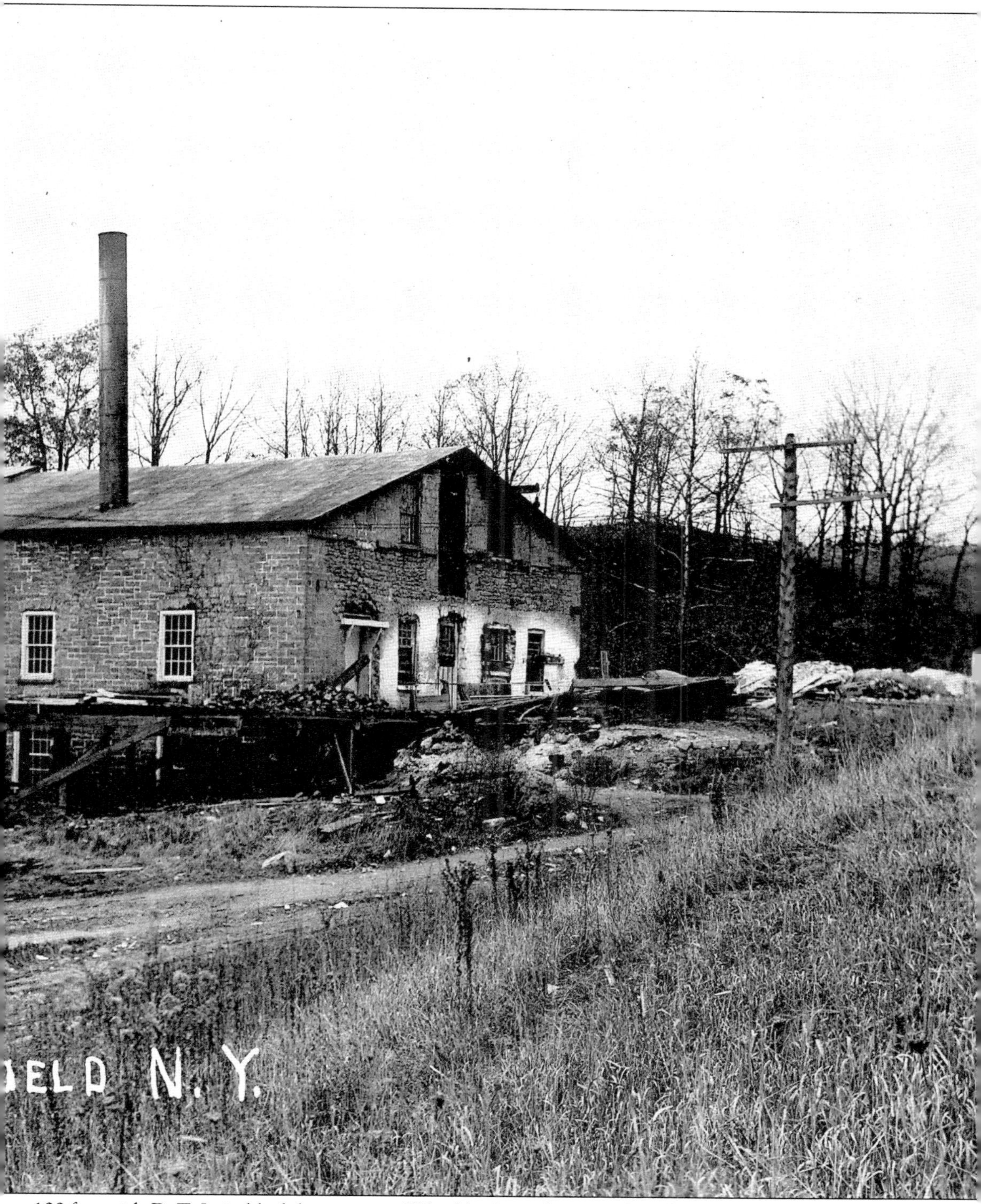

100 feet with D. T. L. in black letters on it. Why [the letters] weren't [Irish] Green was beyond me."

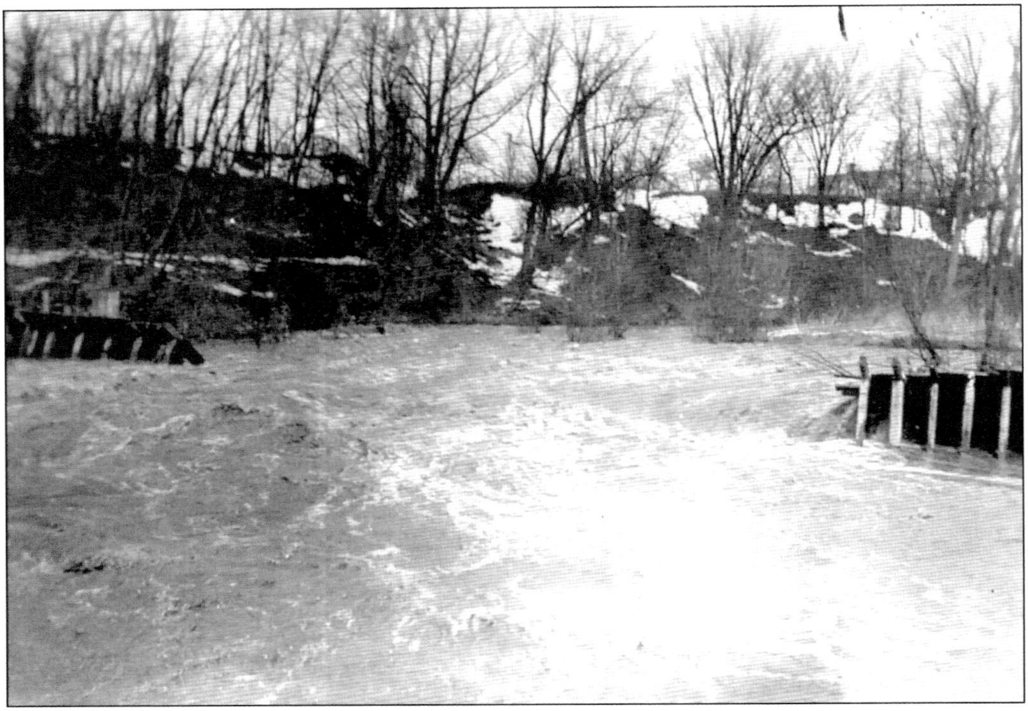

In 1916, the Lincoln Dam broke and the Penfield Mill dam was ruined.

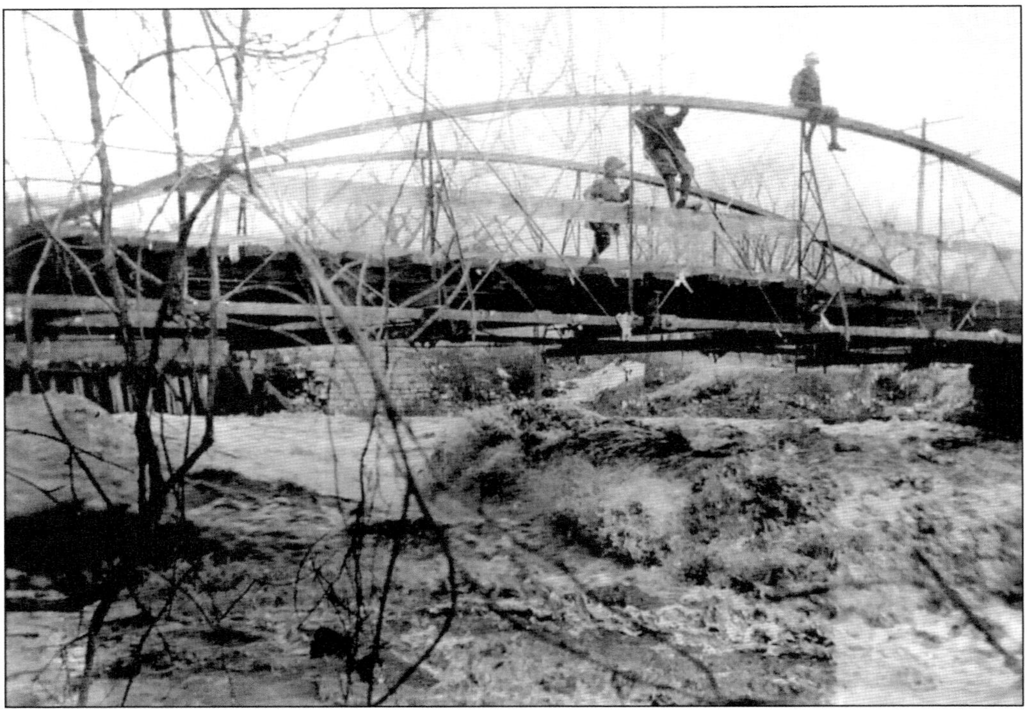

During the same flood, neither the old Penfield Mill nor the old Washington Street Bridge was damaged. Here, some boys can be seen playing on the bridge during the flood.

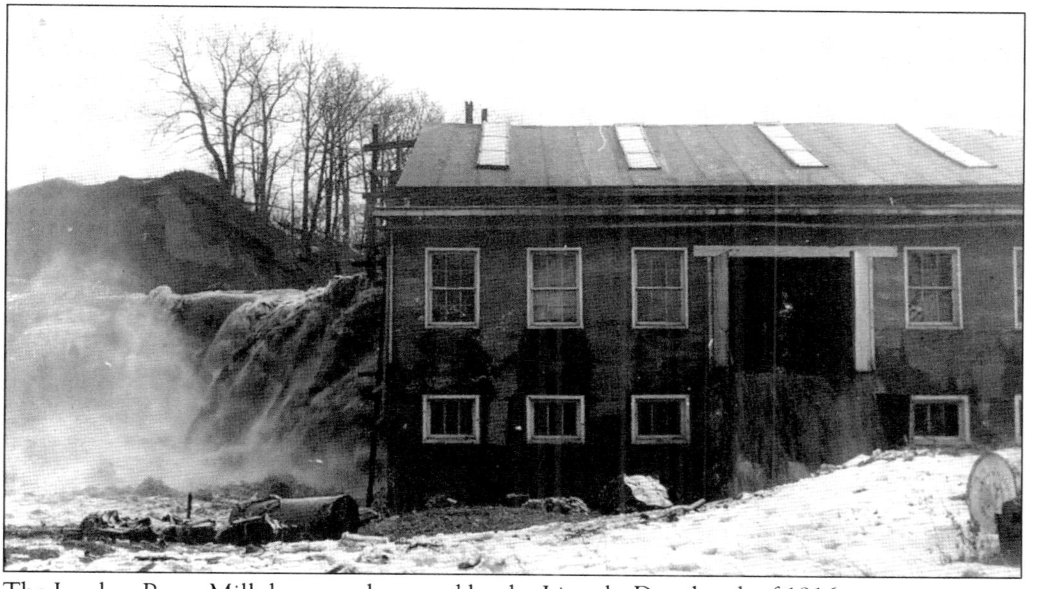

The Lawless Paper Mill dam was destroyed by the Lincoln Dam break of 1916.

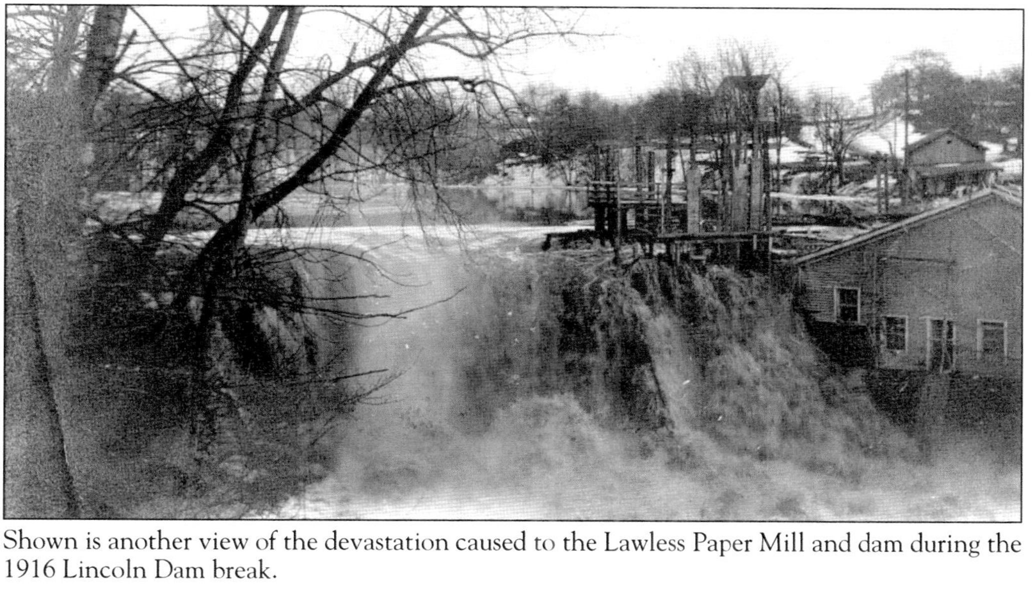

Shown is another view of the devastation caused to the Lawless Paper Mill and dam during the 1916 Lincoln Dam break.

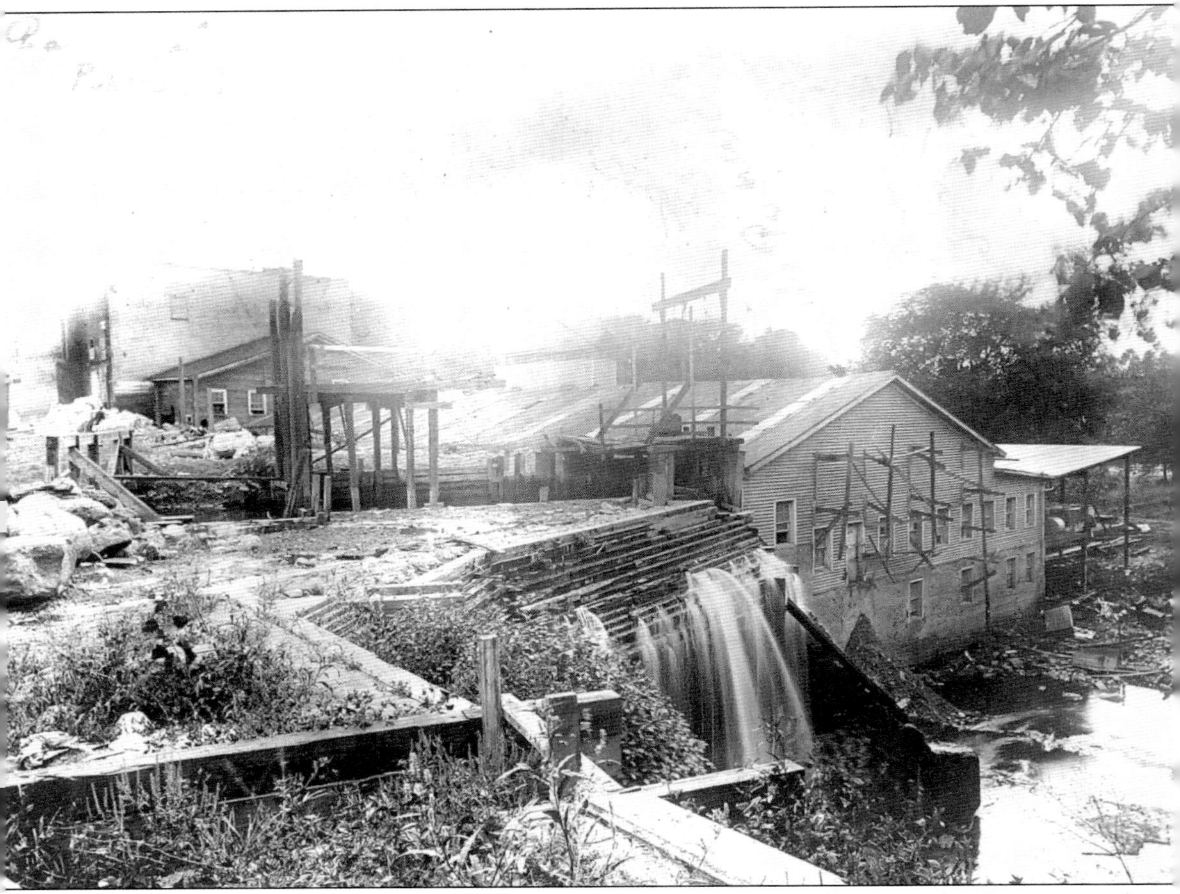

David T. Lawless rebuilt after the flood of 1916, and the paper mill remained in business until the morning of Saturday, October 25, 1924, when the mill burned and was left in ruins. The company then relocated to Despatch-East Rochester. Lawless died at his home in 1929 and was buried in the St. Joseph Cemetery.

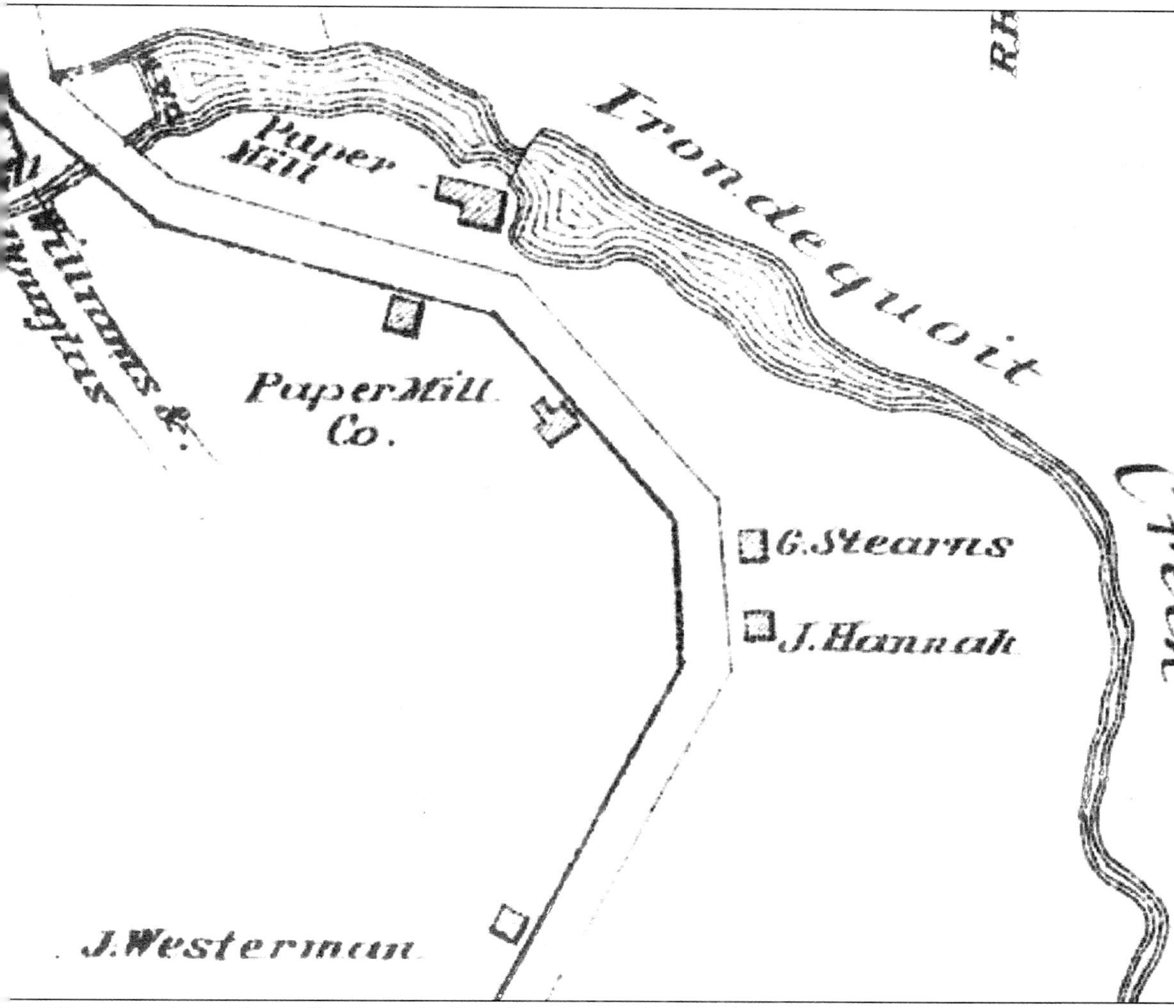

This map shows the mills along the Irondequoit Creek. It is from the 1872 *Atlas of Monroe County*, N.Y., by F. W. Beers and Company. The road down to the mills was referred to as Paper Mill Road.

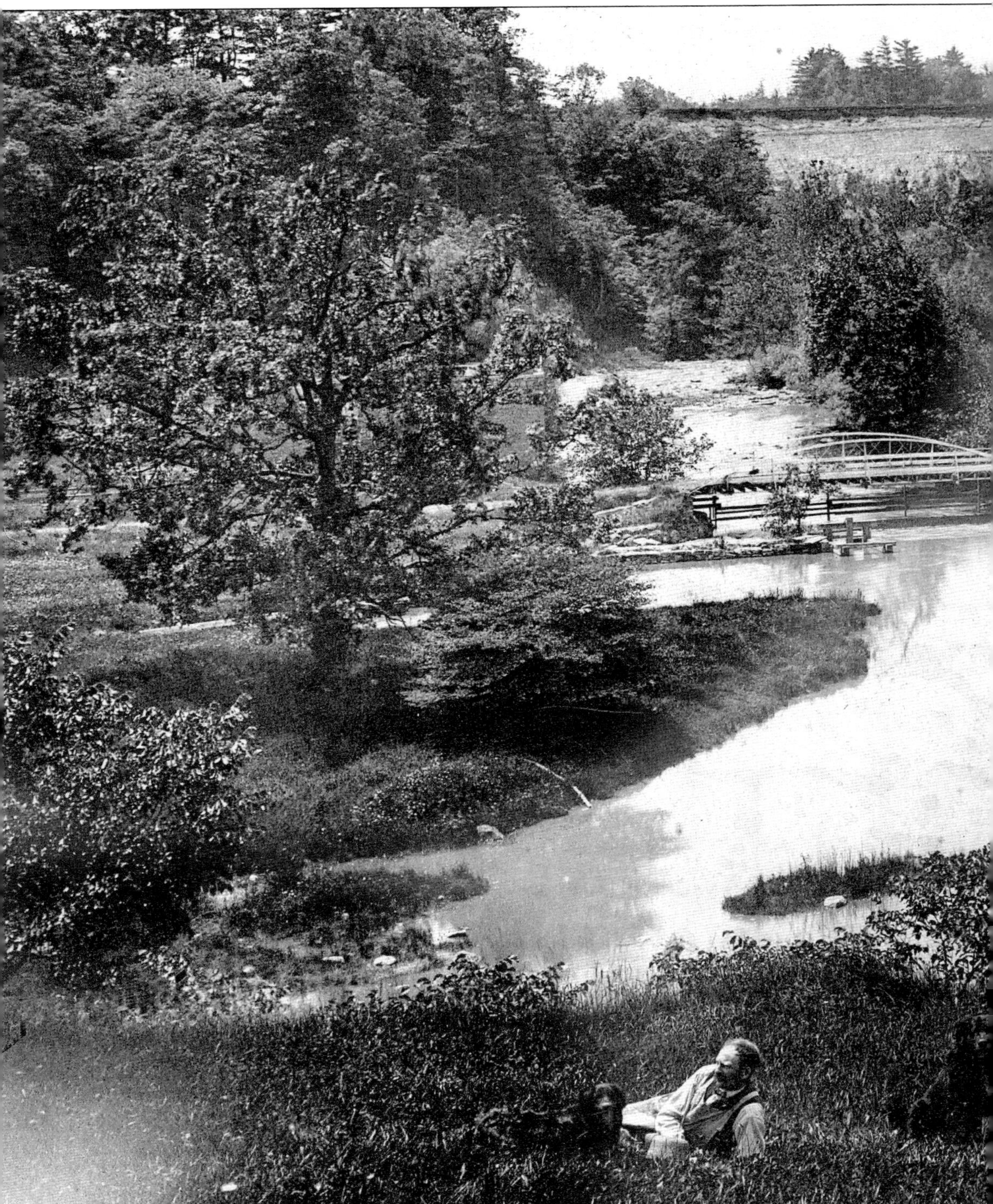

The Penfield Mill was built in 1814. Robert Dalzell acquired an interest in the mill after Daniel Penfield's death in 1840. While in Dalzell's ownership, the mill was aptly named the Yellow Mill,

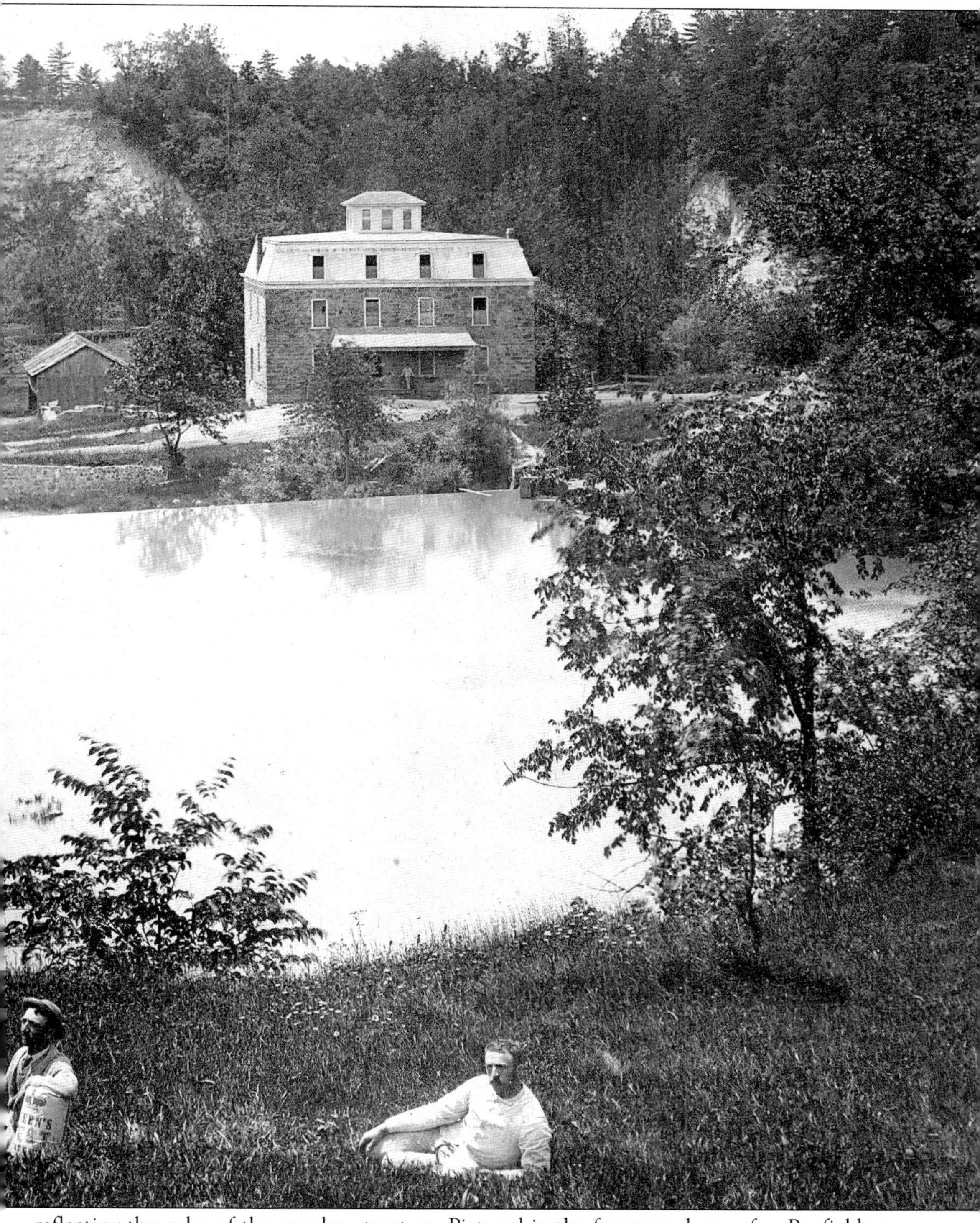

reflecting the color of the wooden structure. Pictured in the foreground are a few Penfielders toting a bag of flour and taking a restful moment to have a photograph taken.

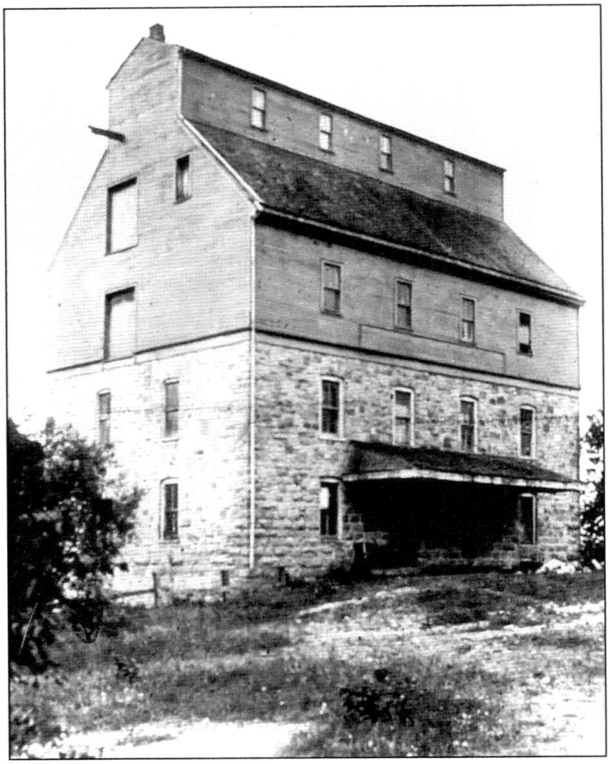

By 1865, Williams and Douglass Company owned and operated the old Penfield Mill. They renovated the building, adding a top story, after a flood in 1864 did $2,000 worth of damage to the mill. The company also repainted the mill white and renamed it the White Grist Mill.

CASH PAID FOR WHEAT

DELIVERED AT THE

WHITE GRIST MILL.

This mill has recently been put in the best of repairs and is now as perfect in every particular, as any mill in the country, Thomas Douglas so long known as Lincoln's head miller, having purchased an interest in this mill, would be pleased to see all of his old friends, and all others who wish their work done in a superior manner.

WILLIAMS & DOUGLAS

Penfield May 25 1865

This White Grist Mill advertisement appeared in the May 25, 1865, issue of the *Penfield Extra*.

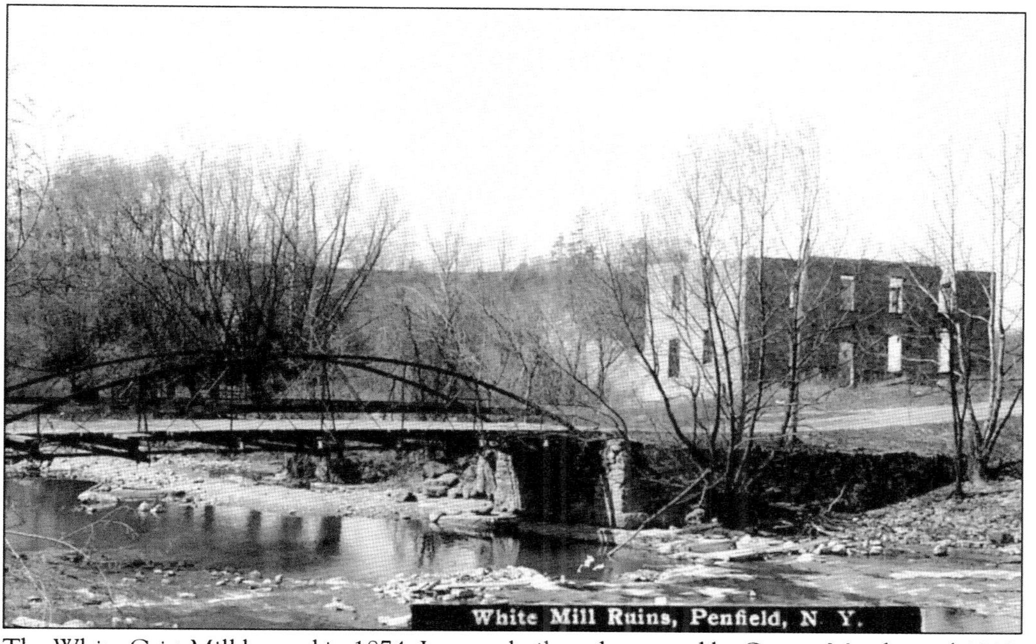

The White Grist Mill burned in 1874. It was rebuilt and operated by George March until 1919, when the mill burned again and was left in a state of ruin.

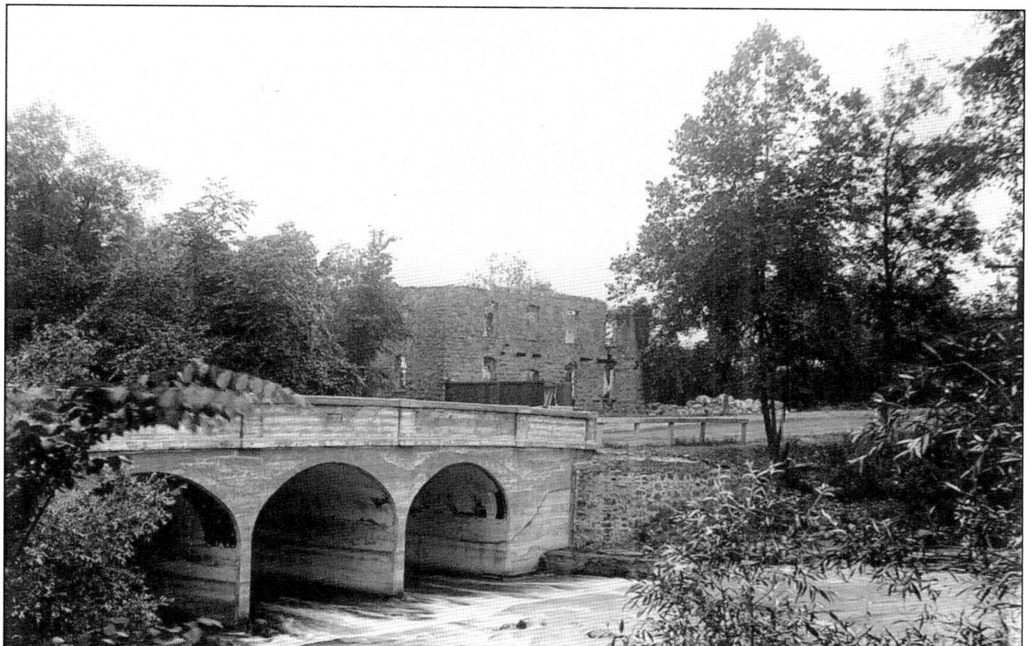

The old steel bridge was replaced in 1917 by a large cement bridge built by the town's superintendent, John Weicher. This bridge still spans the creek in Linear Park. In 2003, Linear Park was renamed the Channing H. Philbrick Park in honor of Penfield's town supervisor, who served from 1993 to 2003.

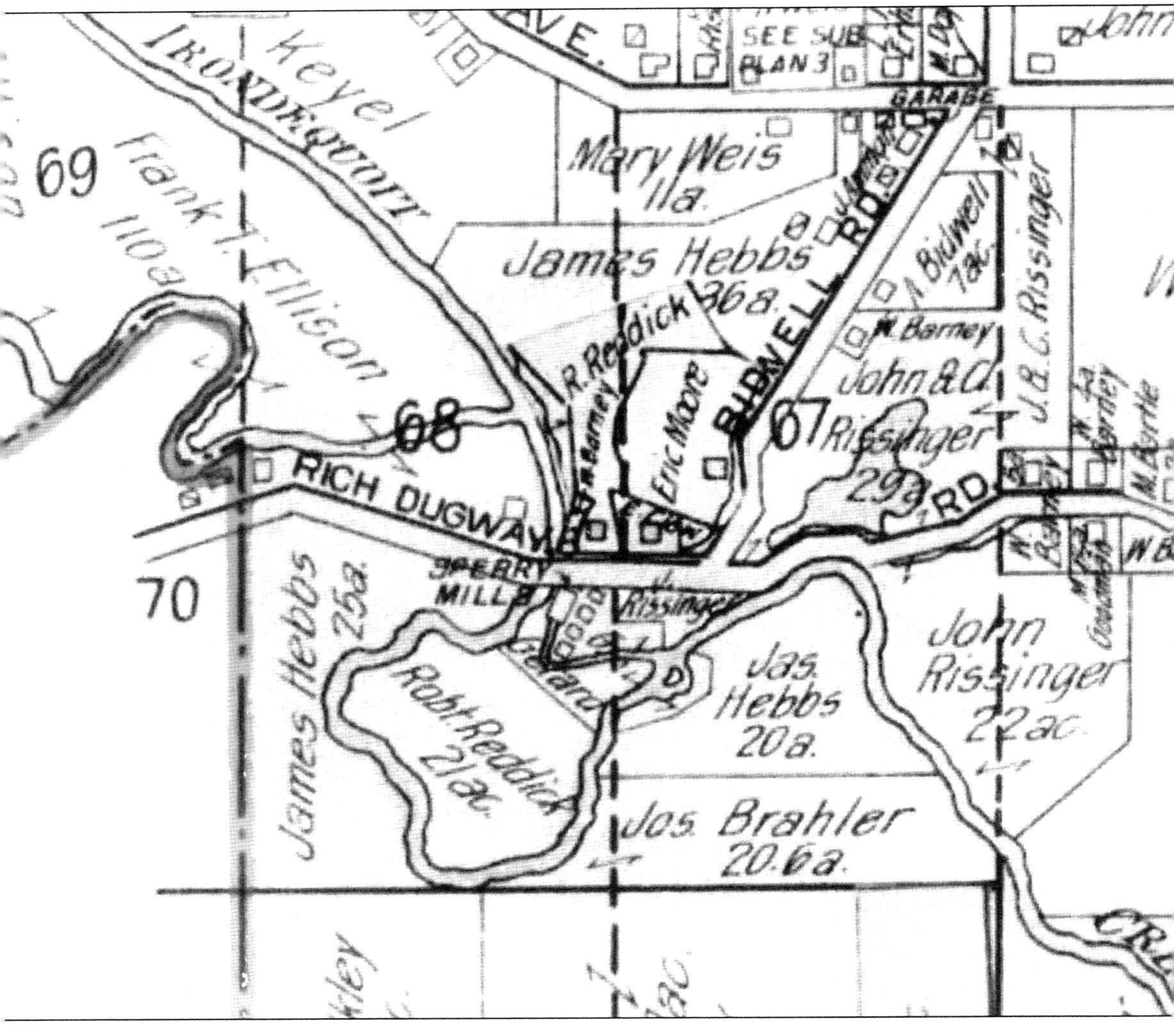

This map of the Irondequoit Creek and the Sperry Mills is from the 1924 *Plat Book of Monroe County, N.Y.*, by G. M. Hopkins and Company. The Sperry Mills were originally built by Samuel Rich. The road carved out of the woods by Rich heading to his mills was aptly named Rich Dugway.

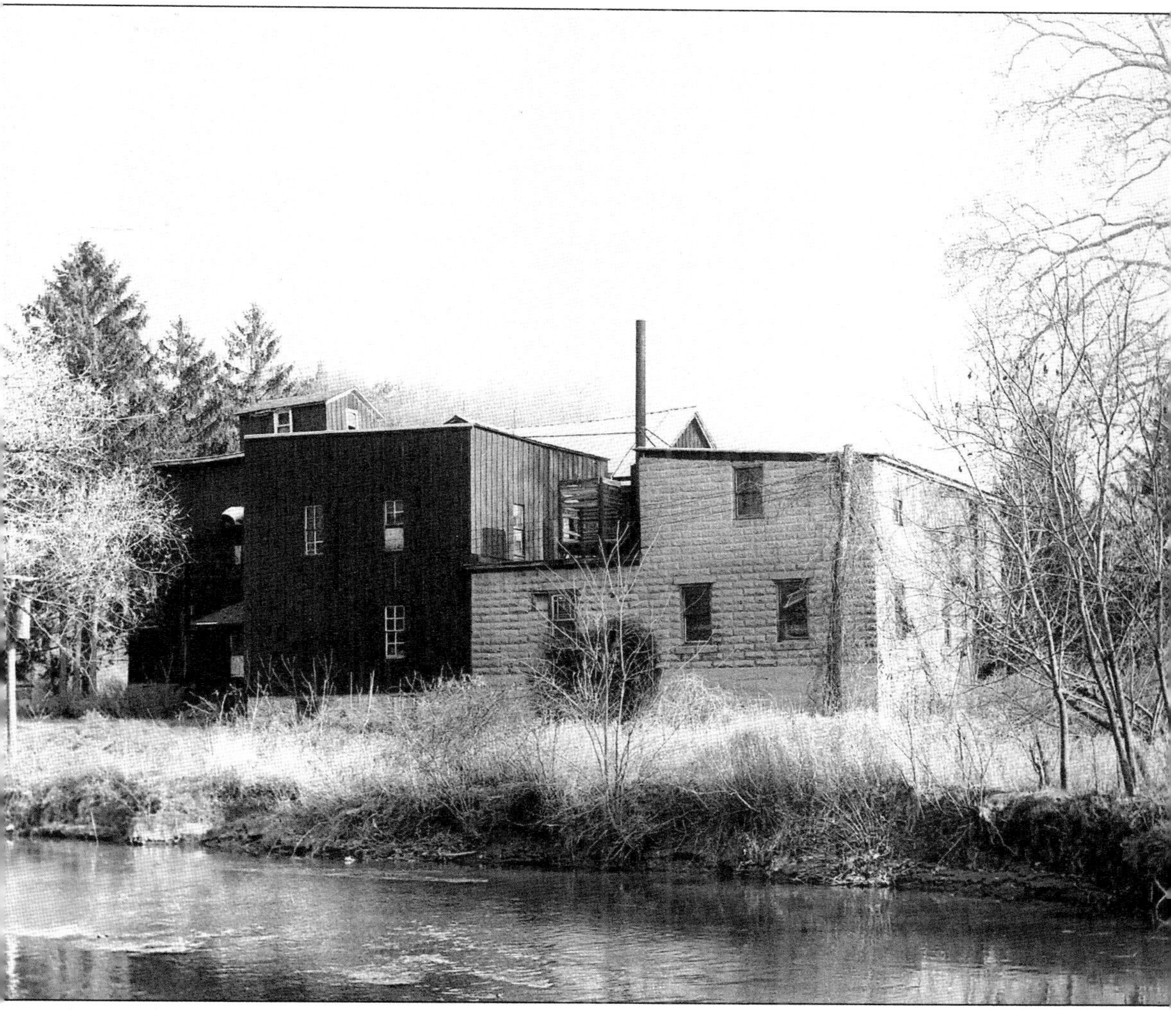

After Rich's death in 1875, the Rich Mills passed through different owners, one being H. Sperry. The mills continued in business as flouring mills and produced pastry flour until 1972. The Rich-Sperry Mills became listed on the National Register of Historic Places in 1972 and, in 1974, became a designated Penfield landmark.

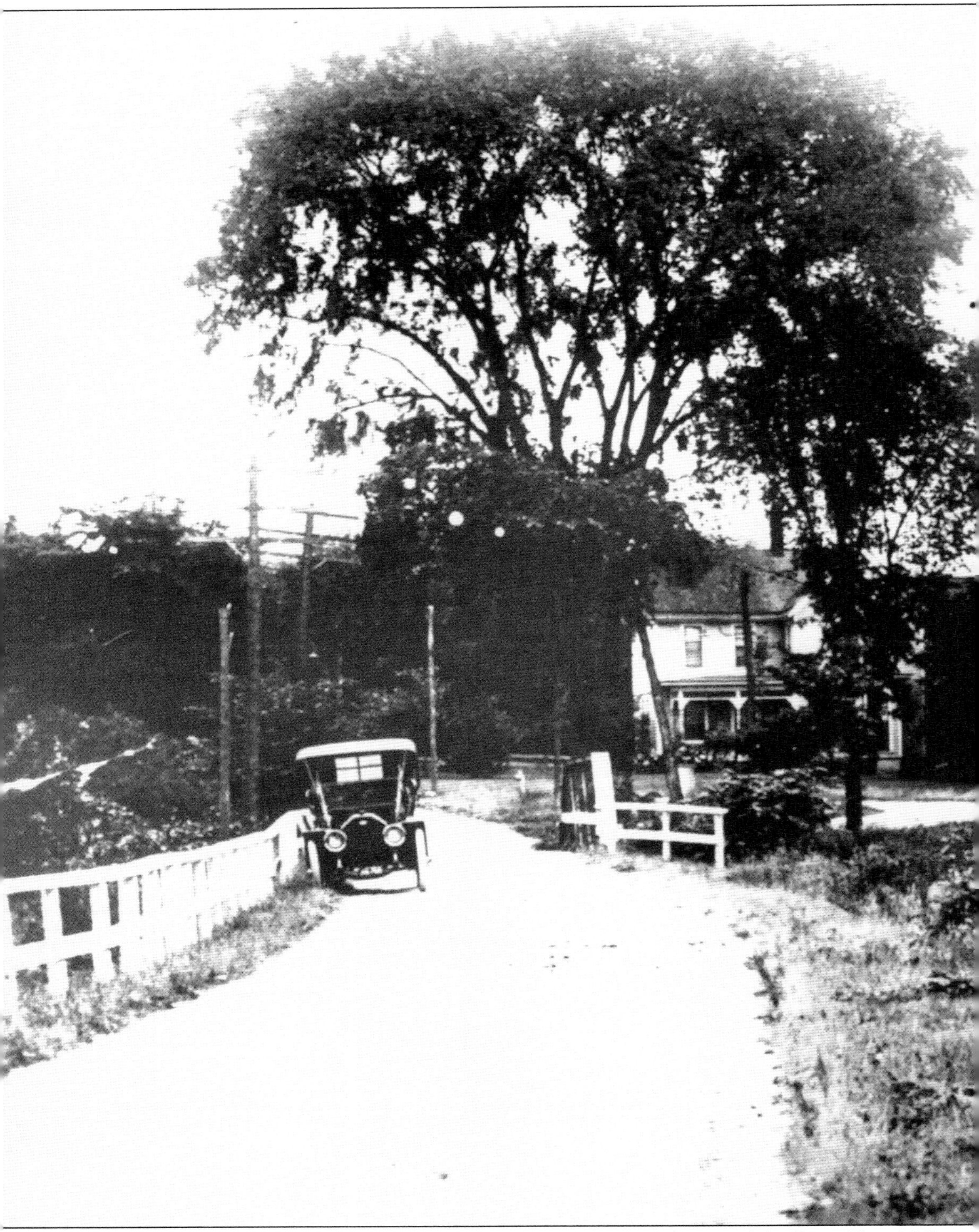

Years after the mills closed, the buildings became a restaurant aptly named the Daisy Flour Mill.

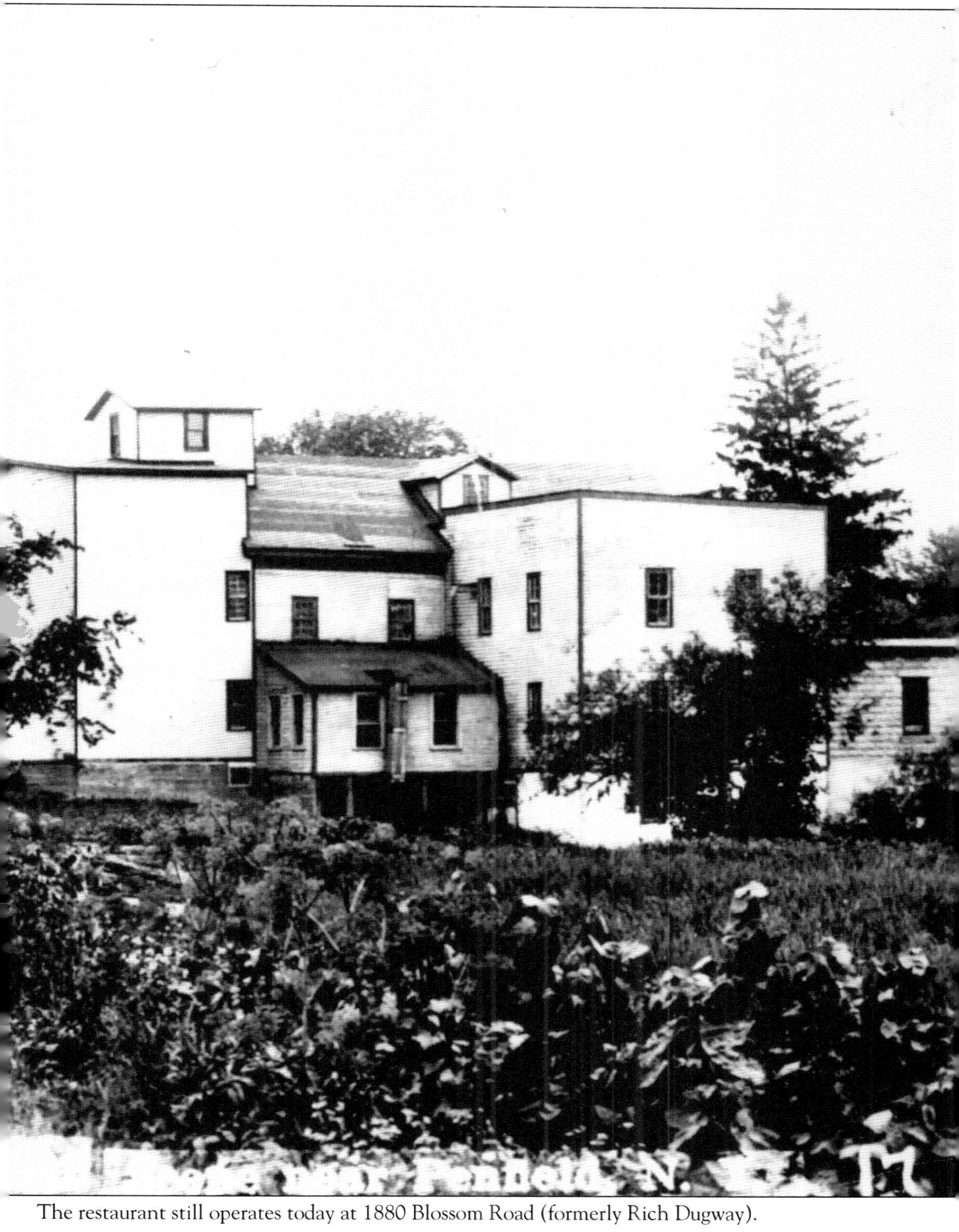

The restaurant still operates today at 1880 Blossom Road (formerly Rich Dugway).

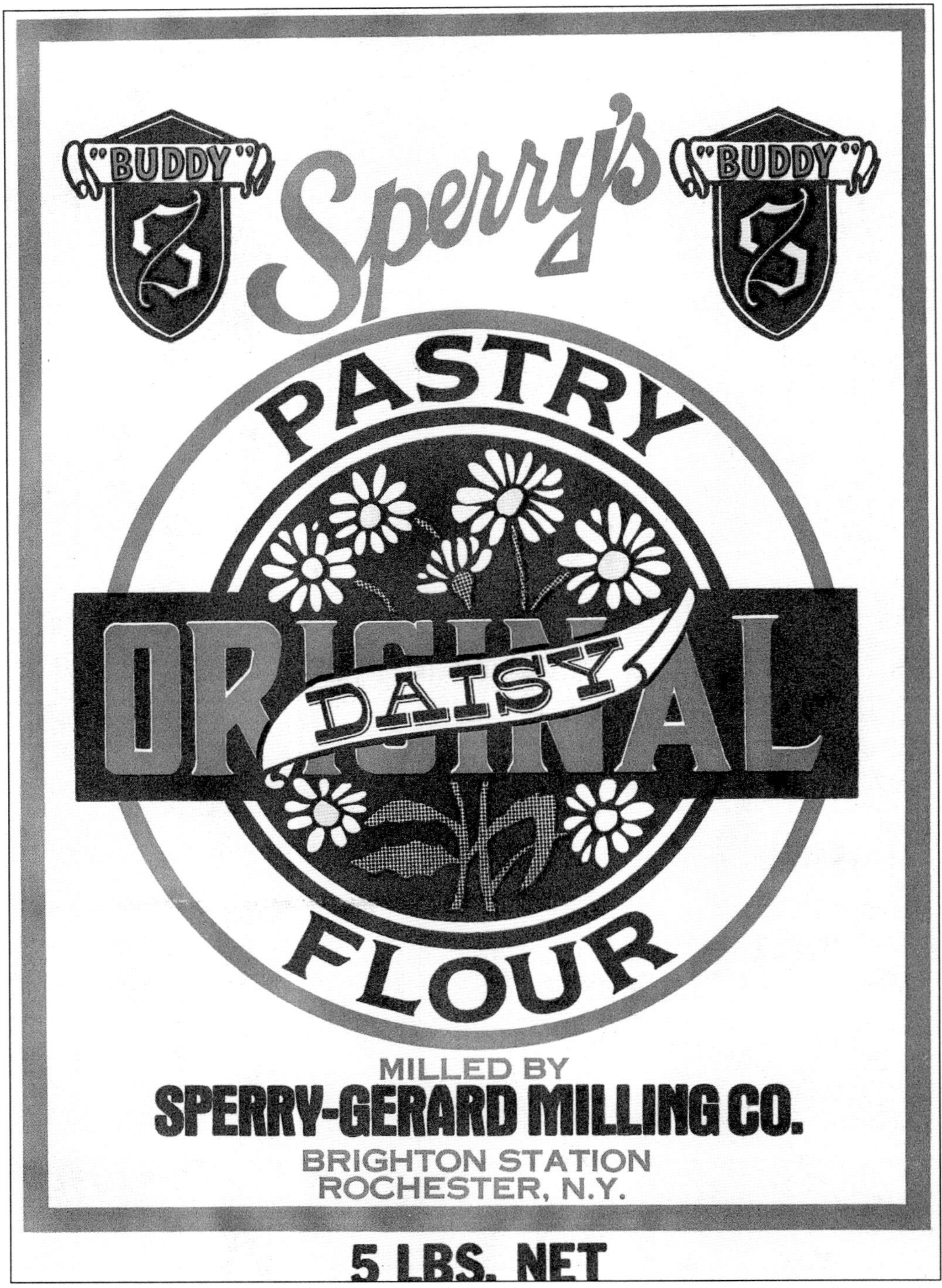

Shown is a Sperry-Gerard Milling Company five-pound flour bag used during the 20th century.

Four

Beyond the Four Corners

Penfield then was a cross roads village. How long the east road seemed and how pleasant . . . as I stayed at home on rainy days and in the winter, my memories are all of sunny days, pleasant unhurried living.

—Clara Hammond Schermerhorn,
I Remember When . . . Penfield,
by Verna K. Brahler, 1961

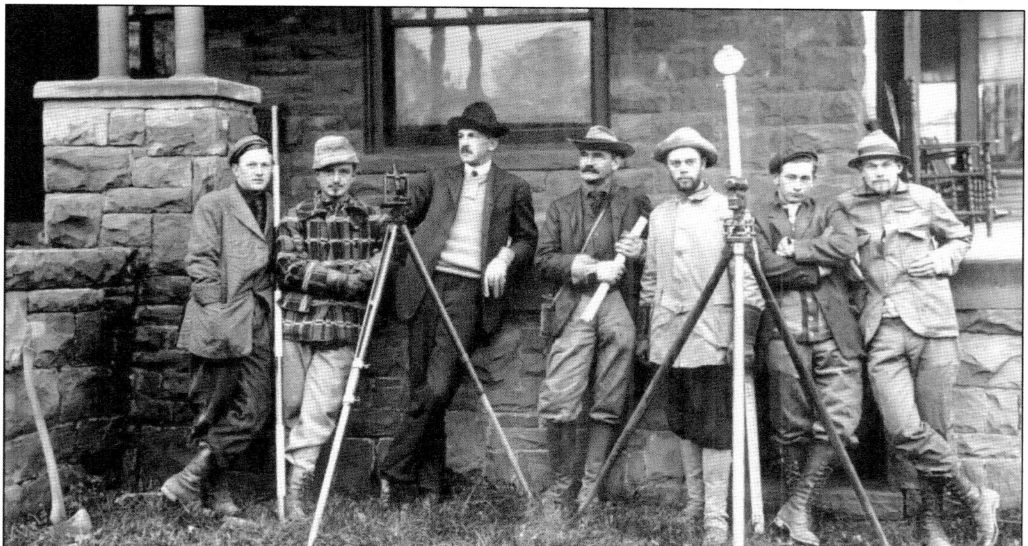

In 1907, a group of surveyors and engineers (pictured here outside the Humphrey House) were commissioned by the Buffalo, Rochester, and Eastern Railroad Company to survey the land in Penfield for a potential site of a new railroad through the town. Upon the completion of their survey, the company decided to bypass Penfield altogether. This decision kept the town very secluded, with a population of around 3,000. By 1950, suburban housing developed around Penfield, and the town grew into one of Rochester's premier suburbs. Today, Penfield has about 35,000 residents.

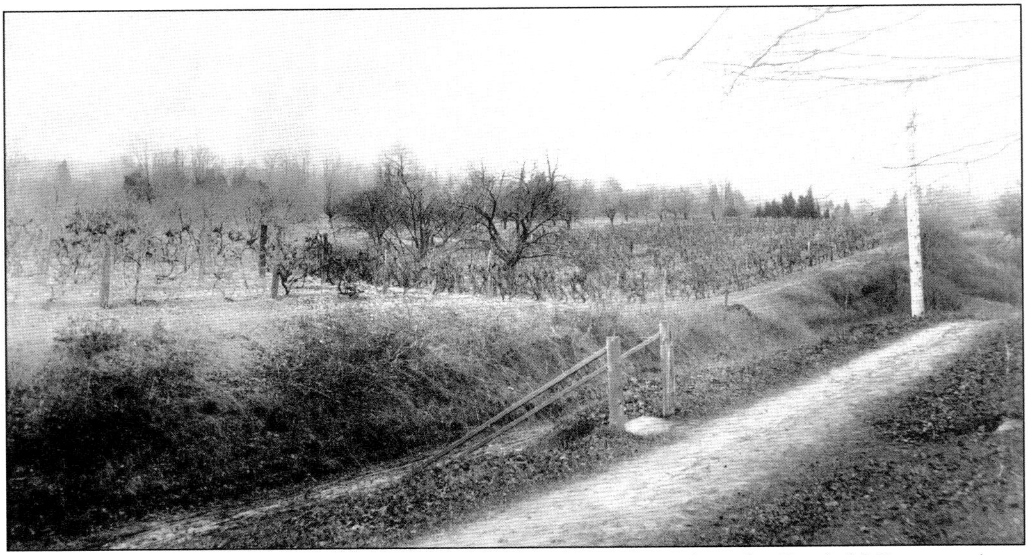

Charles C. Raymond's vineyards once lined Five Mile Line Road on the Penfield-Perinton line. His daughter Grace Raymond recalled in *I Remember When . . . Penfield*, by Verna K. Brahler, "The sad story where in one season [my] father's whole farm, a fruit nursery, was ruined by a hail storm. Only about three trees survived. This was about 1880."

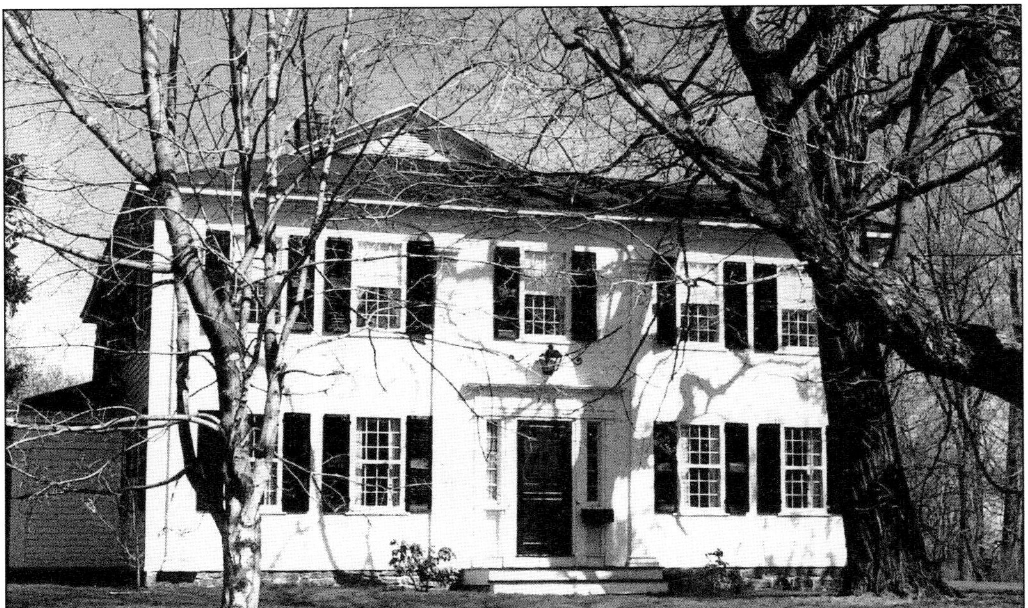

Built in 1816 for Samuel Rich, this house stands at 2204 Five Mile Line Road. Rich's daughter, Mary Ann Rich, married Isaac Raymond and moved into this house after Rich moved his milling interests downstream in 1846. One of Isaac and Mary Ann's sons, Charles C., took on the ownership of the house after Isaac's death in 1849. The house was enlarged over the years. The Rich-Raymond House was designated as a Penfield landmark in 1974 and became listed on the National Register of Historic Places in 1987.

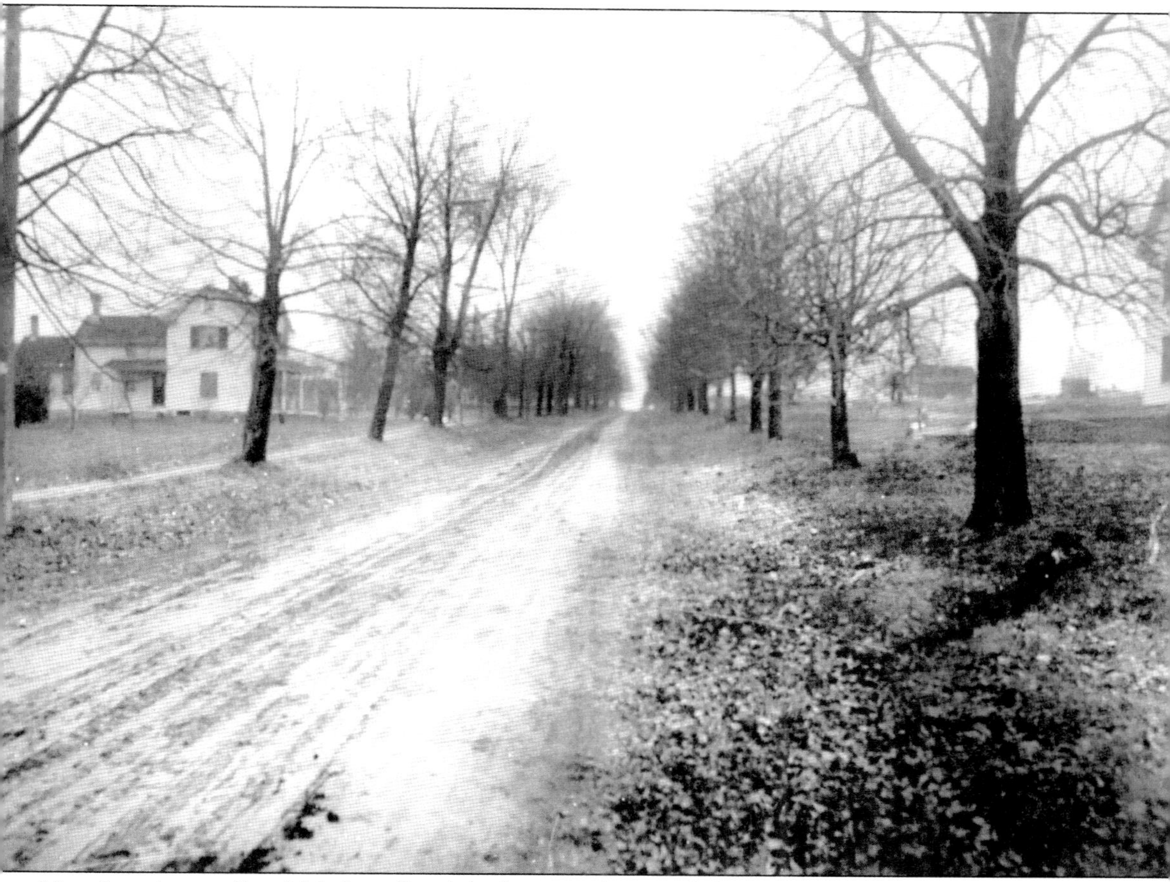

Here is a view up Five Mile Line Road, looking north toward the Whalen Road intersection in 1907. This path was made famous by a war campaign Marquis de Denonville took in 1687 on orders from King Louis XIV of France. He led his troops down from Canada to the Irondequoit Bay and carved a path southeast through Penfield and Perinton to present-day Victor in an effort to annihilate the Seneca Indians and eliminate them as competitors in the fur trade. This path is known today as the Denonville Trail.

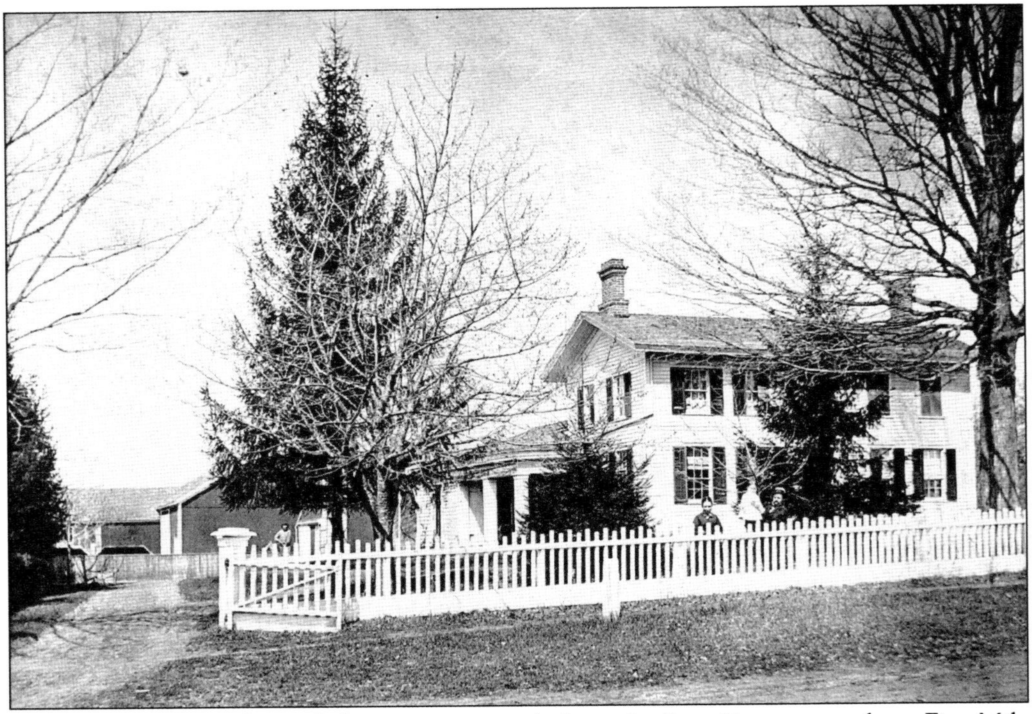

This house was once located about a quarter-mile from the Four Corners, north up Five Mile Line Road. It was owned by Eugene Covey, the son of Alvah Covey, an early settler in Penfield and an abolitionist. In the 1890s, Eugene Covey owned the Penfield Nurseries.

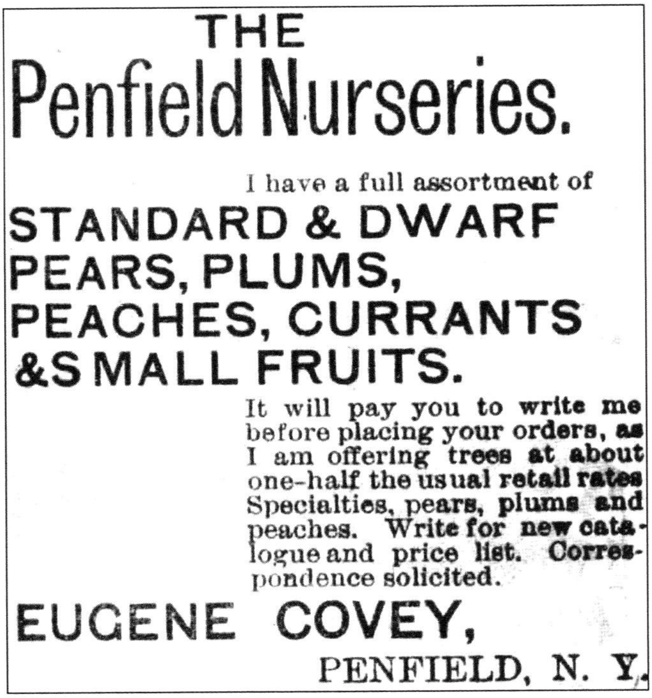

This advertisement appeared in the April 15, 1893, issue of the *Penfield Press*.

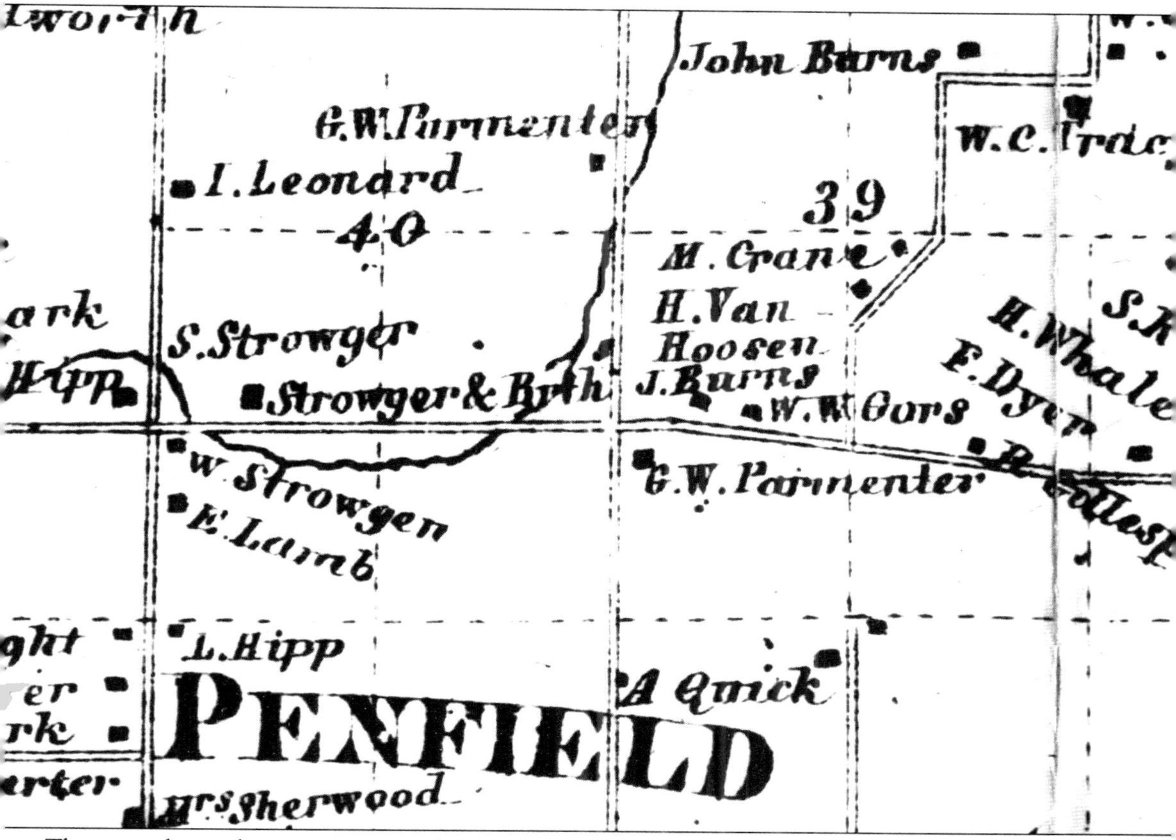

This map shows the intersections of Five Mile Line and Whalen Roads and the surroundings in Penfield in 1852. According to the *Penfield Extra* issue of June 27, 1863, the intersection was referred to as Strowger's Corners since John Strowger, Daniel Penfield's first miller, settled at the southeast corner. Strowger's sons, Samuel and William, also owned property at the corners. The intersection of Whalen and Baird Roads can also be seen. G. W. Parmenter owned a large house at the southeast corner.

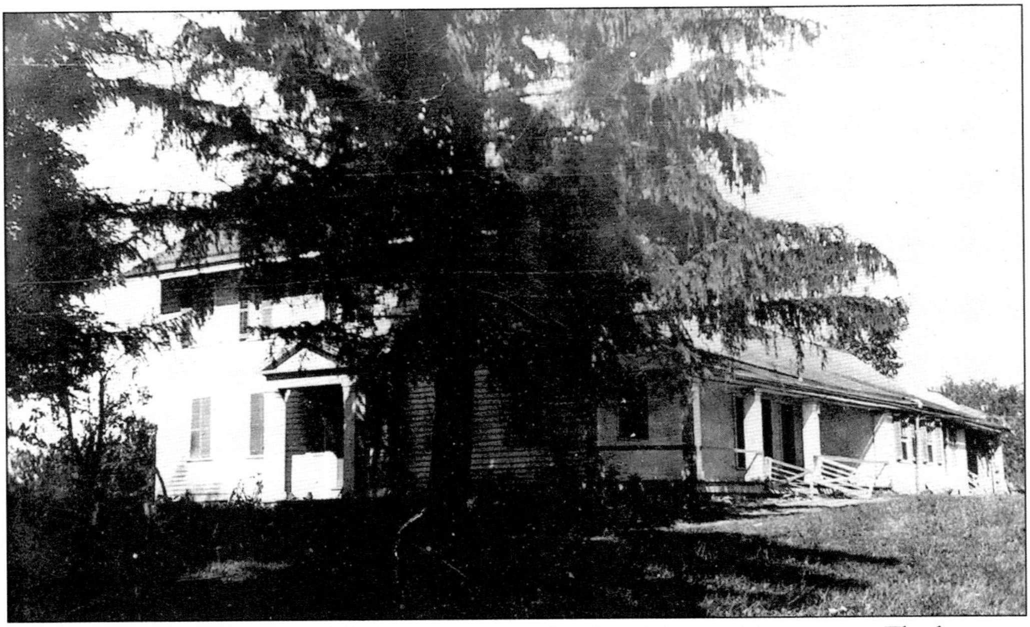

In 1687, Denonville's army of 3,000 set up camp for the night on this property. The house at 1960 Clark Road was built c. 1832 by Alpheus Clark. In 1854, his son, George, purchased the house. The property stayed in the family for more than 100 years. Dora, George's daughter, married Charles Brown, a nurseryman, and they lived in the house for a time. Their son Donald was the owner of the Brown Brothers Nursery. By 1939, Donald Clark (no relation) purchased the house and named the property Tamarack Farm.

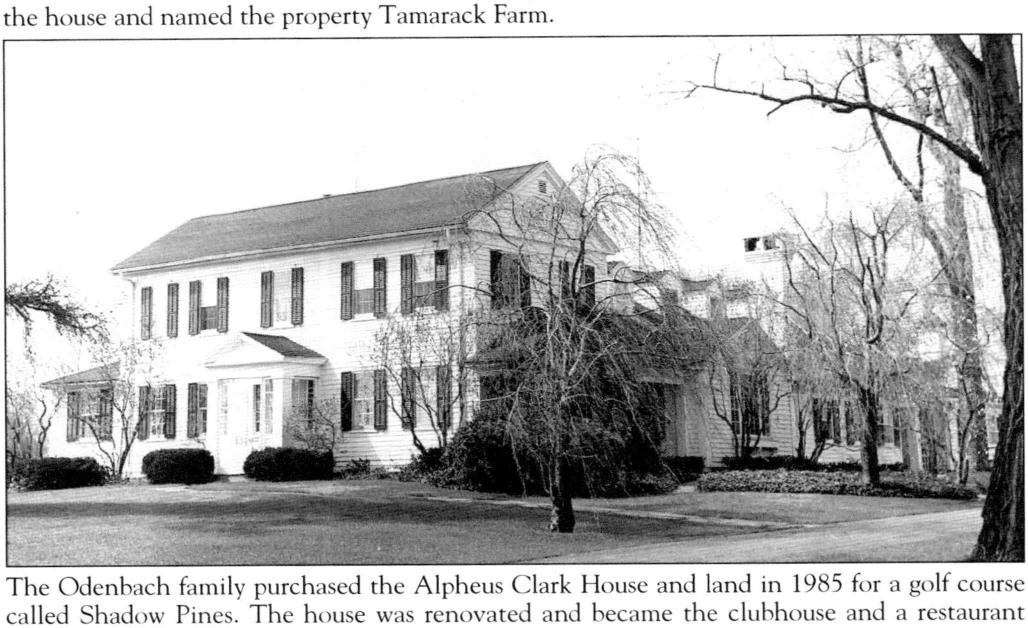

The Odenbach family purchased the Alpheus Clark House and land in 1985 for a golf course called Shadow Pines. The house was renovated and became the clubhouse and a restaurant aptly named the Clark House, which became a Penfield landmark in 1986. In 1928, John M. Odenbach came to Penfield with his company, the Dolomite Products Company. The company was instrumental in providing rock for pavement around the area, and it continues in business with many other quarry locations around New York.

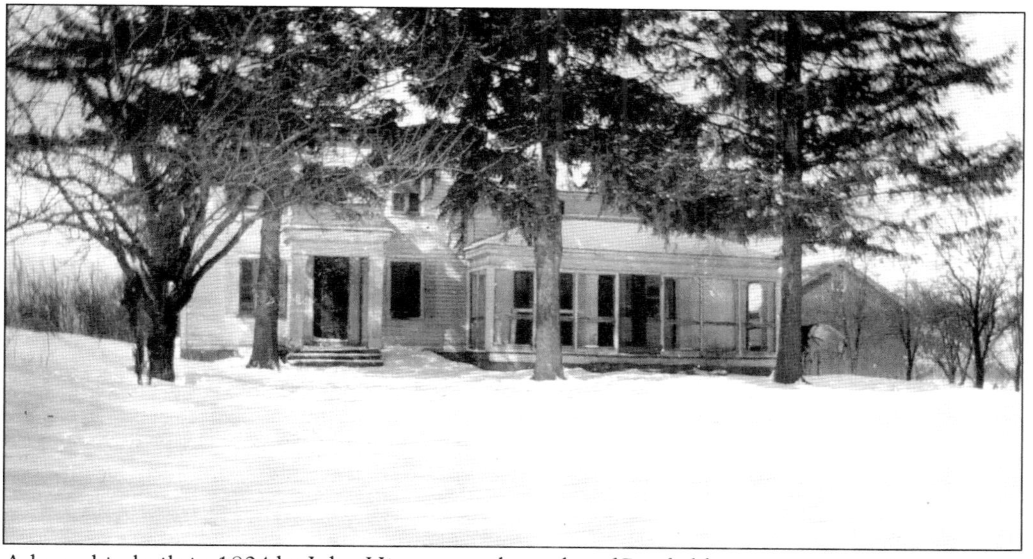

A log cabin built in 1804 by John Hipp, an early settler of Penfield, was constructed on this site. His cabin is still incorporated into the house. A creek that flows around the intersection of Five Mile Line Road and Whalen Road, and crosses the Hipp property is aptly named Hipp Brook. The Hipp House, at 1931 Five Mile Line Road, was designated as a Penfield landmark in 1982 and was listed on the National Register of Historic Places in 1994.

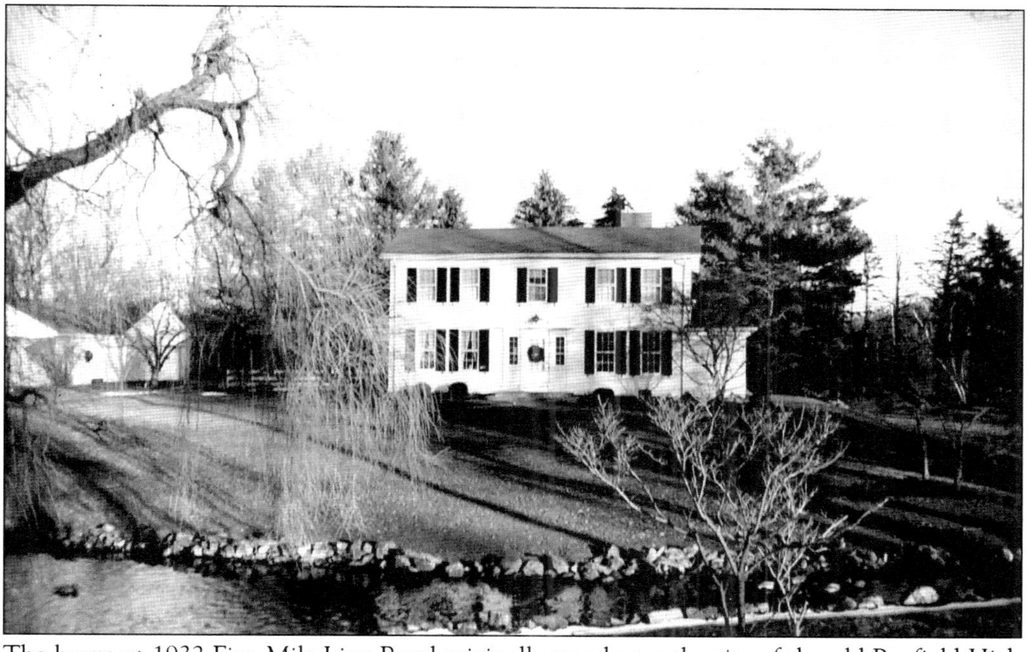

The house at 1932 Five Mile Line Road originally stood near the site of the old Penfield High School. It was built there *c.* 1821 by Horace Bush and Catherine Fellows Bush. Catherine's sister was Mary Fellows Penfield. In 1931, an addition was constructed to the high school, so the house was moved to its present location at Strowger's Corners. The house was designated as a Penfield landmark in 1987 and was listed on the National Register of Historic Places in 1994.

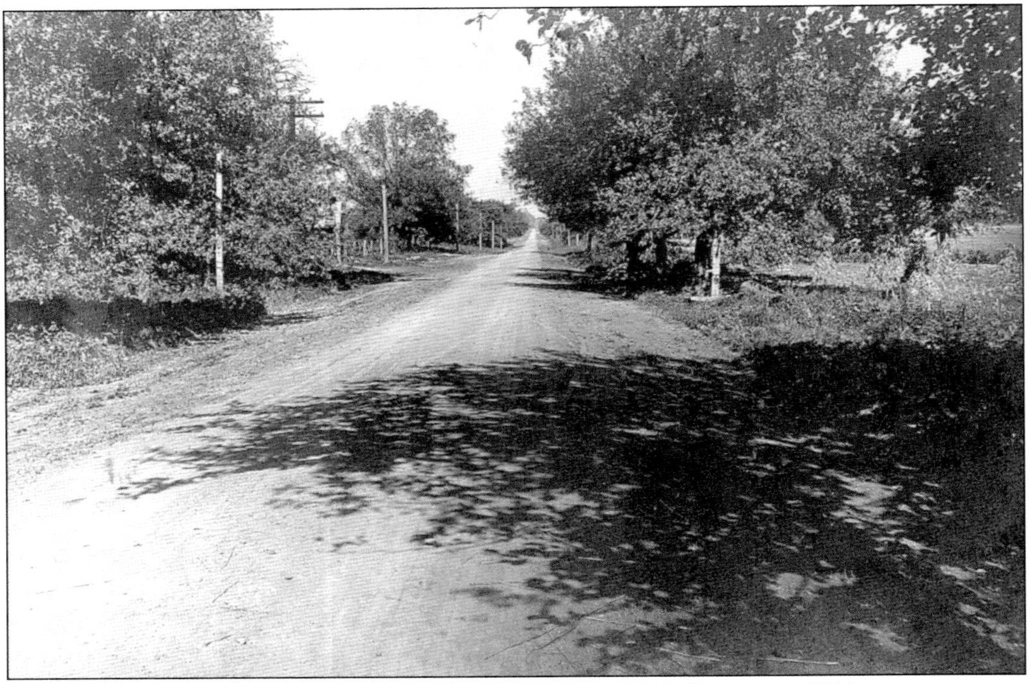

This view looks north up Five Mile Line Road from Strowger's Corners *c.* 1911.

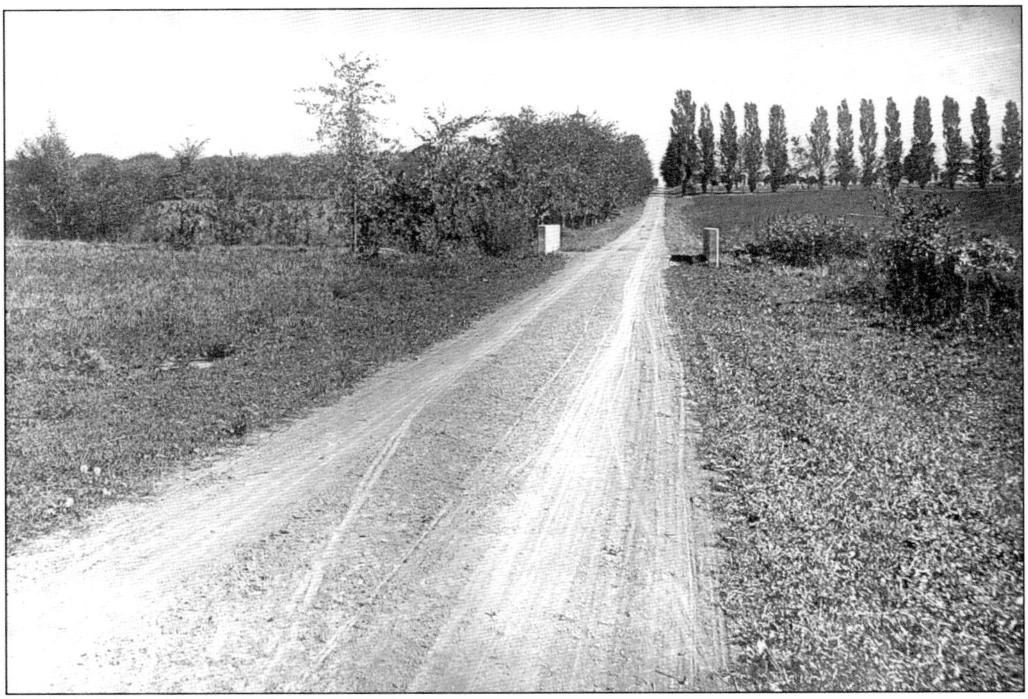

This is a view east from Strowger's Corners on Whalen Road toward Baird Road *c.* 1900.

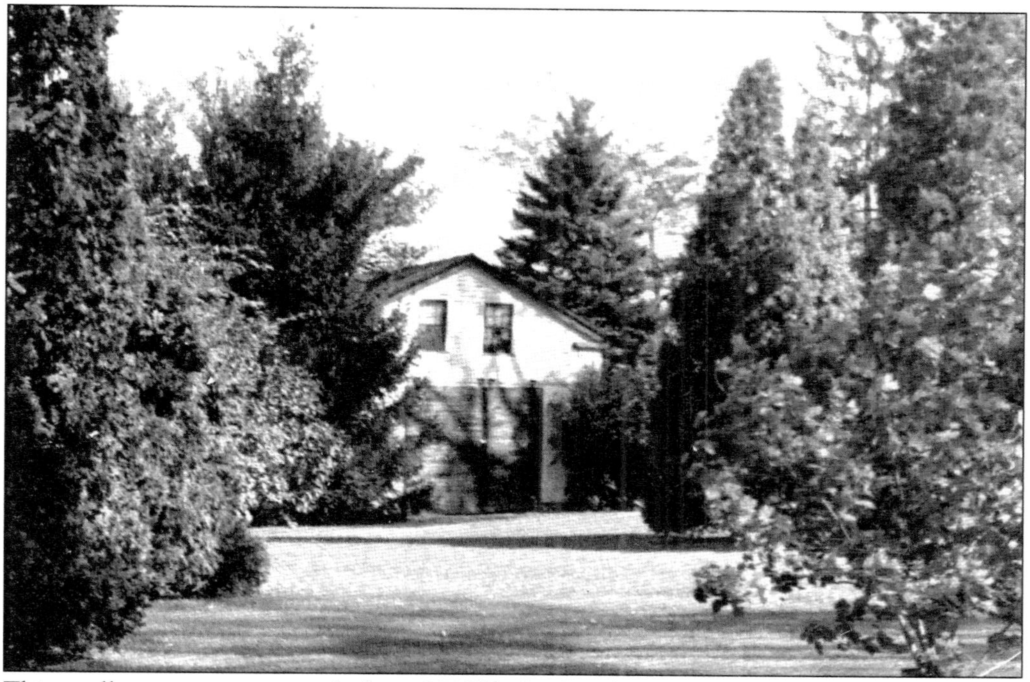

This small structure once stood where 844 Whalen Road stands today. It was the birthplace of Almon Strowger, the inventor of the dial telephone. The house was built before 1850. During the second half of the 20th century, the Strowger House was moved to the back of the property and was converted in to a garage-shed, shown in this photograph.

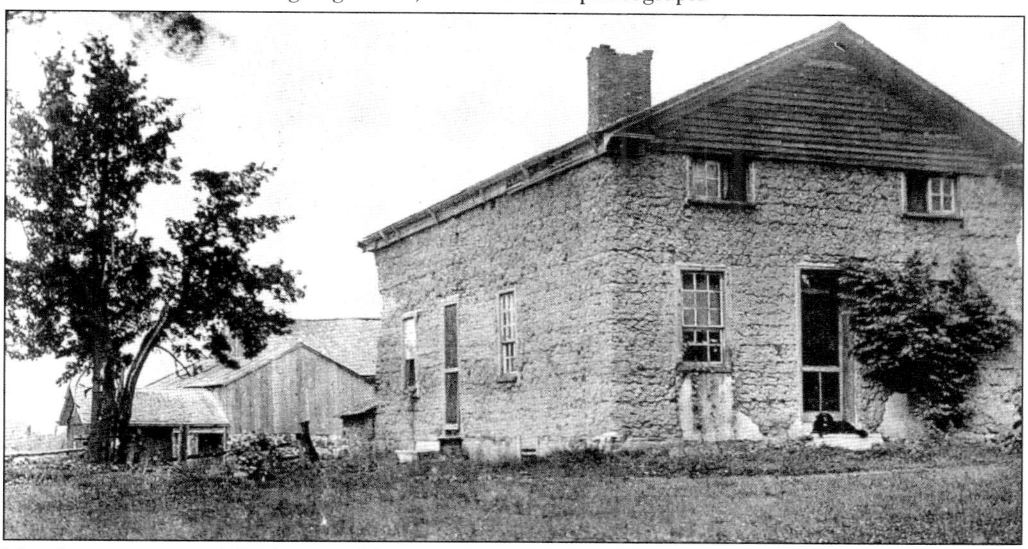

This house is one of the last mud houses standing in New York State today. Made of clay and straw, the house was built by William Gors in 1835. It stands at 992 Whalen Road. By the early 1900s, the Lawless family owned the house and land surrounding it. In 1944, the house became an office for the Brown Brothers Nursery. For many years now, it has been a private residence. The Mud House was listed on the National Register of Historic Places in 1978 and became a Penfield landmark in 1981.

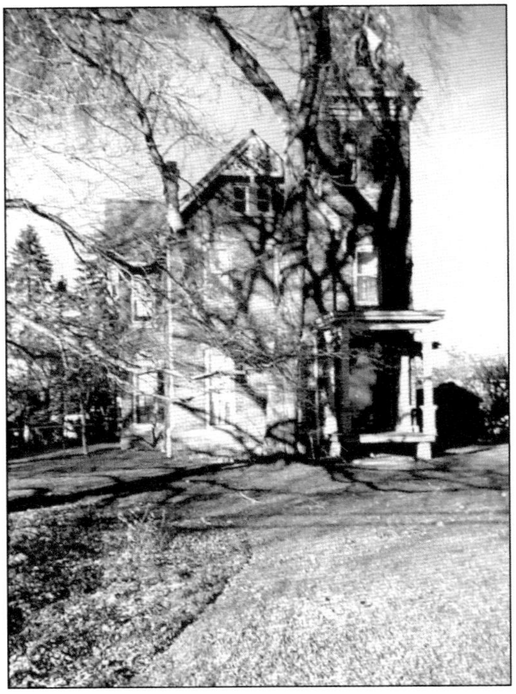

The large brick Victorian at 1140 Whalen Road was built in 1875 by Harvey Whalen. Whalen was born in Penfield in 1855 and became a farmer. The house became a Penfield landmark in 1975 and was listed on the National Register of Historic Places in 1994.

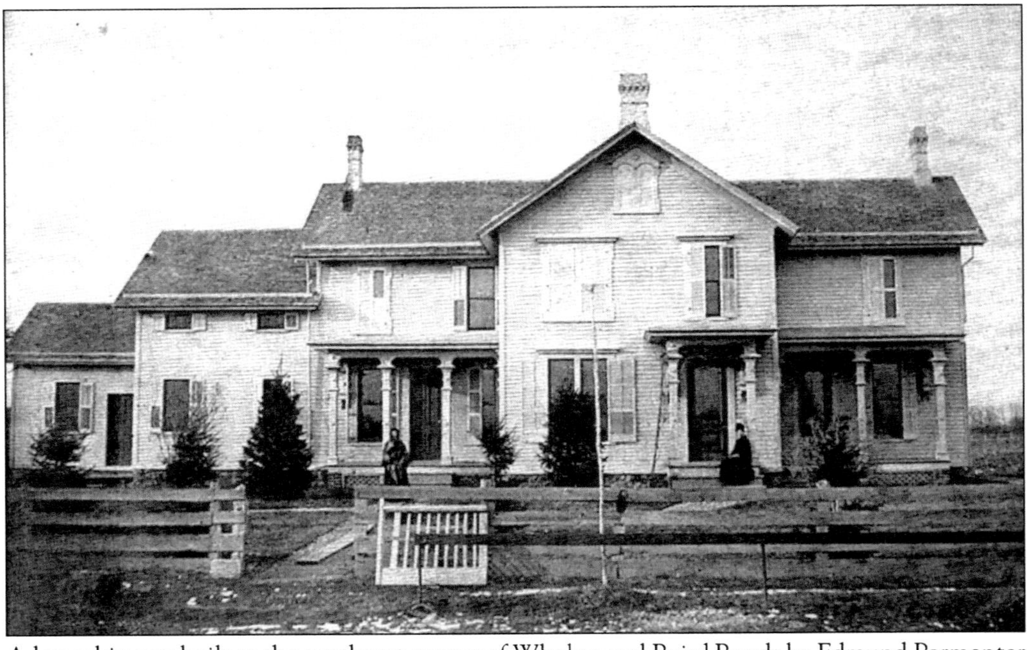

A log cabin was built at the southeast corner of Whalen and Baird Roads by Edmund Parmenter in 1815. Soon afterward, Parmenter replaced the cabin with this large house. He married Sara Ann Fassett, Jonathan Fassett's daughter. His son, George Parmenter, took over the ownership of the house and property after his father's death. Clara Hammond, George's much younger cousin, also lived with the family as a child in the 1860s and 1870s. Clara married George Schermerhorn, who was the town clerk for 30 years. The house burned in 1932.

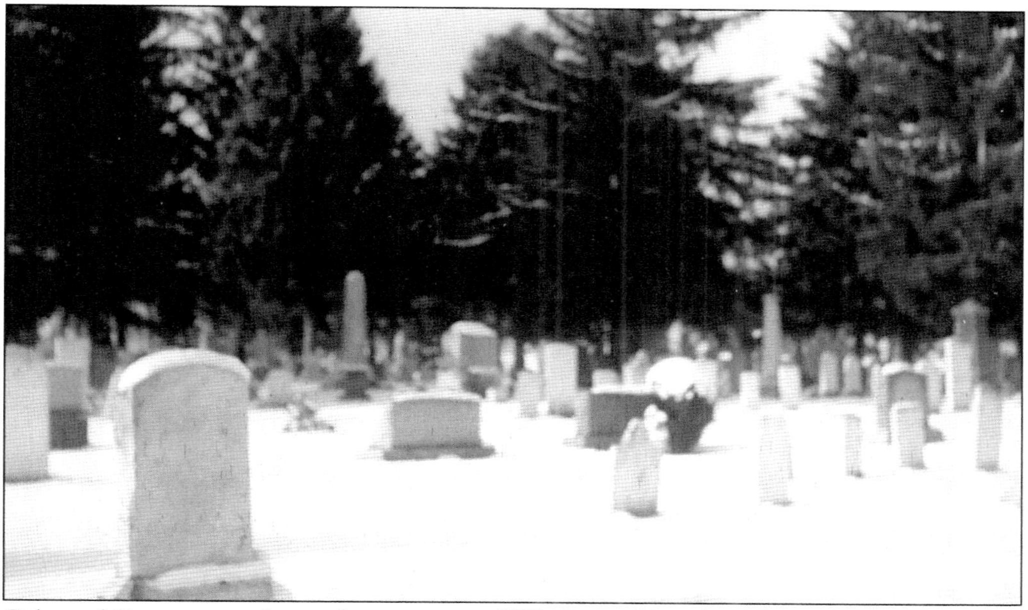

Oakwood Cemetery, at the southwest corner of Whalen and Baird Roads, was one of the earliest cemeteries in Penfield. John Strowger, Daniel Penfield's first miller, was the first person buried in the cemetery with a marked grave. Strowger died in 1812 at the age of 45.

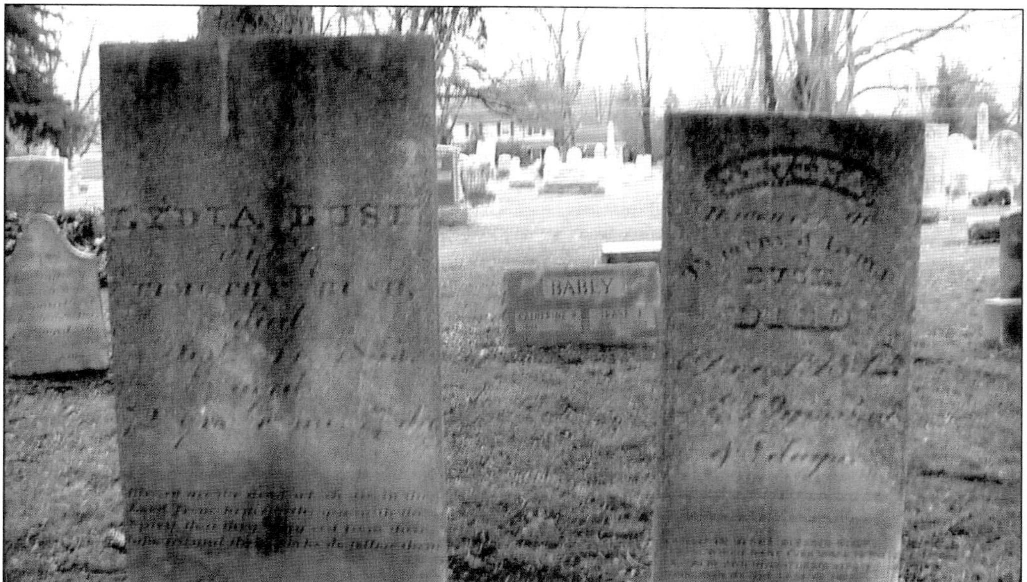

These are the grave plots in Oakwood Cemetery of Timothy and Lydia Bush, the great-great-great-great-grandparents of Pres. George W. Bush. Timothy Bush came to Penfield in 1833 with his family and lived in the Four Corners area. He was a blacksmith in town, and the family belonged to the Baptist church. Lydia Bush died in Penfield in 1835 at the age of 72. Daughter Levina died in 1842 at the age of 49. Timothy Bush lived to be 84 and died in Penfield in 1850. Lydia and Levina have gravestones; Timothy, however, does not. They are direct ancestors of the president of the United States.

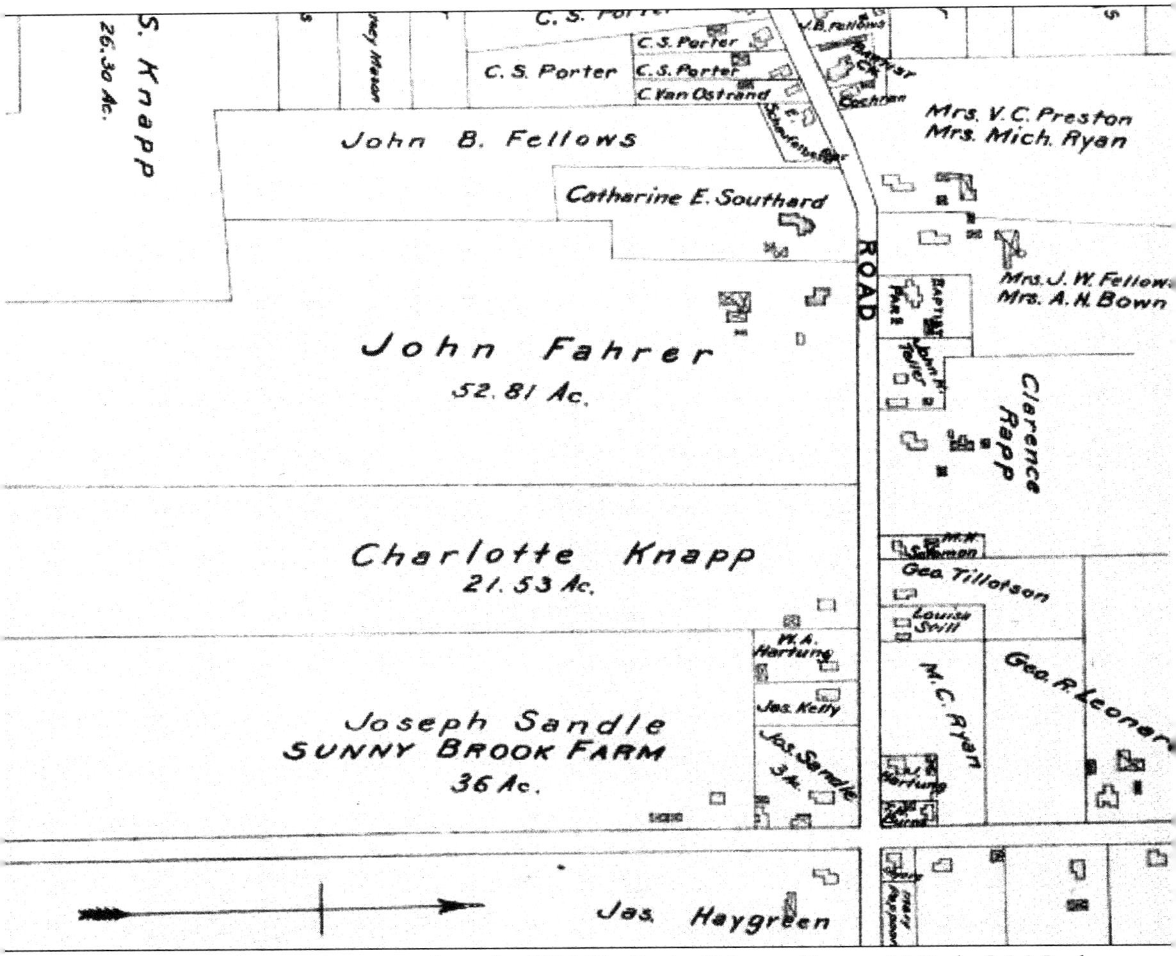

This map of Upper Corners is from the 1902 *Plat Book of Monroe County, N.Y.*, by J. M. Lathrop and Company. Today, this location is at Penfield Road (Route 441) and Baird Road.

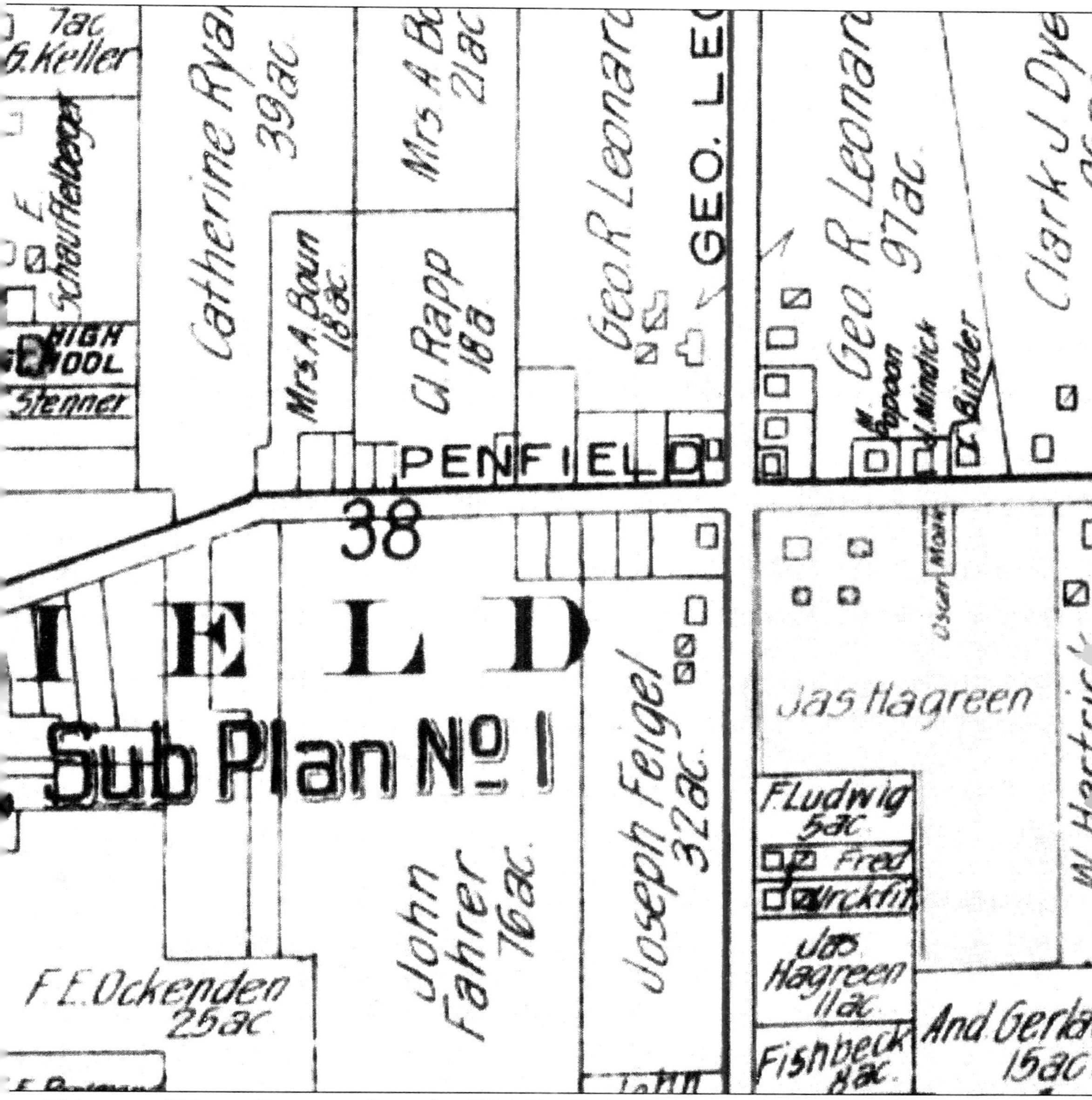

This map of Upper Corners is from the 1924 *Plat Book of Monroe County, N.Y.*, by G. M. Hopkins and Company. Penfield Road was then Rochester Road, and Baird Road was named George Leonard Road.

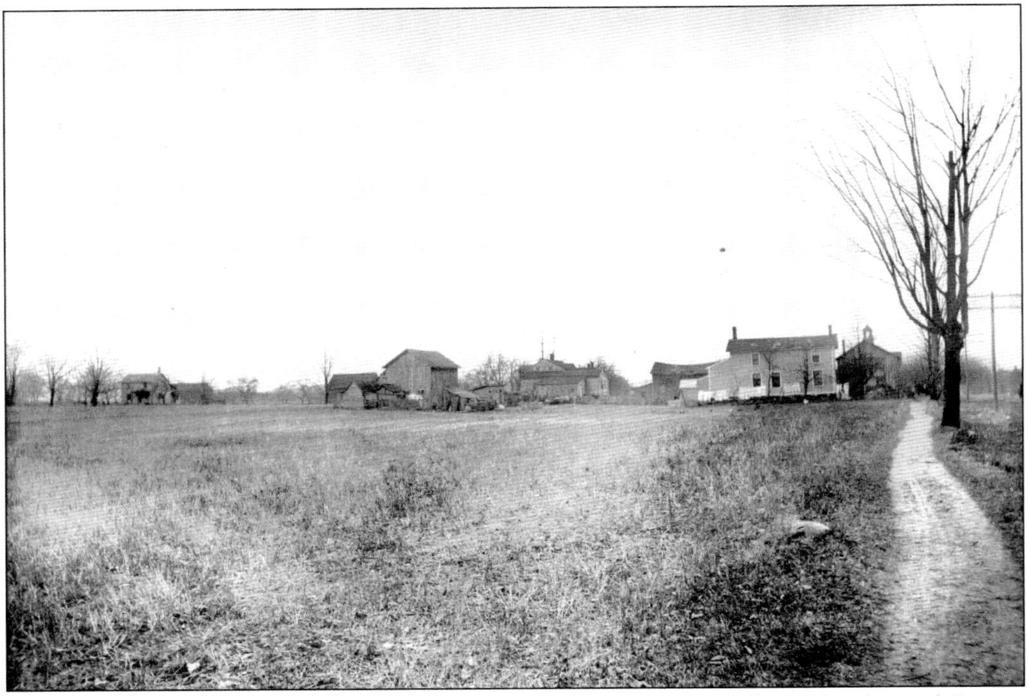

This 1907 view looking north up Baird Road from Upper Corners shows the farm of George Leonard, born in Penfield in 1841. Besides farming his land for many years, Leonard was president of the board of education. His father, Ichabod Leonard Jr., came to Penfield in 1823 from Pittsfield, Massachusetts, and settled on this farmland at Upper Corners. Leonard played an integral role in the local education and was one of the originators of the Penfield Seminary. Today, the land that was once the Leonard Estate is now part of the Baird Road Community Center and a housing development built in the 1960s. Aptly, the road running through it is named Leonard Crescent.

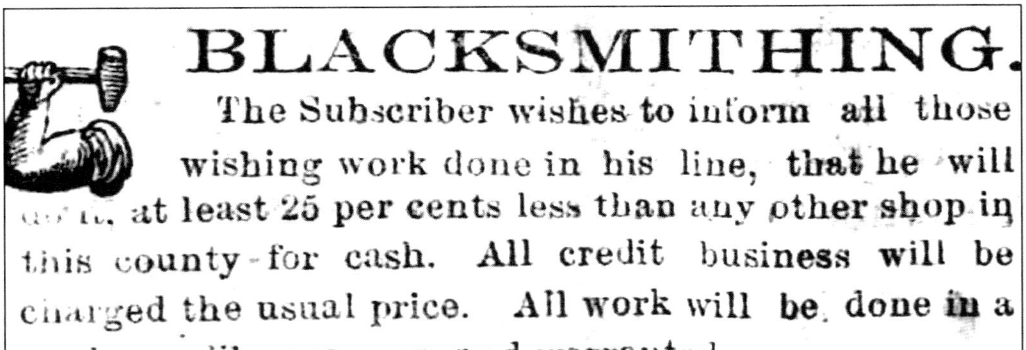

BLACKSMITHING.

The Subscriber wishes to inform all those wishing work done in his line, that he will do it, at least 25 per cents less than any other shop in this county for cash. All credit business will be charged the usual price. All work will be done in a workman like manner, and warranted.

Penfield, Upper Corners, B C. SWEET.

Feb. 5th, 1866.

This advertisement for blacksmithing at Upper Corners is from the February 5, 1866, edition of the *Penfield Extra*.

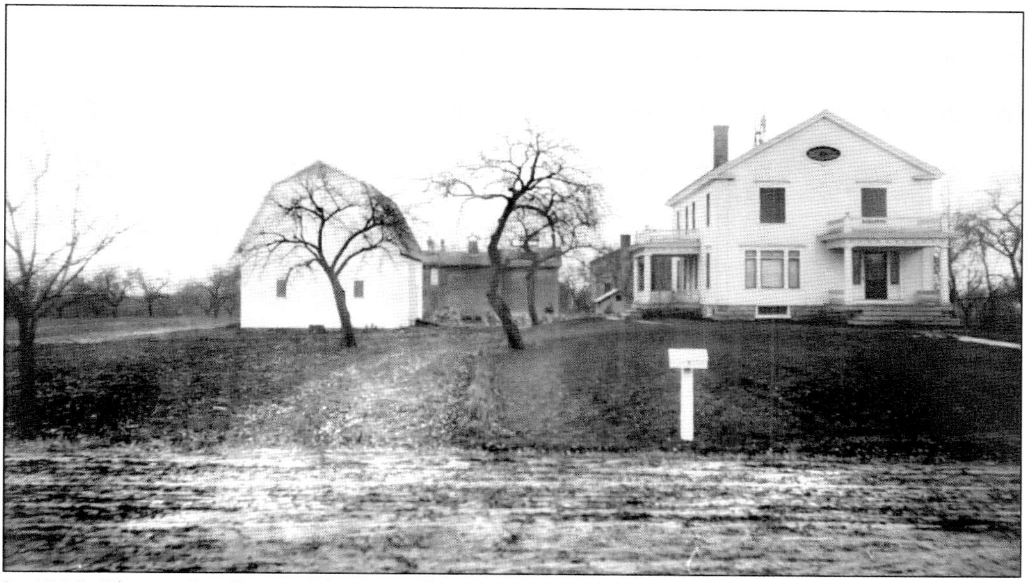

In 1806, Christopher Brizee (also Brisee) came to Penfield and bought this property from Daniel Penfield. Brizee built a small structure at the southwest corner of Upper Corners and farmed his property. By 1822, he built this house at 1941 Penfield Road. He then became a tavern keeper and ran an inn for travelers on the stage. Brizee died in 1841. By the 1870s, the farmland behind the house was a nursery owned by William Fellows, and the house was owned by T. King. Joseph and Ida Sandle purchased the house and farmland in the 1880s, naming it Sunny Brook Farm. The Brizee Tavern Stand was designated as a Penfield landmark in 1976.

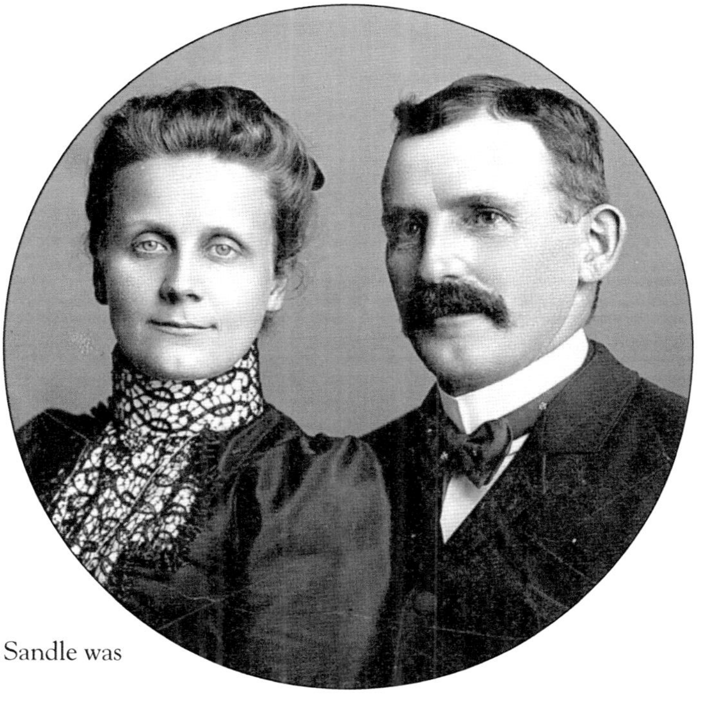

This portrait of Ida and Joseph Sandle was taken c. 1890.

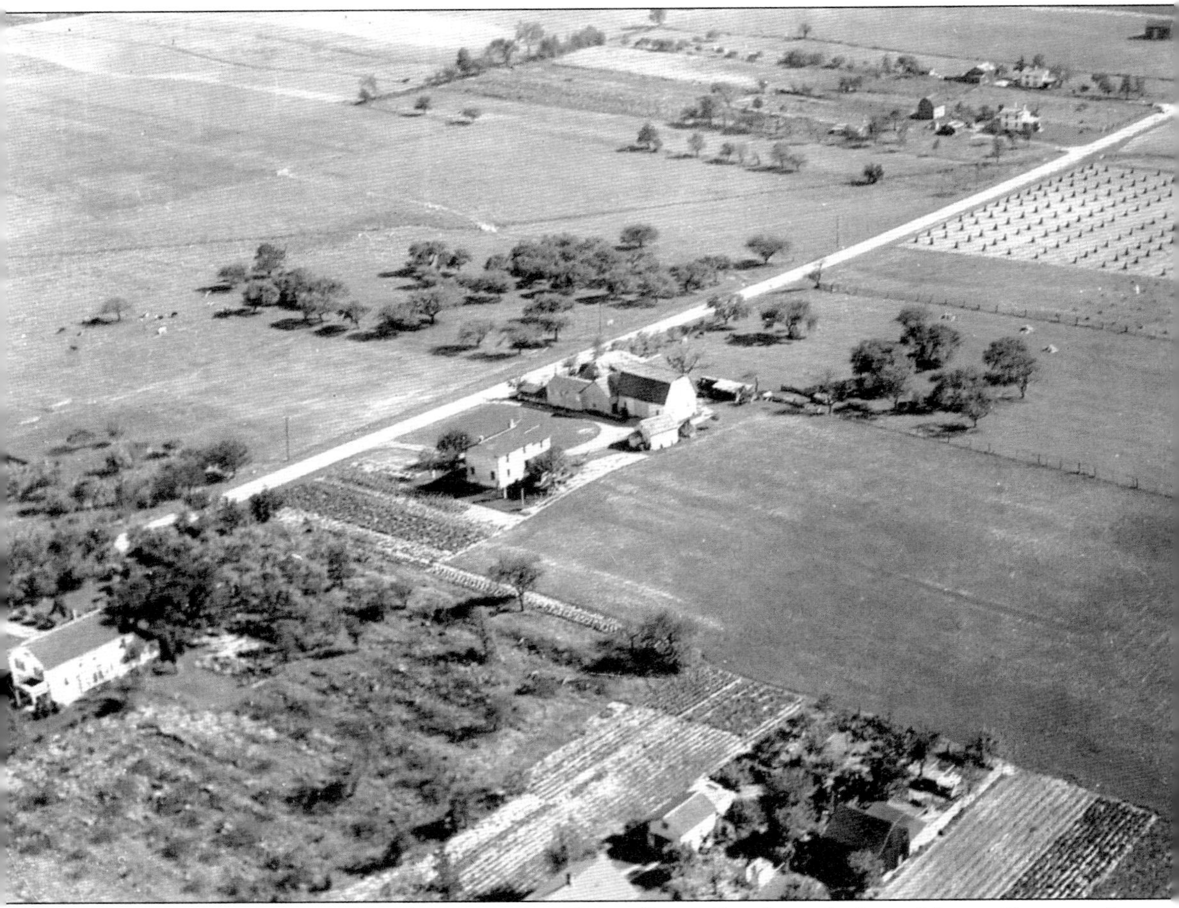

This aerial photograph, taken c. 1940, shows Baird Road south from Upper Corners. In the lower left corner is the Brizee-Sandle House. The Feigel Farm is in the middle of the photograph, and in the upper right are the Ludwig and Urckfitz Farms.

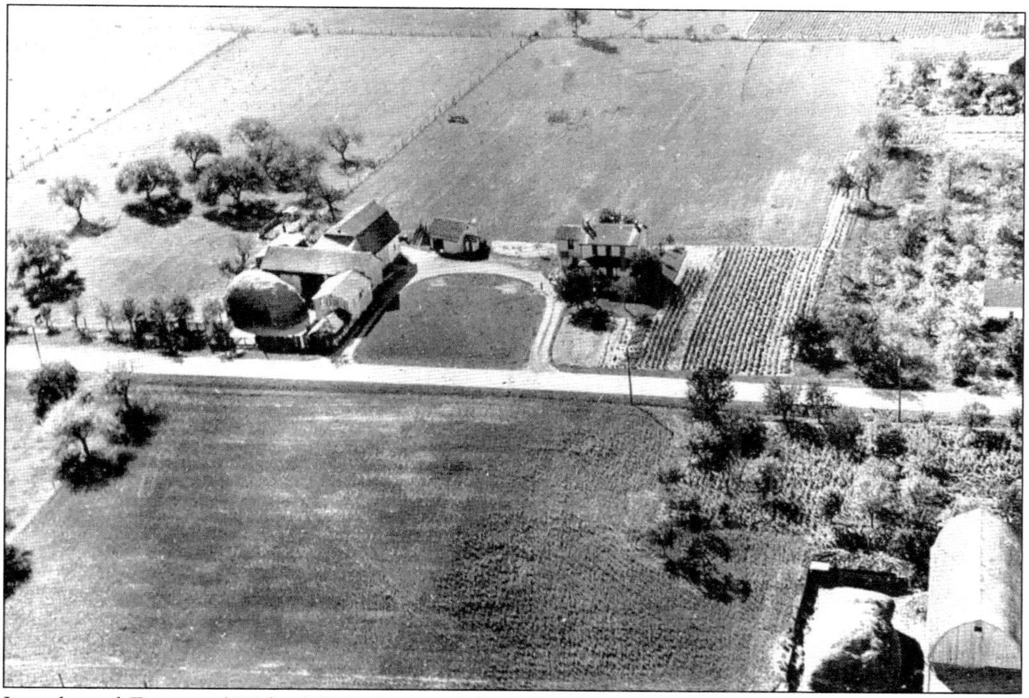

Joseph and Frances (Weber) Feigel moved from Rochester to Penfield in 1911 and purchased Sunny Brook Farm from Joseph Sandle. In the 1950s, the farmland was sold for the development of suburban housing. This house stood at 2121 Baird Road. It was built c. 1850 and was razed in 1962. At that time, Feigel's second son, John, moved the smallest barn down the road to 2145 Baird Road, which still stands today on this property.

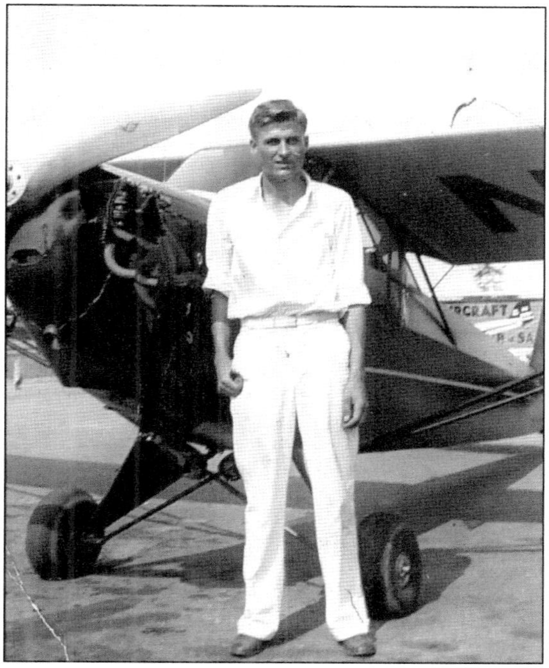

Joseph Feigel's first son, Joseph, had a love for aviation. He learned to fly airplanes in his late teens at the old Brizee Field in East Rochester. He was taught by the famous pilot Spencer Punnet, "a pilot's pilot." Feigel was one of the youngest commercial pilots in Rochester. In later years, as an instructor, he taught hundreds to fly. Today, one of the biplanes flown by Feigel in World War II is on display at the Smithsonian in Washington, D.C. (Image courtesy of Tom Feigel.)

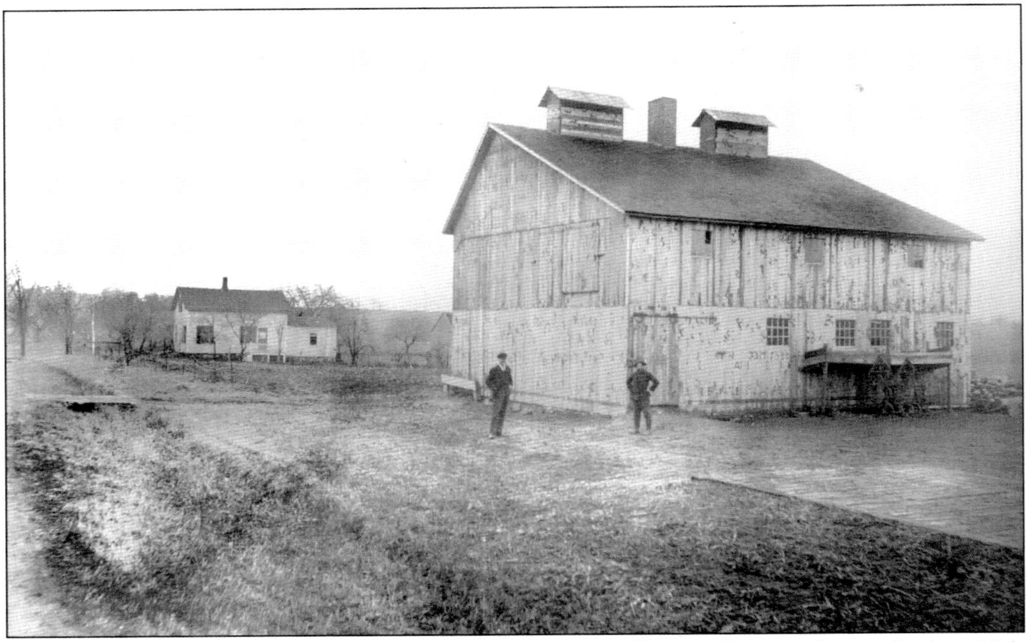

James Hagreen and family lived on the southeast corner of Upper Corners during the late 19th century and into the 20th century. Hagreen was a farmer with about 75 acres of land off Baird Road. He may be one of the men standing in this picture, along with his fruit evaporator. The Hagreen House can be seen in the background.

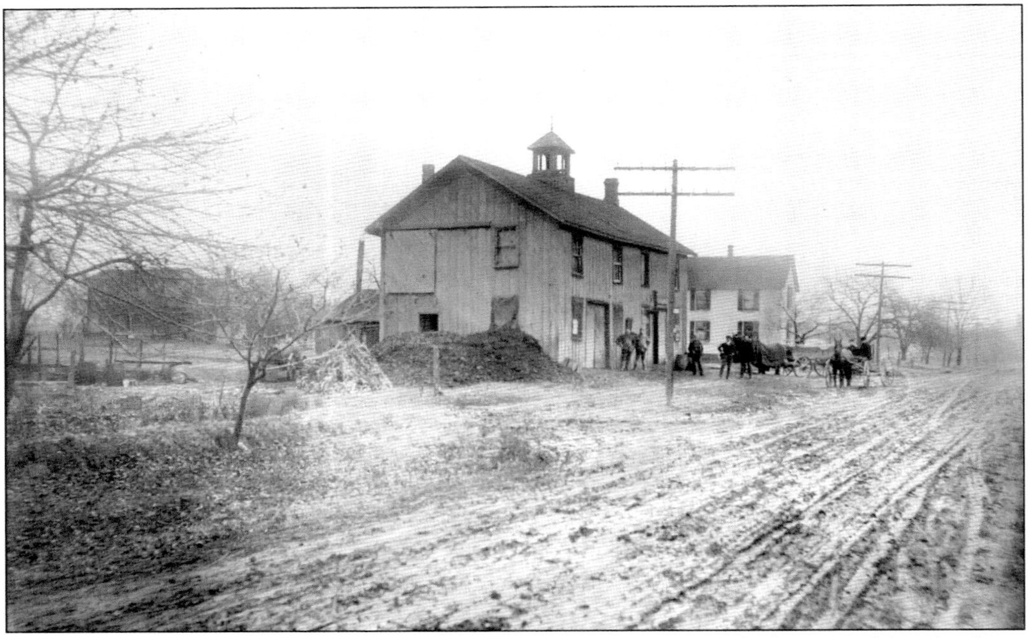

In the early 1900s, Clayton VanOstrand leased from George Leonard a house and farmland just north of the Upper Corners, off Baird Road. The house and barn can be seen in this photograph. This barn either burned or was taken down between 1902 and 1924. It is shown on the 1902 map of Penfield but is not shown on the 1924 map.

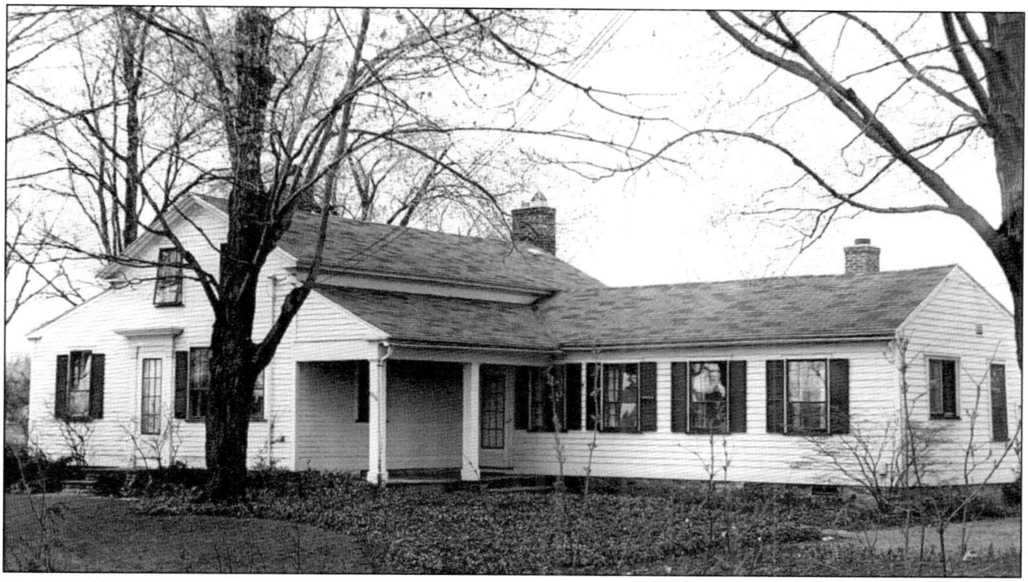

Peter Silliman built this house at 1996 Penfield Road in 1832. In 1839, Horace Ranney and family purchased the home. By 1925, the house was sold to Clark Dye, the principal of the old Penfield High School. In 1943, Donald Brown, owner of the Brown Brothers Nursery, purchased the house. The house was designated as a Penfield landmark in 1975.

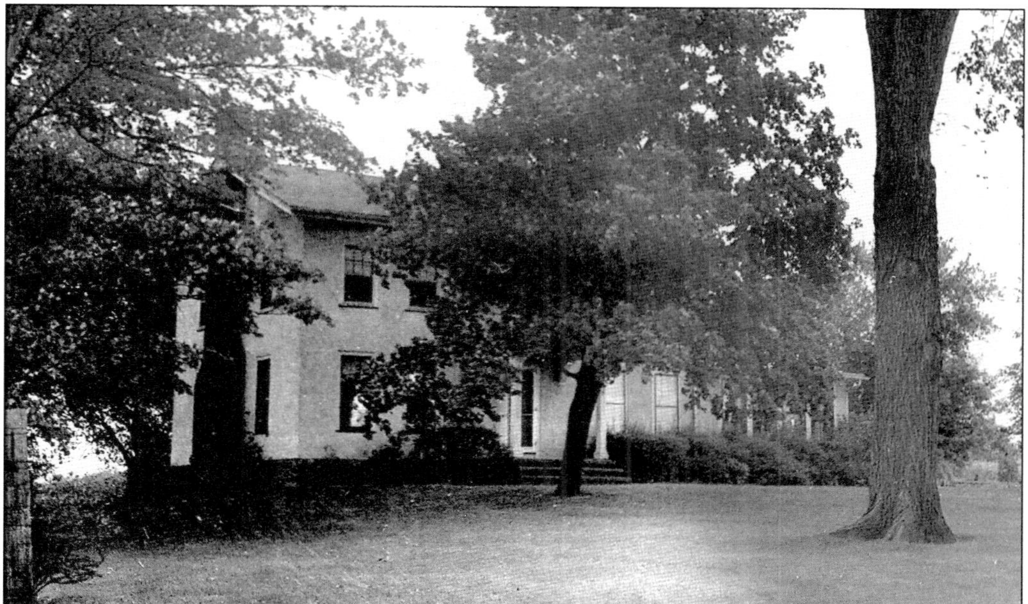

The house at 2040 Penfield Road was purchased in 1856 by James Harris. Harris was born in 1821 in a log cabin in North Penfield (what would become Webster in 1840). His father, William Harris, who settled in North Penfield in 1809, was thought to be the first teacher in the early schools in this area. The farmland of the Harris family, named Grandview Farm, was sold off to the town of Penfield in the 1970s for a school and park, aptly named Harris Hill. The Harris House was designated as a Penfield landmark in 1983.

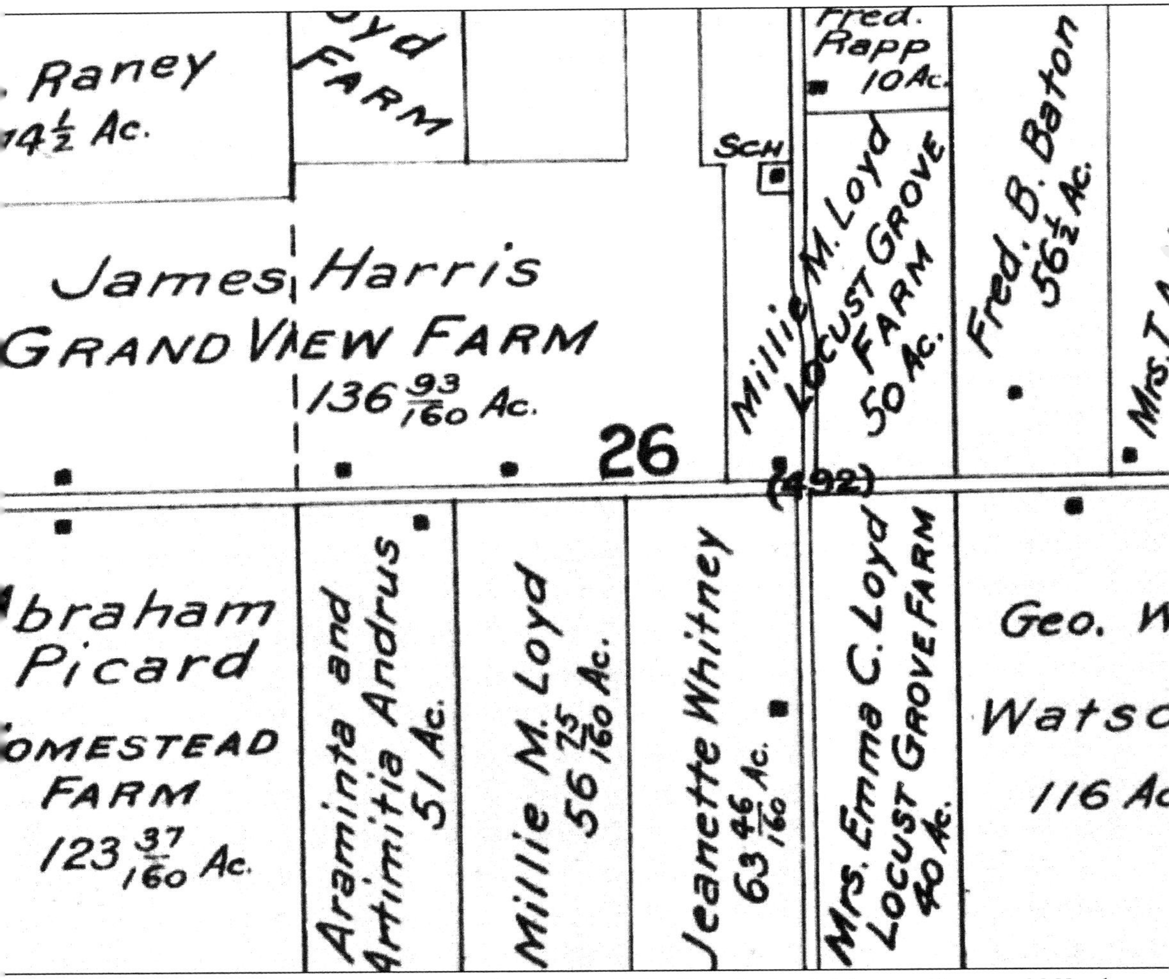

This map of Lloyd's Corners is from the 1902 *Plat Book of Monroe County, N.Y.*, by J. M. Lathrop and Company. This present intersection is at Penfield Road (Route 441) and Nine Mile Point Road (Route 250, also known as Webster-Fairport Road). The Lloyd family farm once stood at 2103 Webster-Fairport Road, and the family also owned land all around the intersection for many years. The Lloyd name is misspelled on this map. The Lloyd farm was named Locust Grove Farm.

Five

LOVETT'S CORNERS

The corners in its heyday was a busy, thriving community of well-kept homes, white picket fences, and beautiful trees. It boasted three blacksmith shops, a cooperage, a store, several nurseries, and a number of saloons.

—James and Dorothy Shedd,
"Lovett's Corners," October 1953

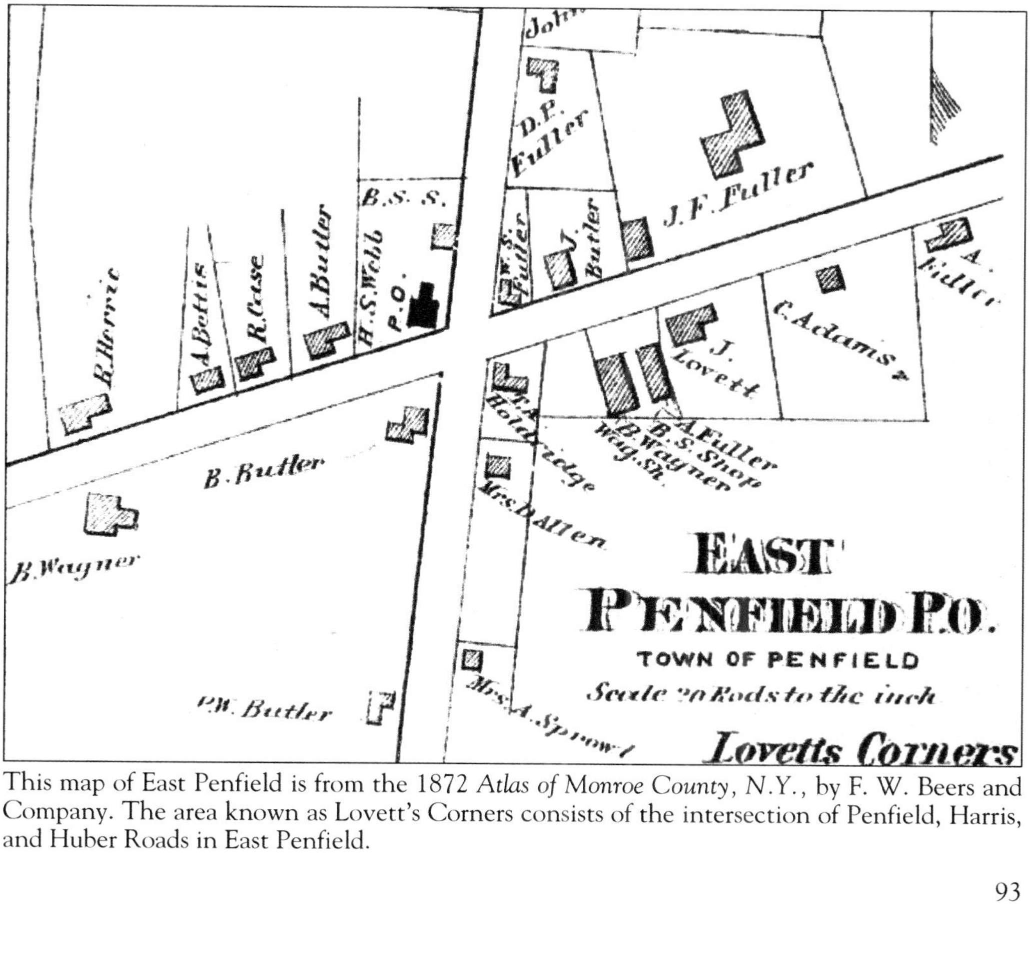

This map of East Penfield is from the 1872 *Atlas of Monroe County*, N.Y., by F. W. Beers and Company. The area known as Lovett's Corners consists of the intersection of Penfield, Harris, and Huber Roads in East Penfield.

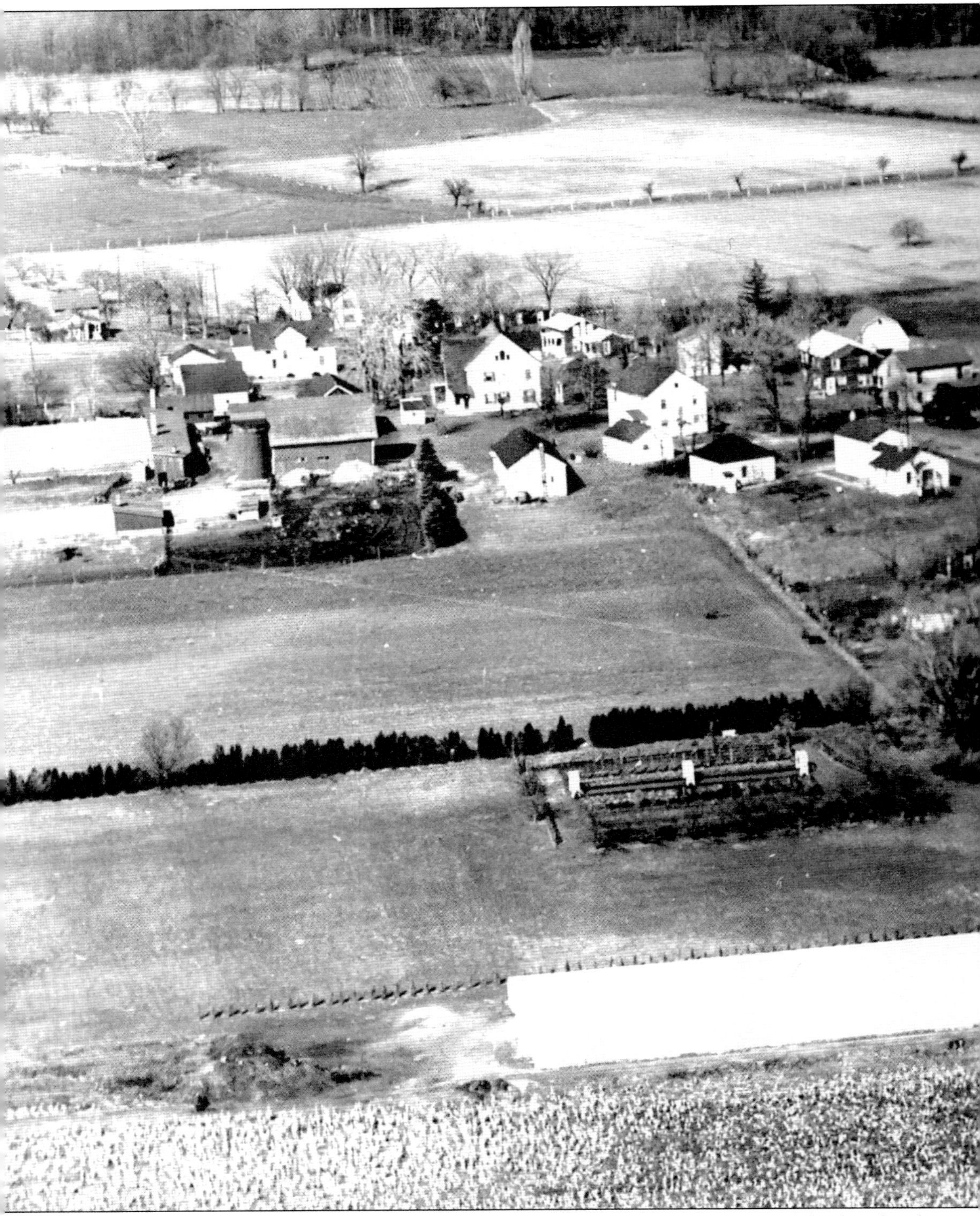

Seen here is the hamlet of East Penfield. Joseph Fuller and family were one of the first families to settle in East Penfield between 1800 and 1804. The Fullers built a log cabin on their property,

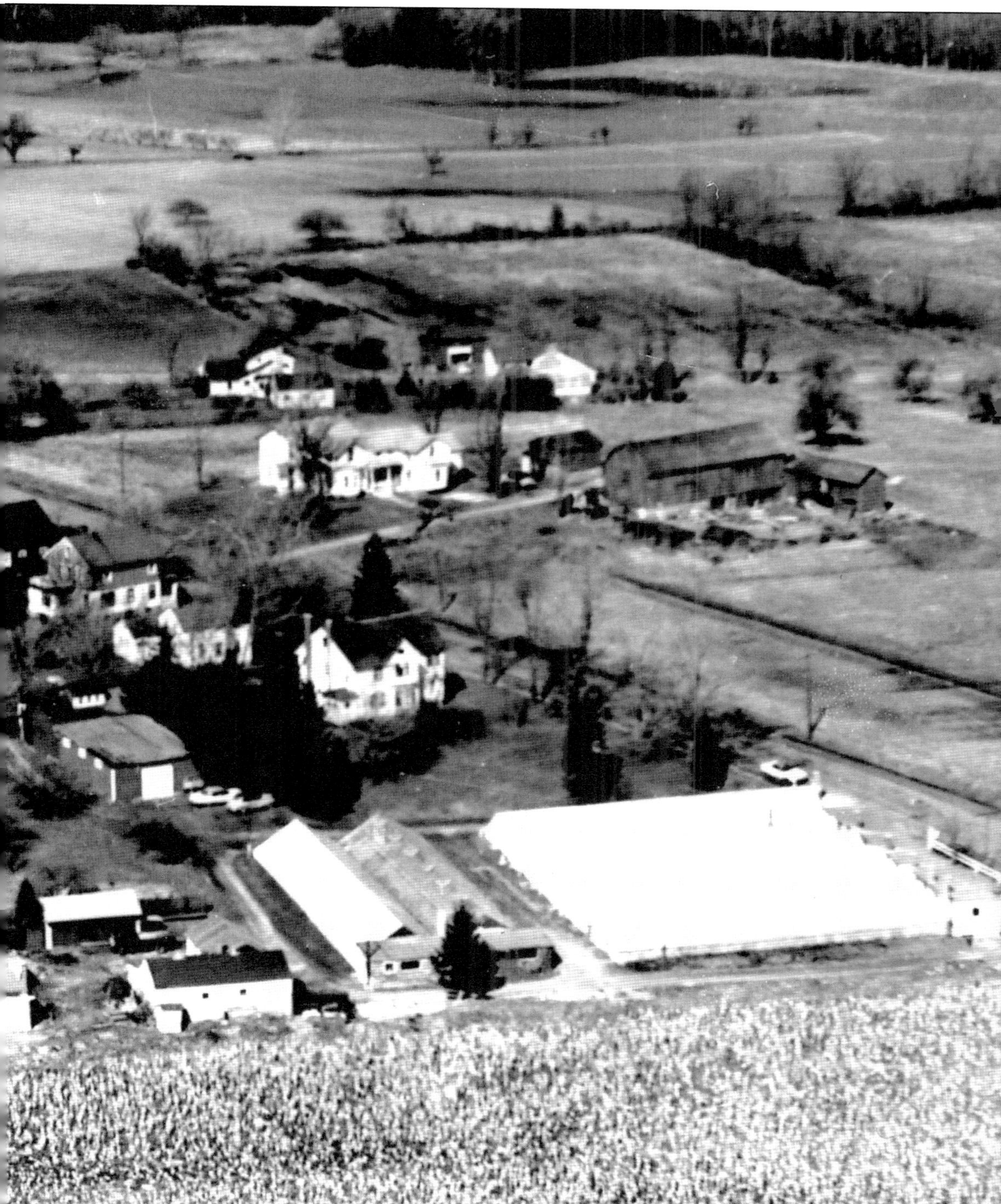

just east of the corners.

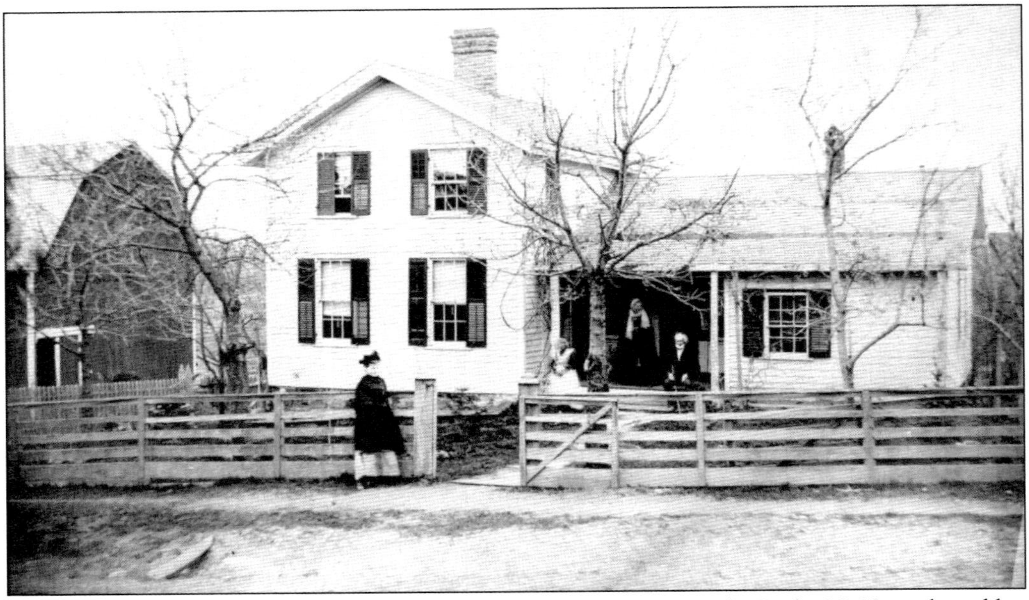

The Herrick Homestead, at 2468 Penfield Road, was built *c.* 1846 for Rufus N. Herrick and his wife, Lucinda Crippen. After Lucinda died in 1860, Herrick married Sarah Ann Lovett (James Lovett's daughter). In 1868, the couple had a son named Rufus Jr., who married Edith May Johnson in 1886. By 1902, Rufus Jr. took over the ownership of the house, and it stayed in the family for many years. Today, the house has been extensively remodeled and is no longer owned by the Herrick family.

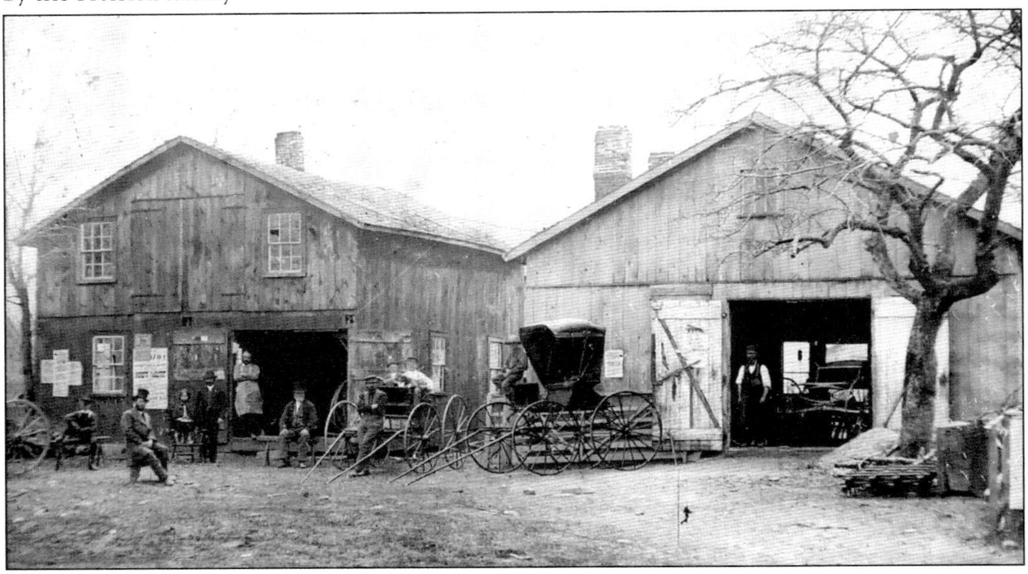

The William Wagner blacksmith shop stood on the south side of Penfield Road, just east of Huber Road. This was once the site of the first "smithy" in East Penfield, built by Artemus Fuller. It was then sold to Barney Wagner and passed down to his son, William. The blacksmith shop operated until 1925, doing types of jobs such as horseshoeing and wagon work. The person sitting in the left barn doorway is James Lovett. He can easily be identified by his long white beard.

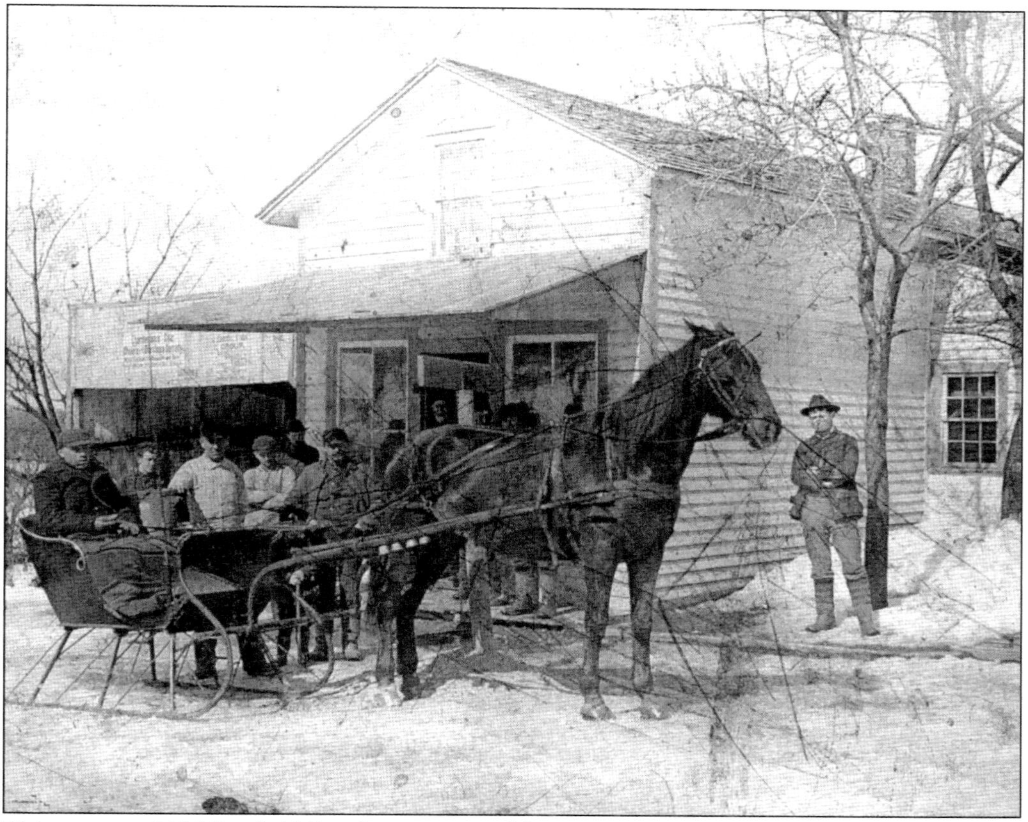

This store at 2476 Penfield Road was operated by Henry Gifford c. 1900. Gifford owned the store for almost 50 years. Prior to that, in the 1850s, J. W. Conklin owned the store. Even earlier, the building was used as a trading post, owned by Nathan Buck. The store continued in business until 1969. The building still stands today and is a residence.

It is now conceeded by all that
J. W. Conklin
of East Penfield is the best
Auctioneer
In this section of the country. That he will sell goods and chattles for the most money. And that his services can be had at the most reasonable rates.

J. W. Conklin became an auctioneer in the 1860s around East Penfield. This advertisement is from the February 26, 1866, issue of the *Penfield Extra*.

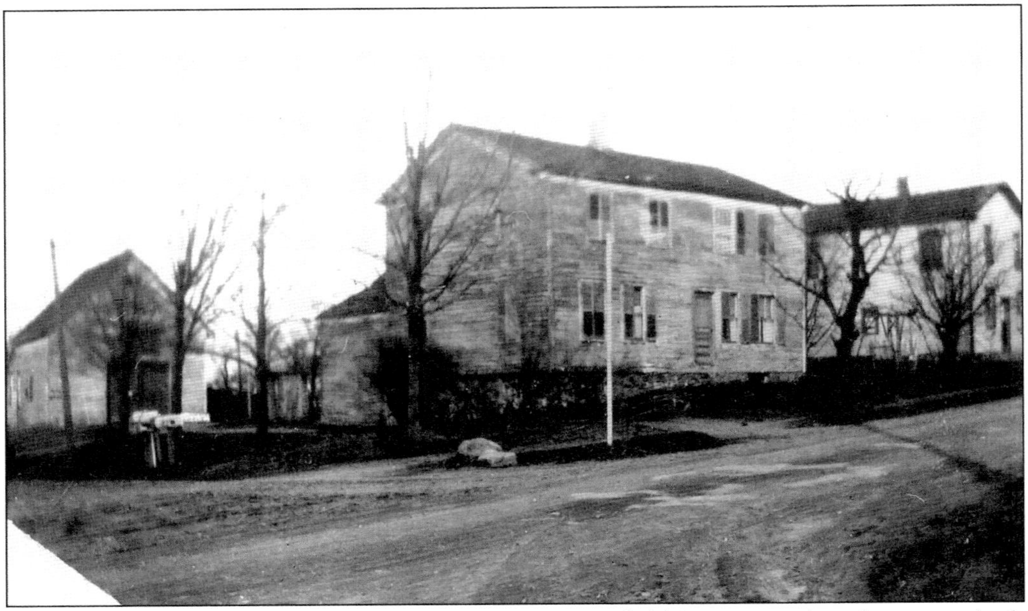

In the 1820s, James Lovett and family settled in East Penfield. Lovett purchased an inn, which he named Lovett's Tavern, from Winslow Heth, another pioneer of East Penfield. Lovett was also a deacon of the Baptist church in East Penfield. Lovett's Tavern is now a private residence, at 2492 Penfield Road.

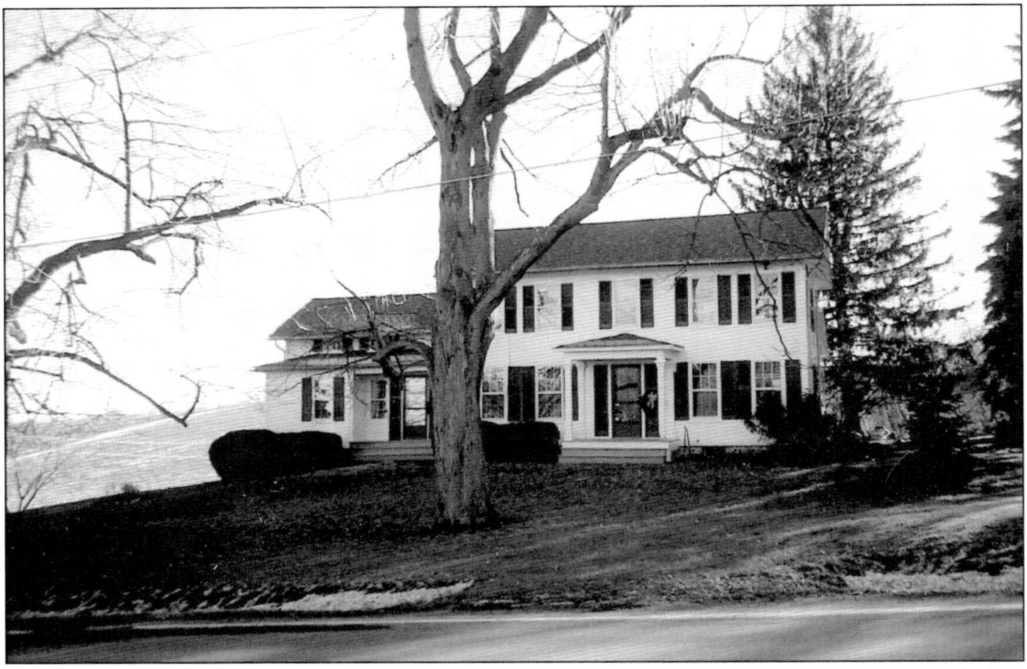

This house at 2701 Penfield Road in East Penfield was built in 1814 for Stephen M. Phelps. Phelps was a pathmaster, designating residents with responsibilities for upkeep of a certain distance of road in front of their homes. The Phelps House became listed on the National Register of Historic Places in 1995.

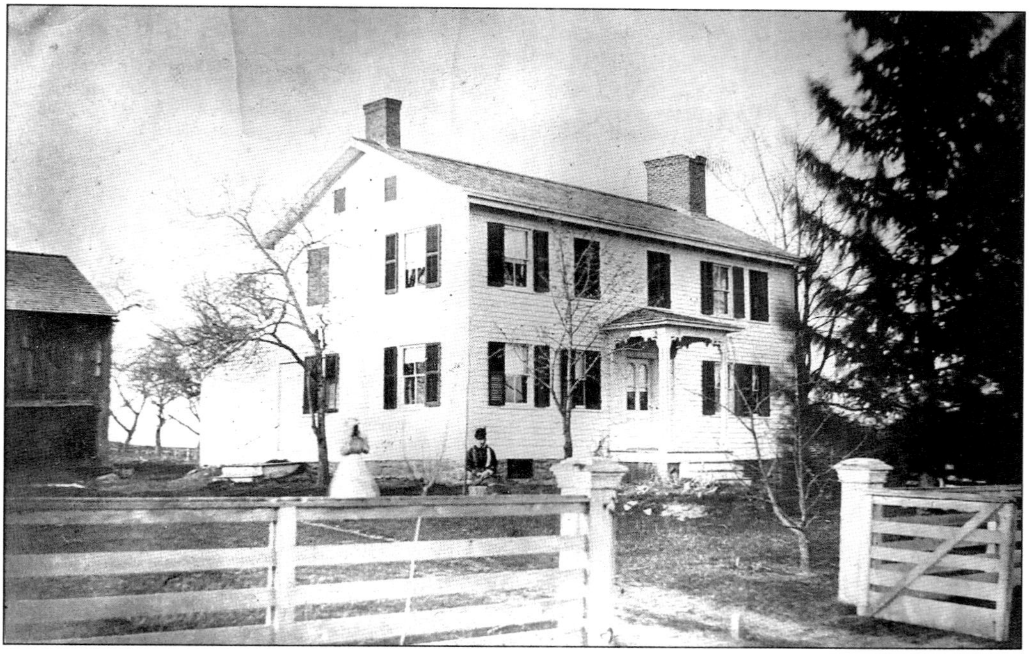

At 2780 Penfield Road, in East Penfield, stands a large house built in 1818 for Abner Brown and family. It was one of the first frame houses to be built in East Penfield. Abner Brown was a pioneer in Penfield, settling *c.* 1807. He was also a clerk, a pathmaster, and a farmer. In 1879, the house and farm were purchased by Benjamin Furman, a blacksmith. The Furman descendants owned the home until 1965. This house was listed on the National Register of Historic Places in 2003.

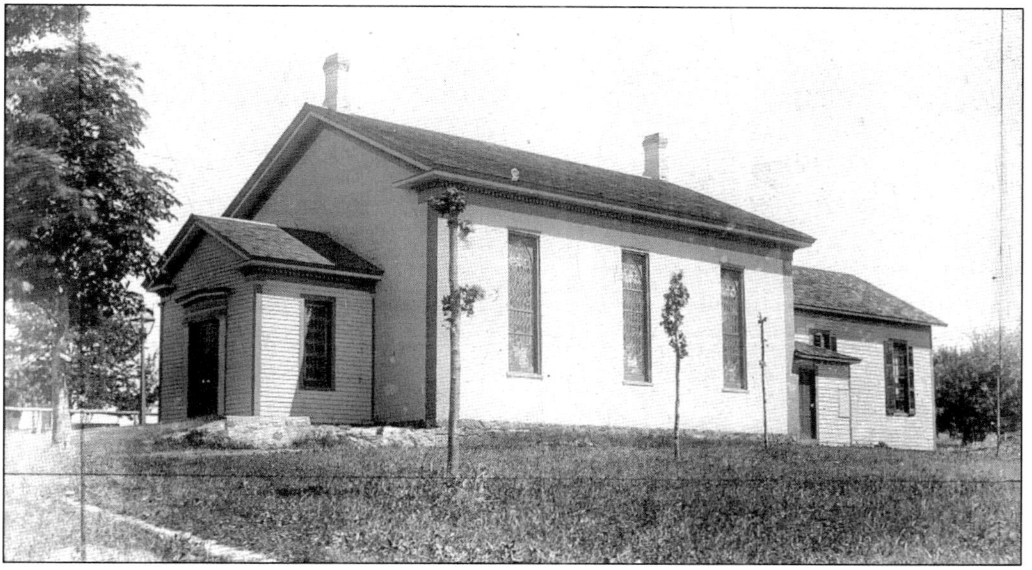

The East Penfield Baptist Church was built in 1836, but the congregation began worshiping in 1826. Mary McLatchey served here from 1896 to 1901. She was one of the first females to join the clergy in Monroe County and in the United States. This church, at 2635 Penfield Road, was designated as a Penfield landmark in 2003.

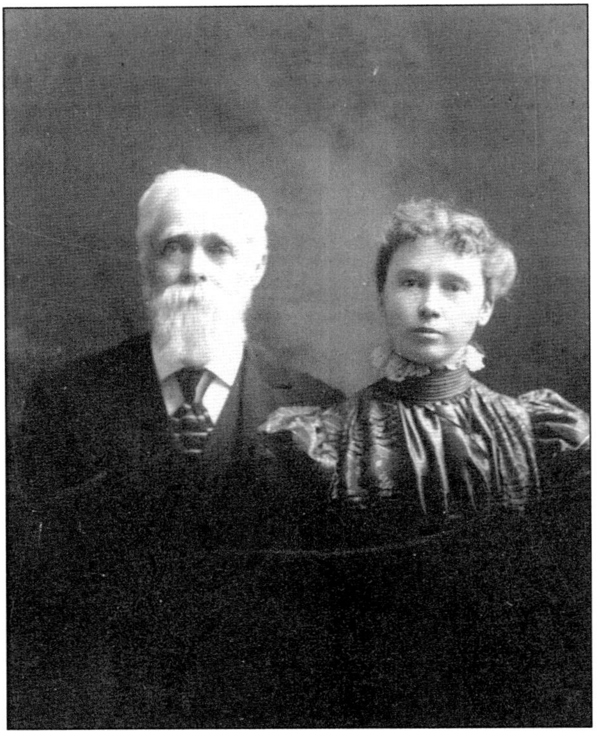

Preston Butler Nurseries stood on the east side of Huber Road in East Penfield. The owner, Preston Butler, is shown here c. 1900 with his daughter, Sara. The nursery was one of the earliest clematis growers in the country and the first in the area.

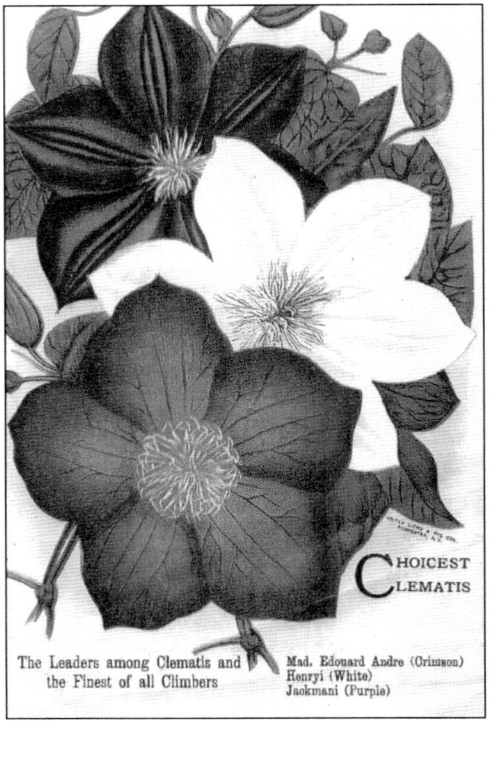

After working as a nurseryman for the Green Nursery Company, David S. George started his own nursery in East Penfield in 1894. He formed a partnership with his brother James I., and together they formed the George Brothers Nursery on land behind Lovett's Tavern. They specialized in growing clematis flowers. Years later, David split off from the company to create the D. S. George Nurseries. James continued to operate the George Brothers' Nursery. Their clematis flowers were shipped all over the United States. The George nurseries were the last nurseries in Penfield. In 1973, the clematis became the official flower for the town of Penfield in tribute to East Penfield nurseries.

Six

GRAVES' CORNERS AND ROSELAND

We are blessed with pleasant showers and the grass and the wheat begins to look beautiful, most kinds of fruit trees are now in blossom, and Penfield again begging to look lovely.

—*Penfield Extra*, May 4, 1866

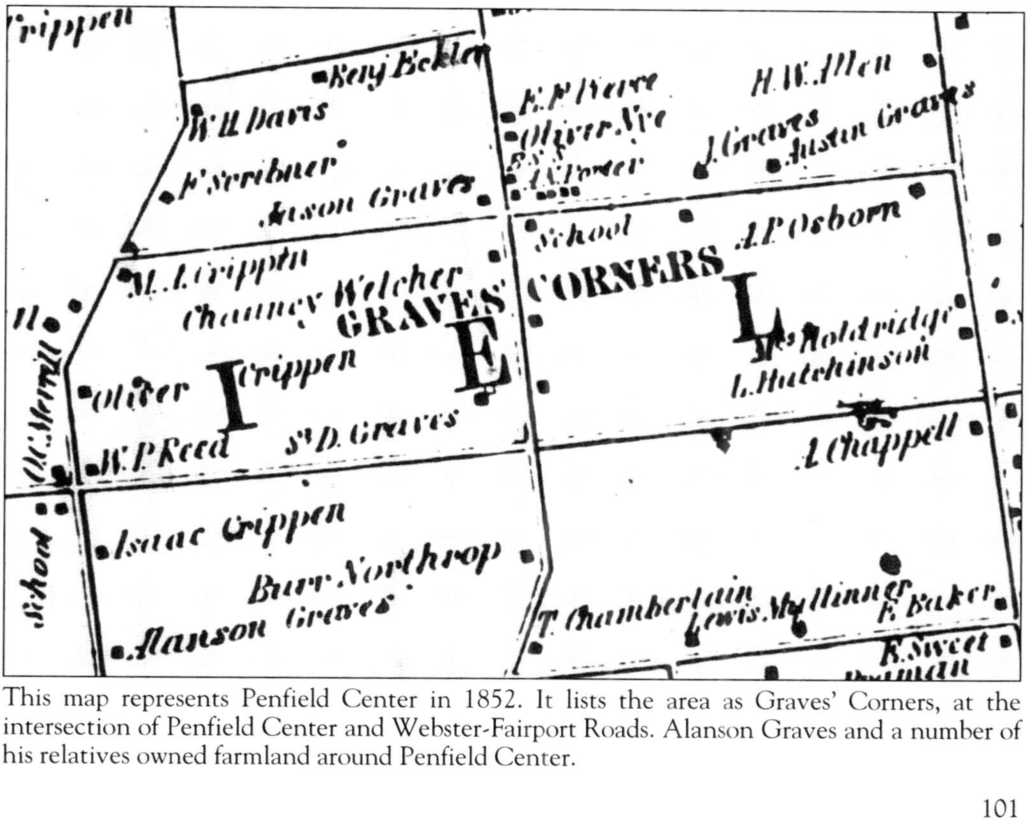

This map represents Penfield Center in 1852. It lists the area as Graves' Corners, at the intersection of Penfield Center and Webster-Fairport Roads. Alanson Graves and a number of his relatives owned farmland around Penfield Center.

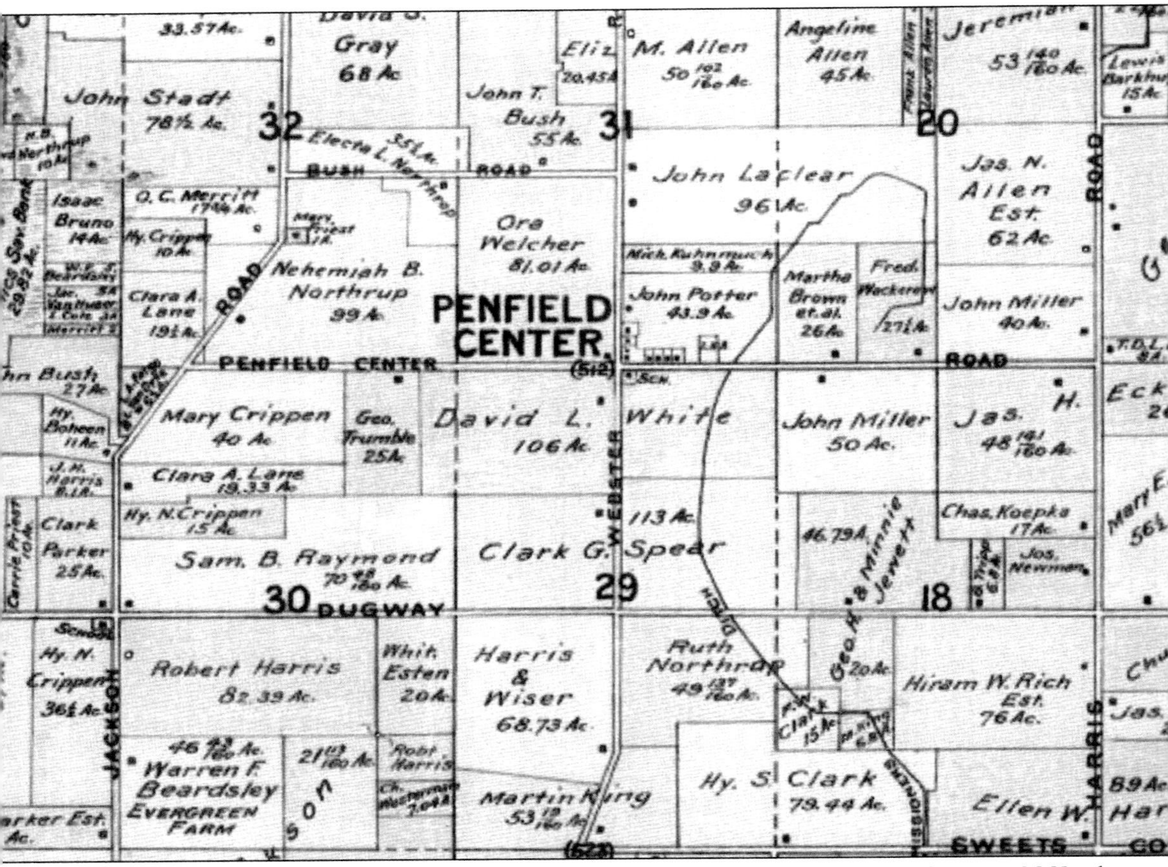

This map of Penfield Center is from the 1902 *Plat Book of Monroe County*, N.Y., by J. M. Lathrop and Company.

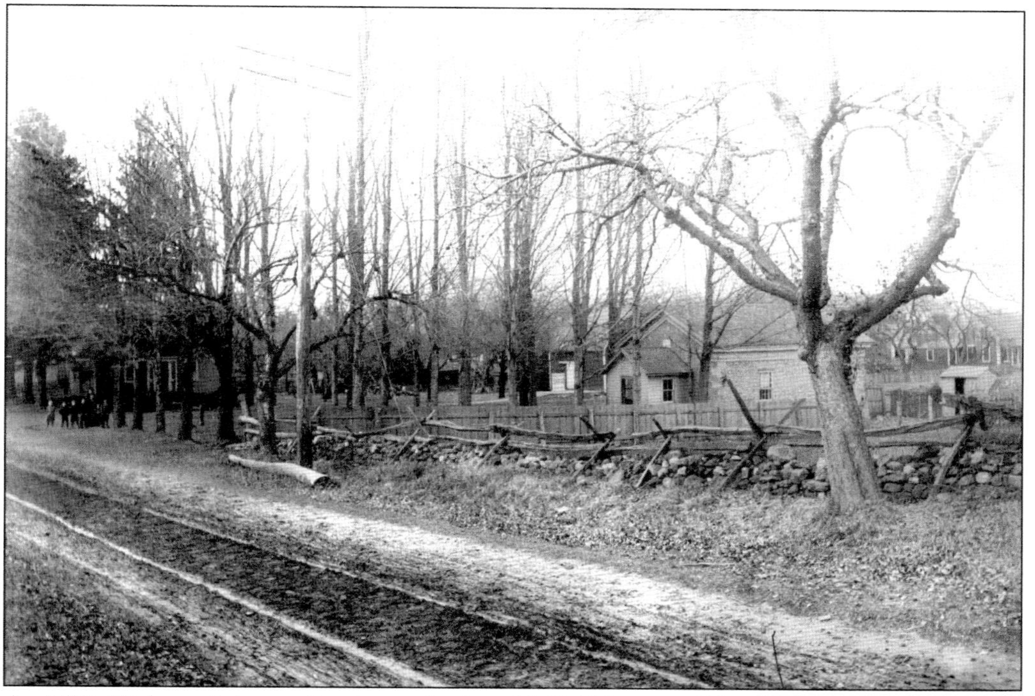

At 1586 Webster-Fairport Road stands the old Cobblestone School, District No. 11. The schoolhouse is at the southeast corner of Penfield Center and Webster-Fairport Roads. The earliest records show the school was opened for teaching in 1849. Today, the old school is a private residence.

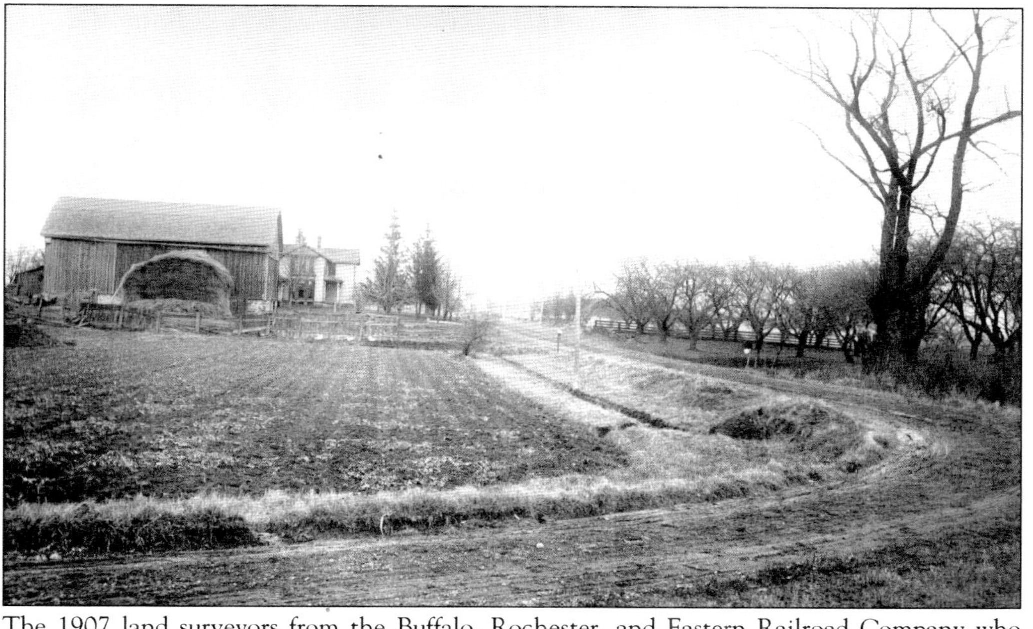

The 1907 land surveyors from the Buffalo, Rochester, and Eastern Railroad Company who came to Penfield to survey for a railroad took this photograph for their survey collection. The surveyors listed this corner as Osborns Corners-Penfield Center area.

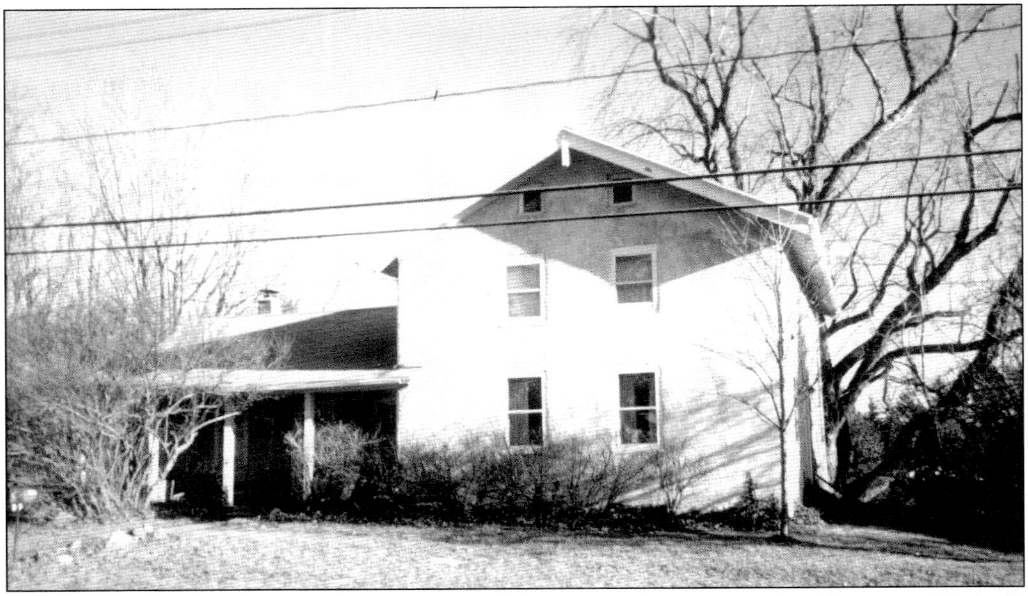

Originally from Rhode Island, Herrington Baker and family came to Penfield *c.* 1804. He built this house at 1778 Webster-Fairport Road *c.* 1809. A veteran of the American Revolution, Herrington married Lydia Jeems (James) *c.* 1775 before removing to Penfield. The Bakers had 12 children. Herrington died in Penfield in 1833 and is buried in Oakwood Cemetery. Lydia died in 1844 and is buried next to her husband. Descendants of Herrington Baker—the Stevens, the Foxes, and the Darlings—all resided in Penfield at one time or another.

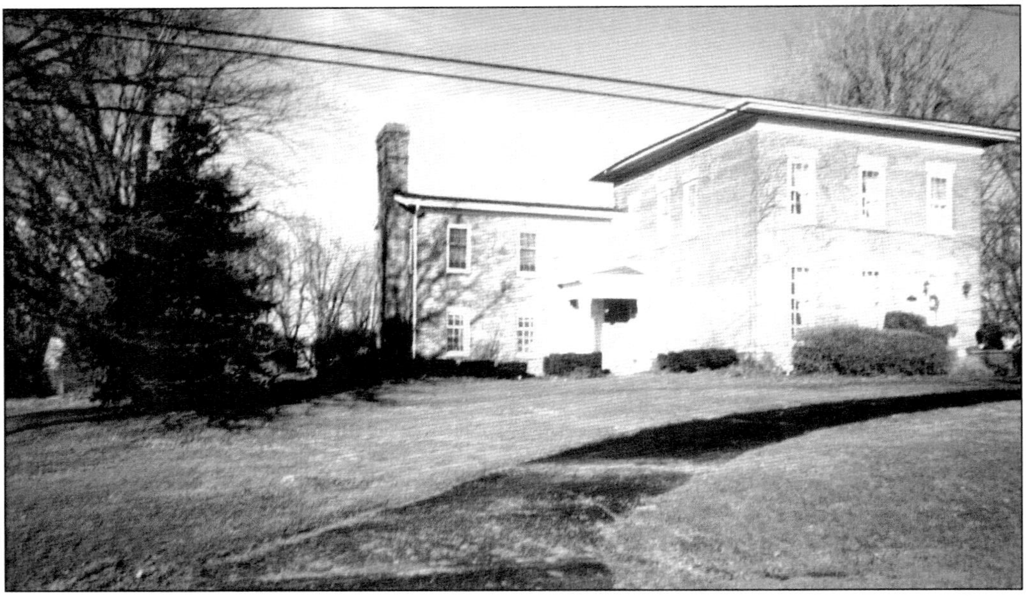

This house at 1720 Sweets Corners Road was built in 1810 for Tiffany Nettleton. Nettleton owned a farm on Harris Road but built this large house a couple of miles from his farm. By 1902, his grandson, Darius, owned the house and the 196 acres surrounding it. In 1904, Frederick Busch purchased the house, and it has remained in the Busch (also Bush) family for 100 years. The Tiffany Nettleton House became a Penfield landmark in 1977.

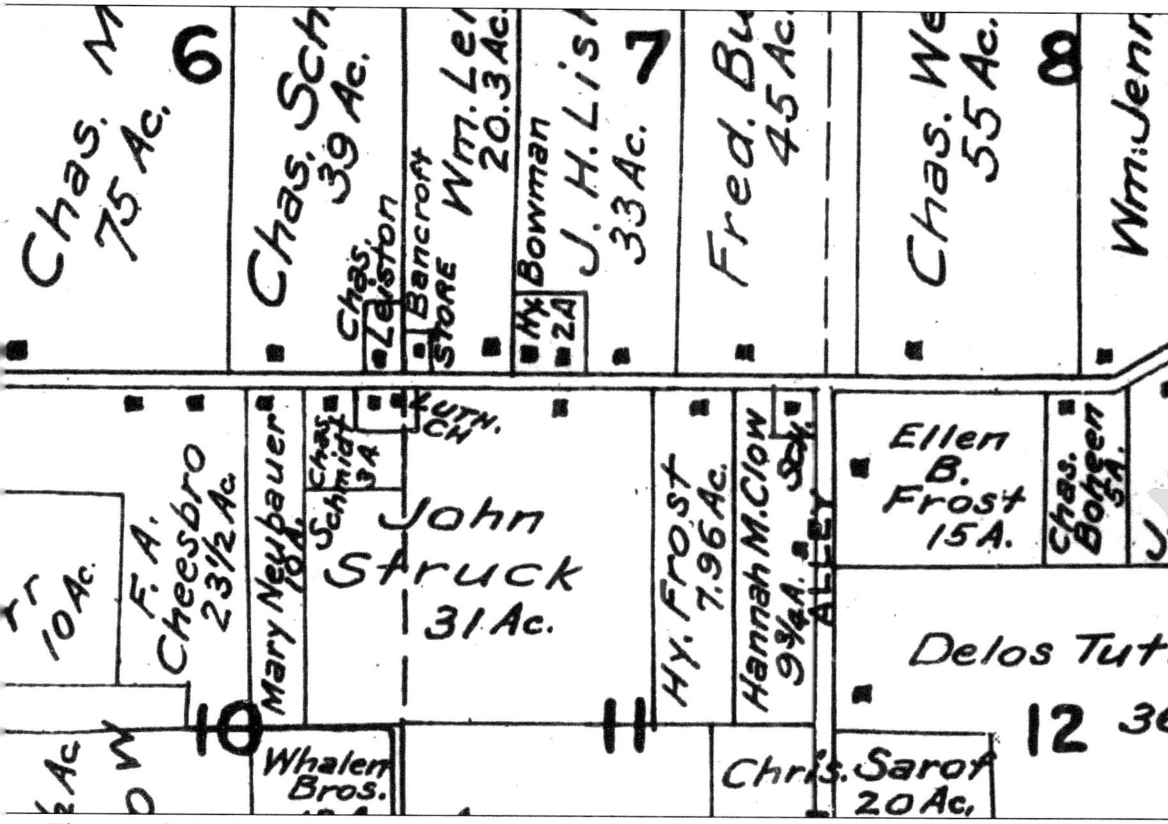

This map shows the Roseland area in northeast Penfield. It is from the 1902 *Plat Book of Monroe County, N.Y.*, by J. M. Lathrop and Company.

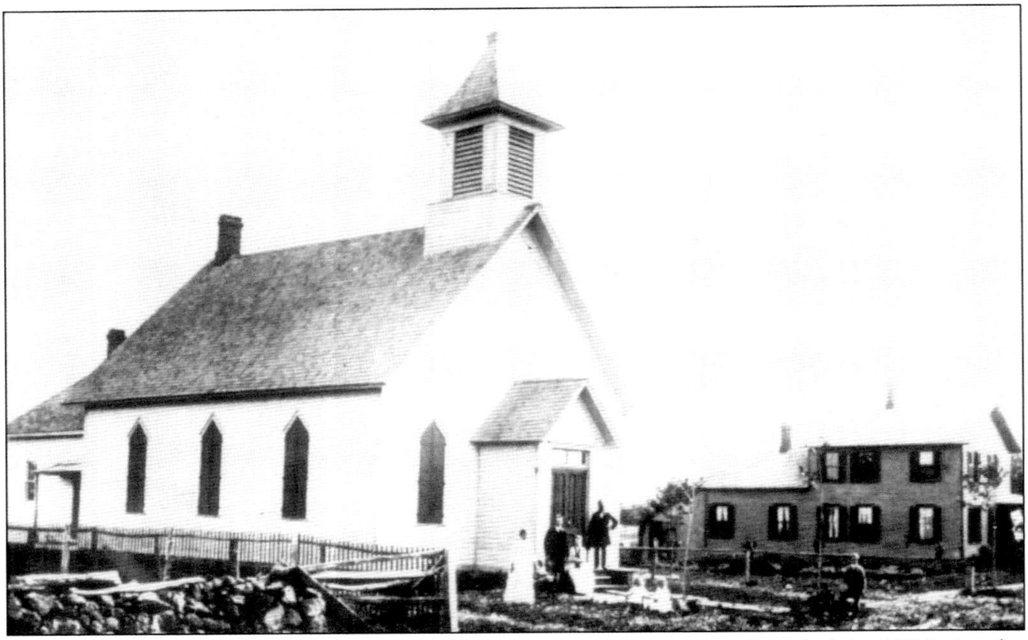

The German Evangelical Lutheran Bethlehem congregation was founded in 1876. In the mid- to late 1800s, many German immigrants settled in this area of northeast Penfield. Services were conducted in German until 1899. The area became known as Roseland around the early 1900s. The church stands at 1767 Plank Road.

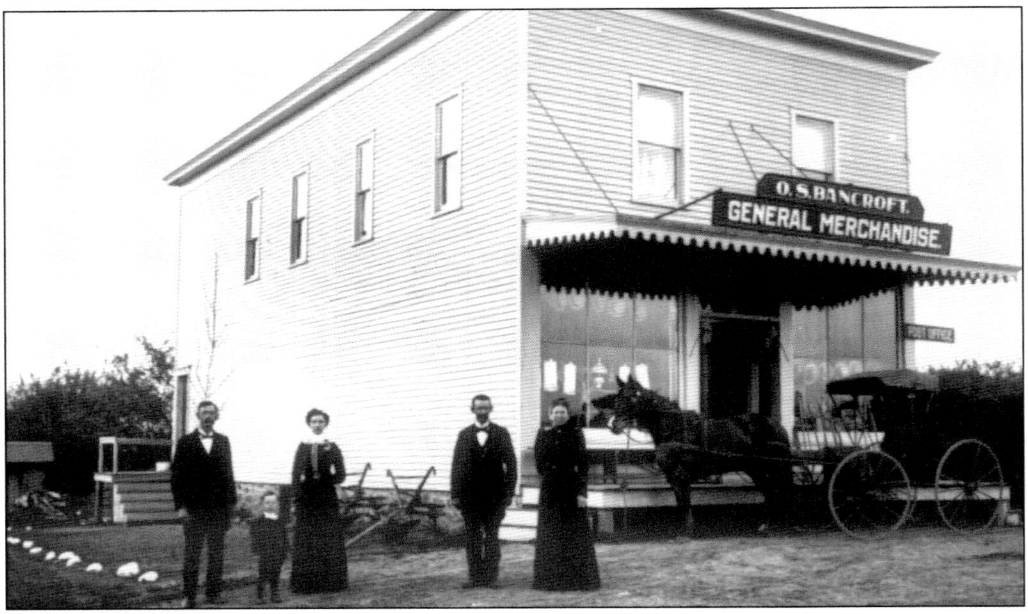

Otis Bancroft built a store on Plank Road, in northeast Penfield, *c.* 1900. He applied for a postal station to be located in his store at 1770 Plank Road. The post office needed a mailing address name within Penfield, so Bancroft and two other local men decided on the name Otisville. They later changed the name to Roseland, after Bancroft's wife, Rose. The post office served the community in east Penfield until 1915. This area has kept the name Roseland ever since.

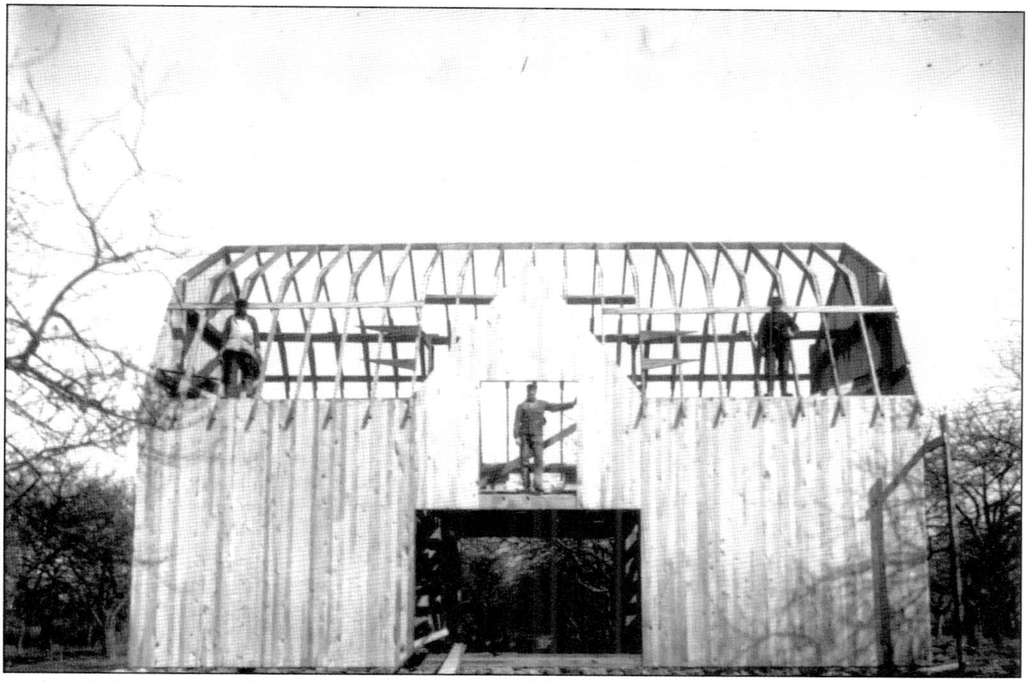

Arthur B. Frost was a farmer in northeast Penfield *c.* 1900. He was also quite a photographer. Frost took many photographs from around northeast Penfield. This is an image of his barn being built *c.* 1902–1903.

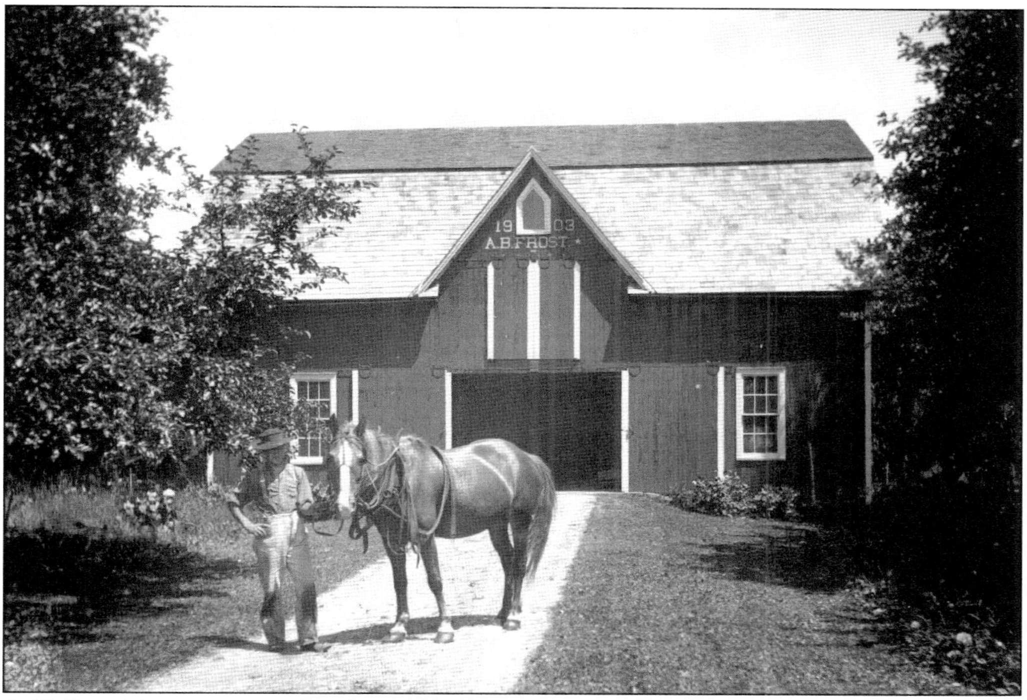

A. B. Frost's barn was completed in 1903. Henry Howe and his horse are pictured here.

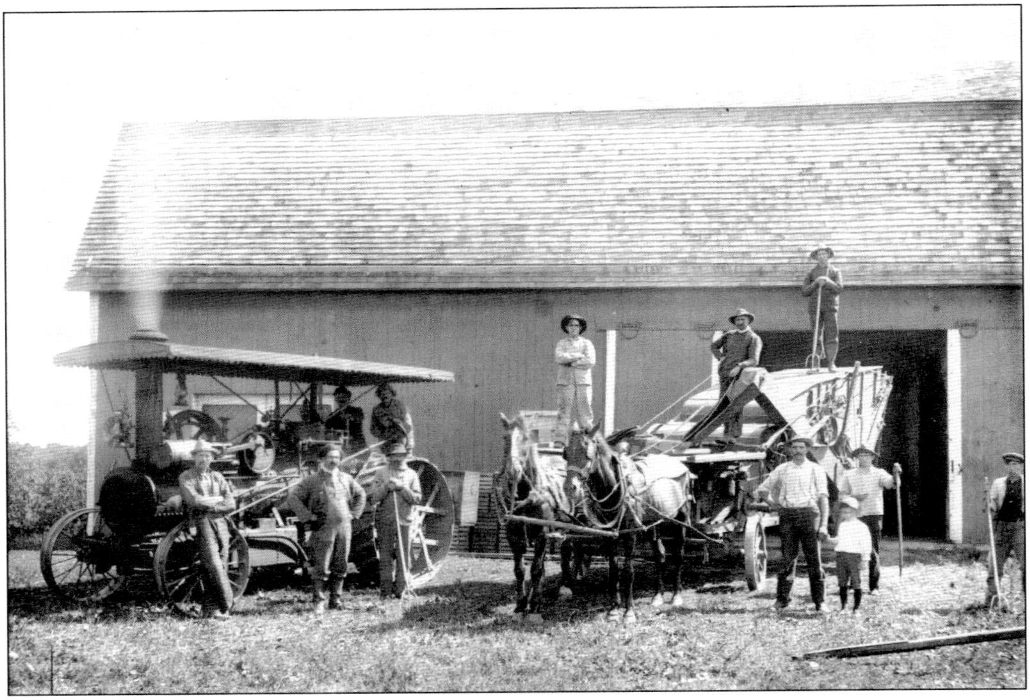

Shown are farming teams in northeast Penfield *c.* 1900.

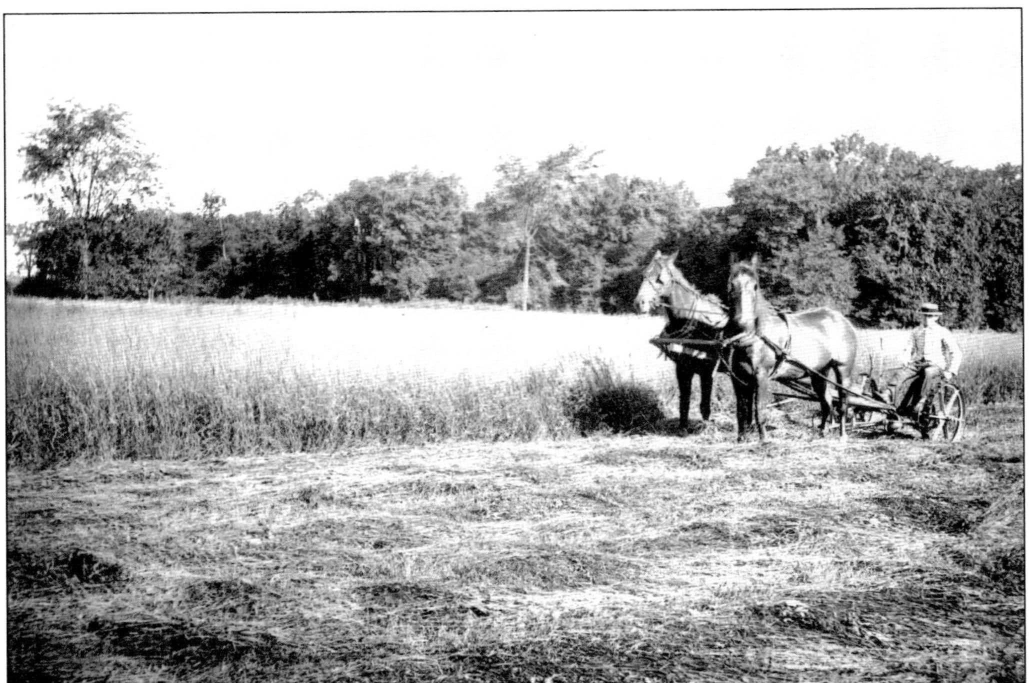

Thrashing wheat takes place on a farm in northeast Penfield *c.* 1900.

Seven

LaSalle's Landing, Dayton's Corners, and Bidwell

SATURDAY MORNING—The sun shines beautifully, and the snow is melting before its rays as fast as it fell on the two previous days.

—*Penfield Extra*, March 12, 1866

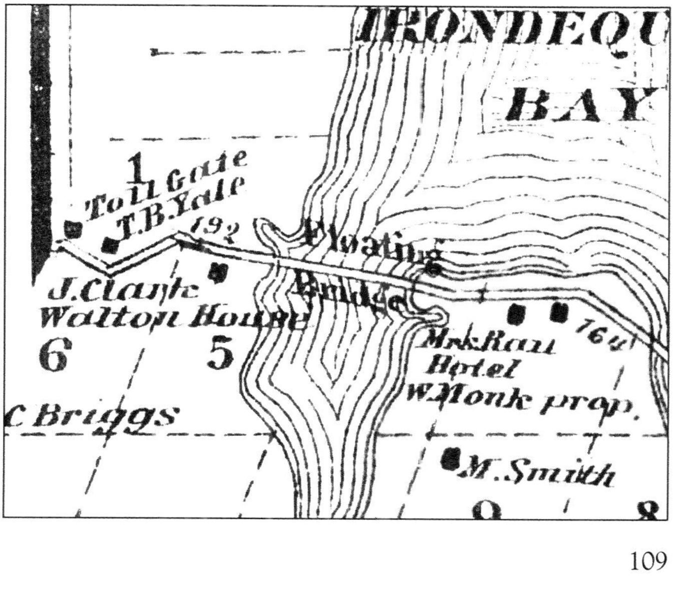

This map showing the head of the Irondequoit Bay, LaSalle's Landing, is from the 1872 *Atlas of Monroe County, N.Y.*, by F. W. Beers and Company. In 1669, Robert Cavelier de La Salle came across Lake Ontario, into the Irondequoit Bay, and through the Irondequoit Creek seeking information from the Iroquois about the trail west—the great Ohio Trail. Today, this area is known as LaSalle's Landing.

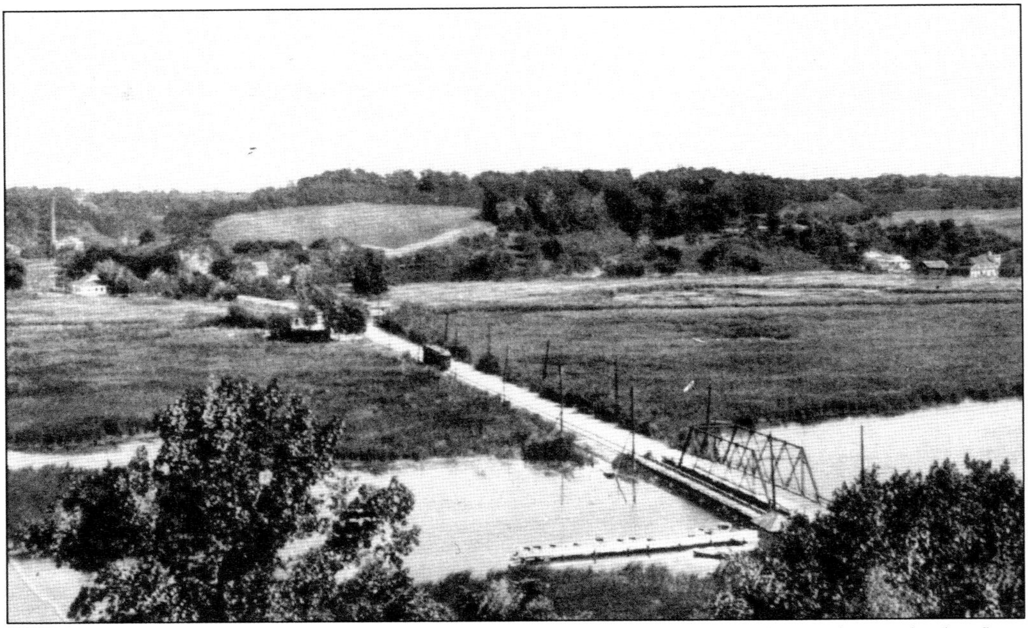

A float bridge once spanned the Irondequoit Creek at the head of the bay. Alongside the float bridge was a set of railroad tracks used by the Sodus Bay Railroad trolley. In 1872, W. Monk was the proprietor of the Float Bridge Hotel, just east of the bridge.

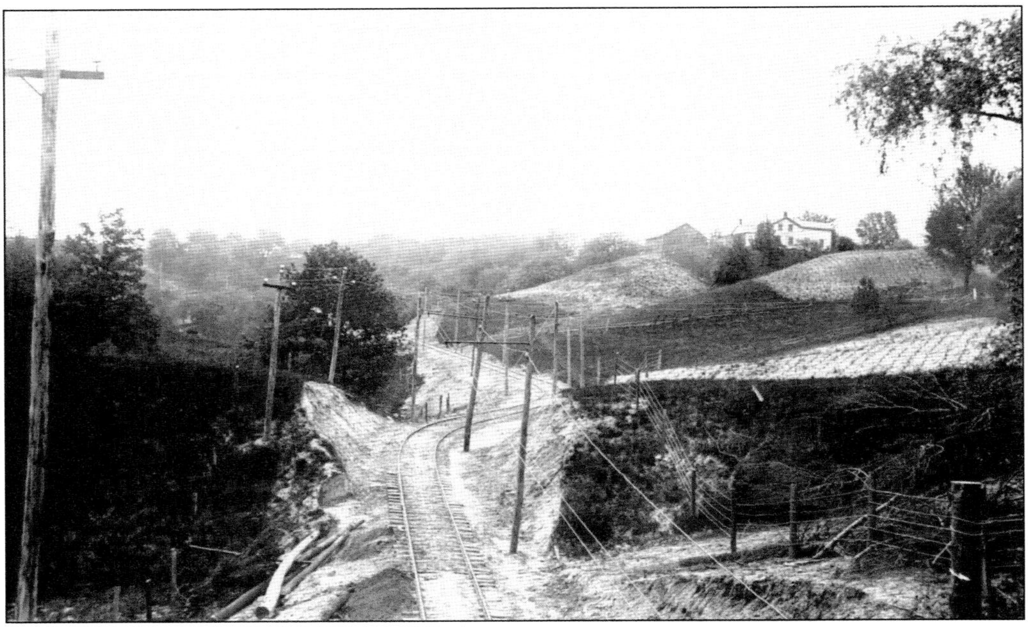

The Sodus Bay Railroad trolley started a passenger stop in 1901 at Dayton's Corners, at present-day Empire Boulevard and Plank Road. The stop was referred to as Dayton Siding 6. The trolley tracks ran along Drake Road (now Bay Road), turning south down Dayton Road (now Empire Boulevard) and meandering through the dunes down to the Irondequoit Bay. The trolley crossed the float bridge at the bay and was off to the city of Rochester.

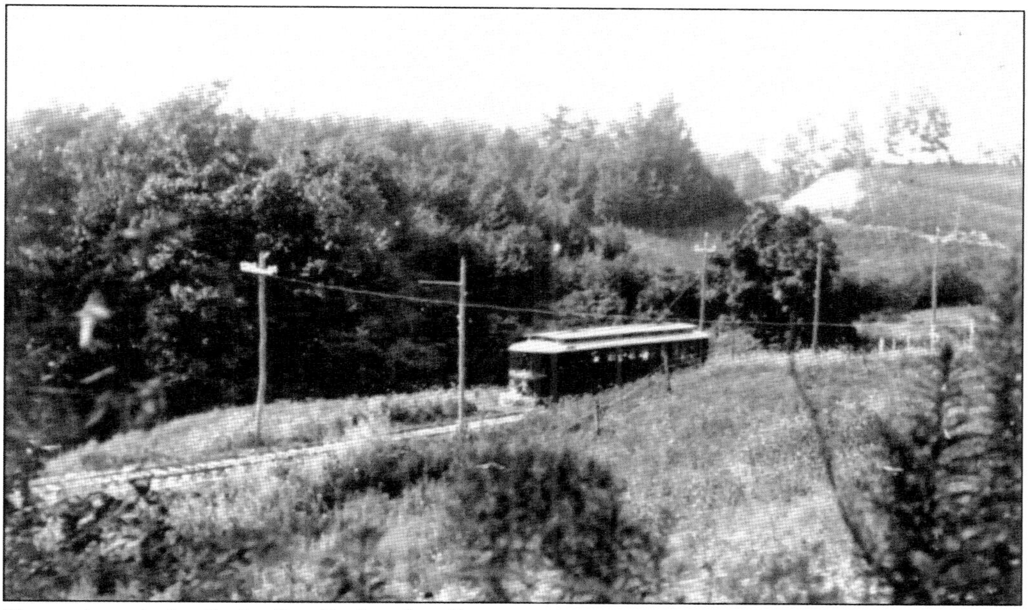

Shown here is the Sodus Bay Railroad trolley.

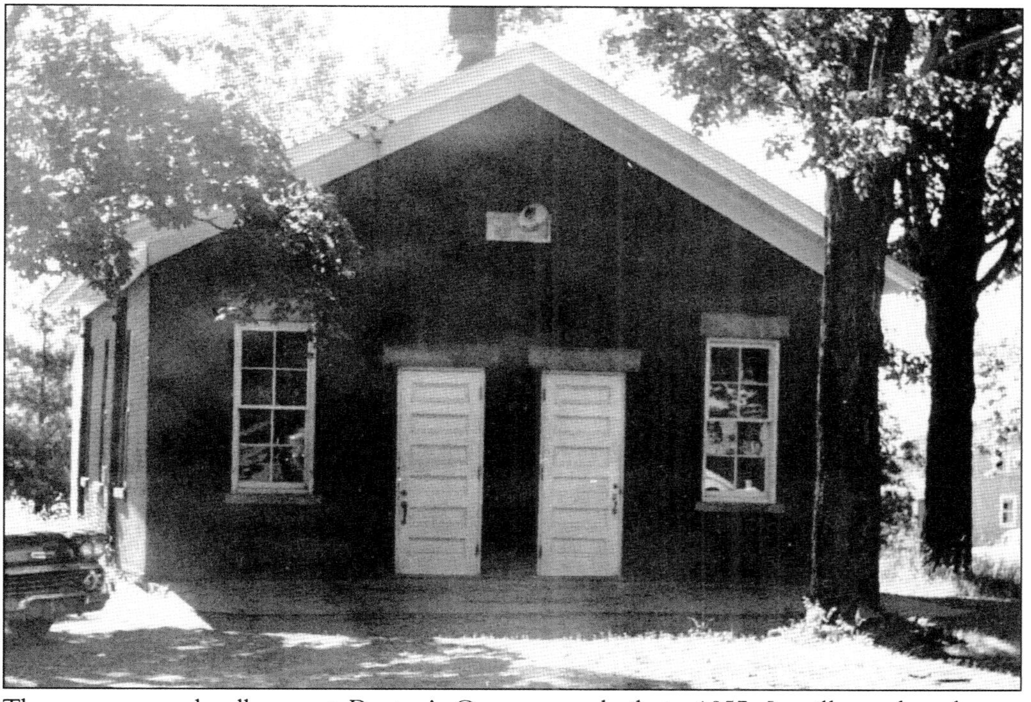

The one-room schoolhouse at Dayton's Corners was built in 1857. It still stands today, at 1363 Creek Street. This was Penfield School District No. 9. From 1948 to the late 1960s, the school was used by the Webster School District for kindergarten and first grade. In 1983, the schoolhouse became a Penfield landmark, and in 2001, it was listed on the National Register of Historic Places. Today, the school is used as a living museum for fourth-grade classes all over the area.

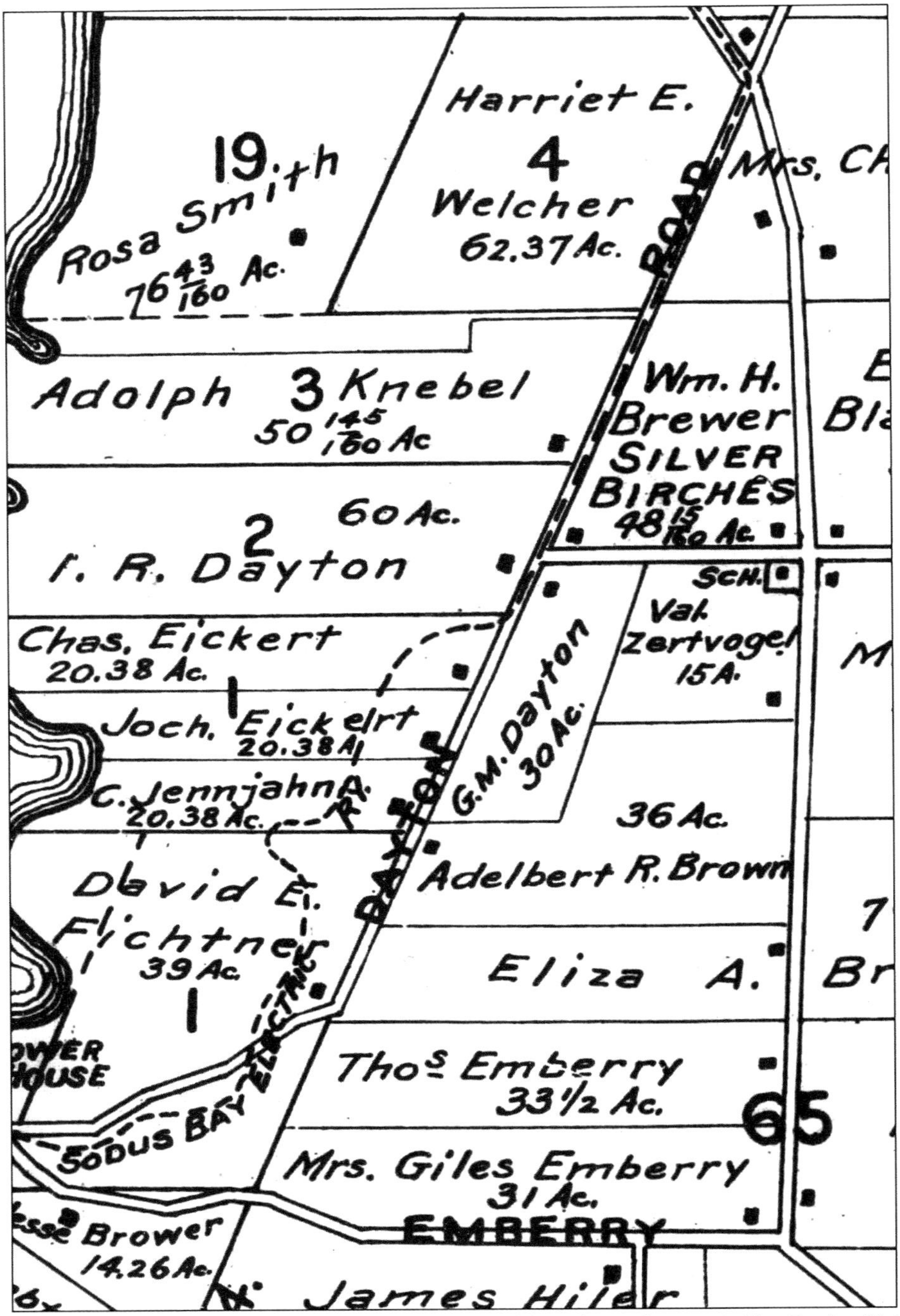

This map of Dayton's Corners, in Northwest Penfield, is from the 1902 *Plat Book of Monroe County*, N.Y., by J. M. Lathrop and Company. The Eli Dayton family settled around the intersection of Dayton Road and Plank Road in the 1850s. Dayton was a farmer who had orchards. Adolph Knebel and family were also farmers who settled at Dayton's Corners in the 1860s. Their farm remained in the Knebel family for over 120 years. Rossman Dayton operated a general store at the corner *c*. 1900.

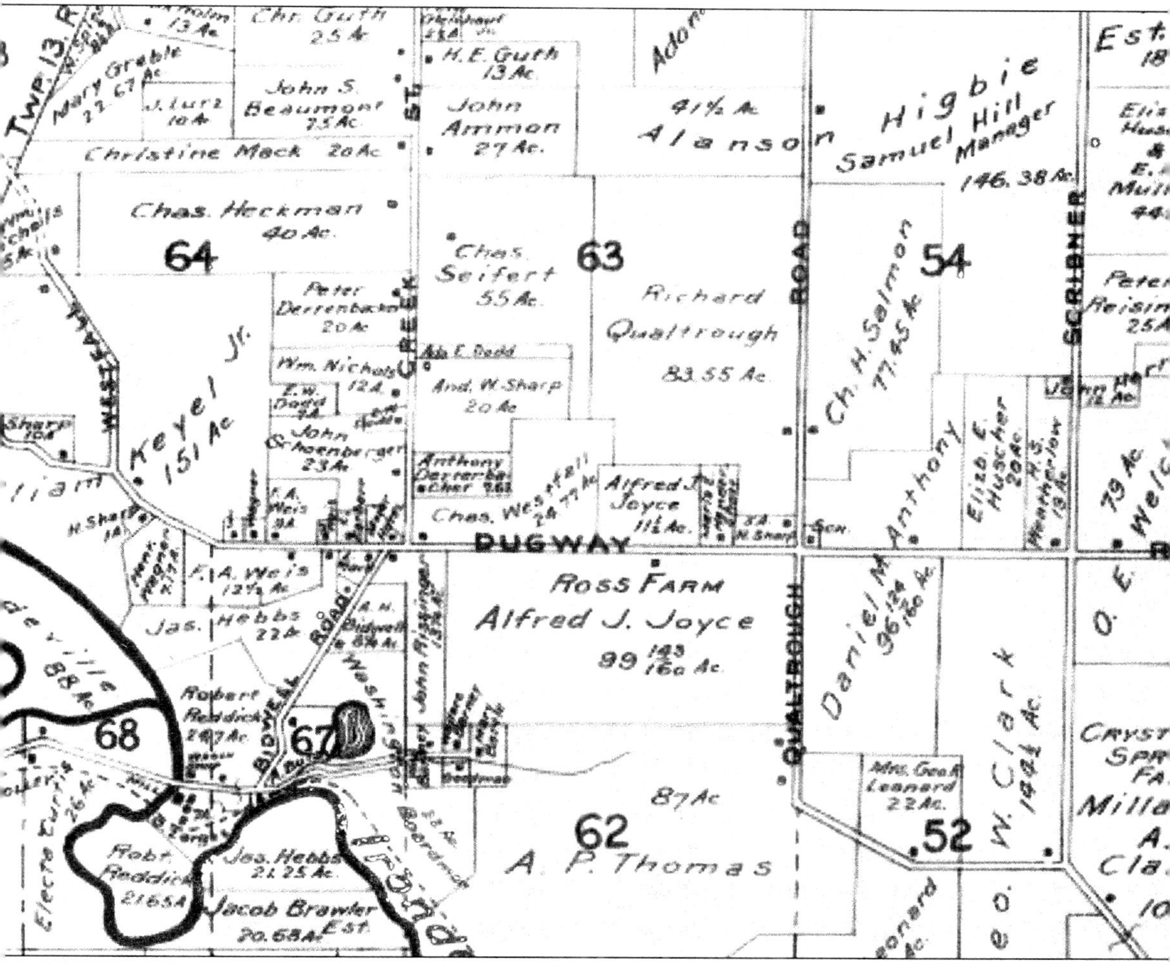

This map of Bidwell and its surroundings in West Penfield is from the 1902 *Plat Book of Monroe County, N.Y.*, by J. M. Lathrop and Company. The crossroads that made up Bidwell was More's Tavern Road north, Atlantic Dugway, and Bidwell Road. More's Tavern Road is now called Creek Street, Atlantic Dugway is Browncroft Boulevard–Atlantic Avenue, and Bidwell Road is called Blossom Road.

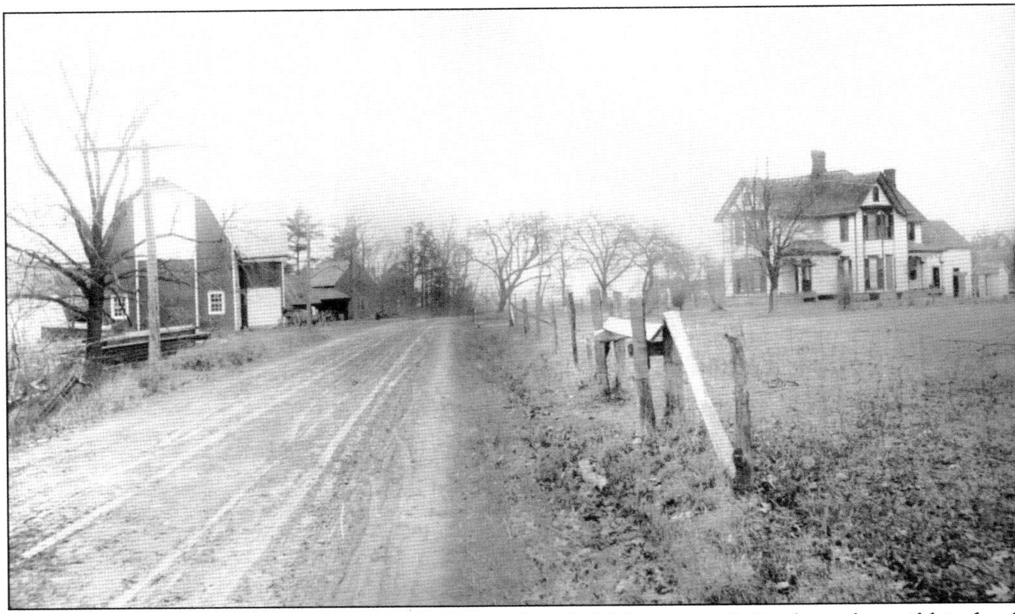

William Keyel Jr. owned this house, which stood at 2406 Browncroft Boulevard, until his death in 1946. He was one of the largest growers of raspberry plants in western New York. His parents moved to Penfield in 1861, when William was just an infant.

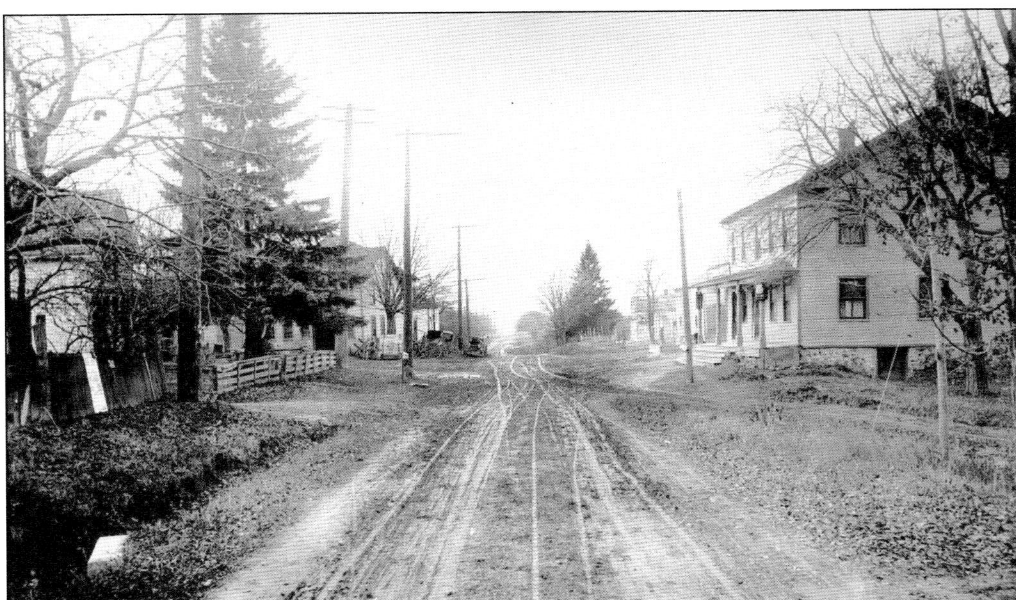

West Penfield was a crossroads community in the early 20th century. The area had its own post office, tavern, blacksmith shop, and a large community of farms. Bidwell was the name given to the area for the post office's mailing address, named after William Bidwell, who lived at 1820 Blossom Road. In 1863, he was listed as a proprietor of a hotel in Bidwell.

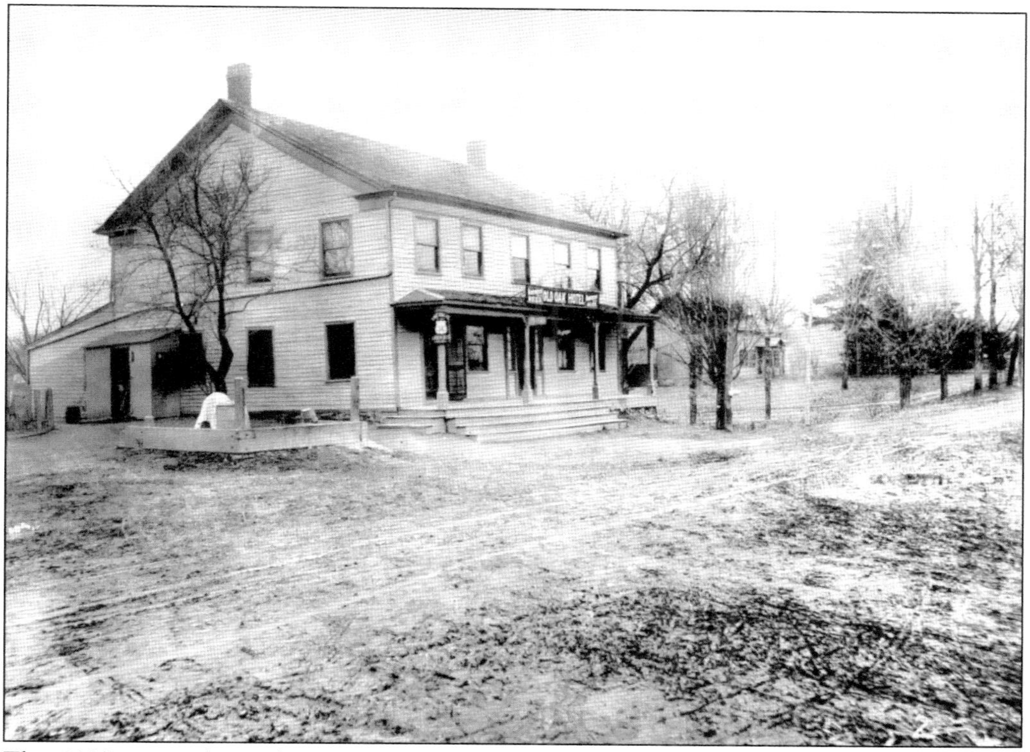

This 1907 image shows the Old Oak Hotel, owned by John Meier, in Bidwell. In the 1850s, this was a tavern called More's Tavern. In 1893, Henry Gress was the hotel's proprietor. Many years later, the building became a house and store owned by John Ammon. In the early 1960s, the building was razed. A new building was constructed in 1966 and still stands at 2494 Browncroft Boulevard.

Old Oak Hotel

West Penfield.

Good entertainment for man or beast at popular prices.

HENRY L. GRESS, Prop'r.

This Old Oak Hotel advertisement is from the April 15, 1893, issue of the *Penfield Press*.

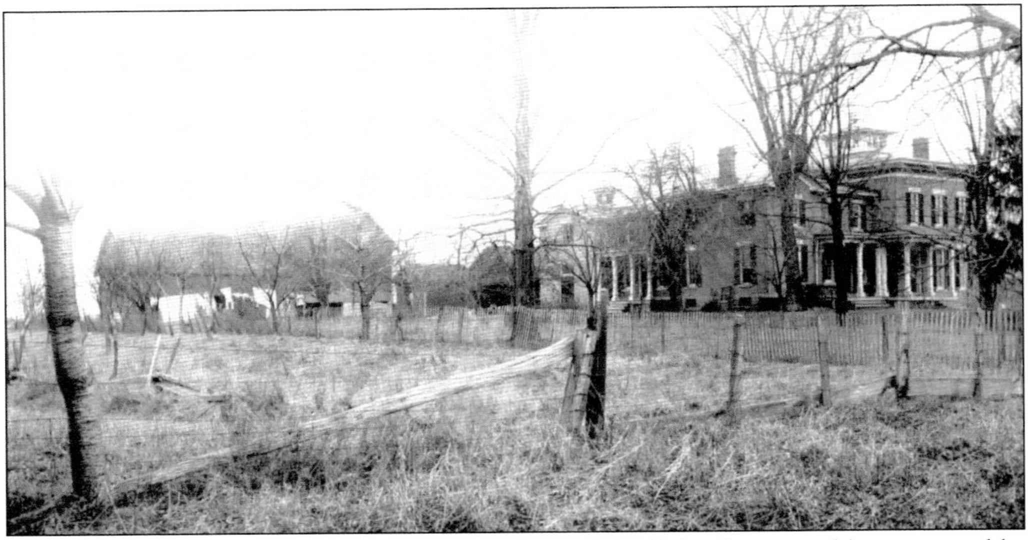

This home, located at 2594 Atlantic Avenue (east of the Bidwell crossroads), was owned by Alfred J. Joyce and family. Joyce was a farmer and owned almost 100 acres of land across Atlantic Avenue. His farm was named Ross Farm.

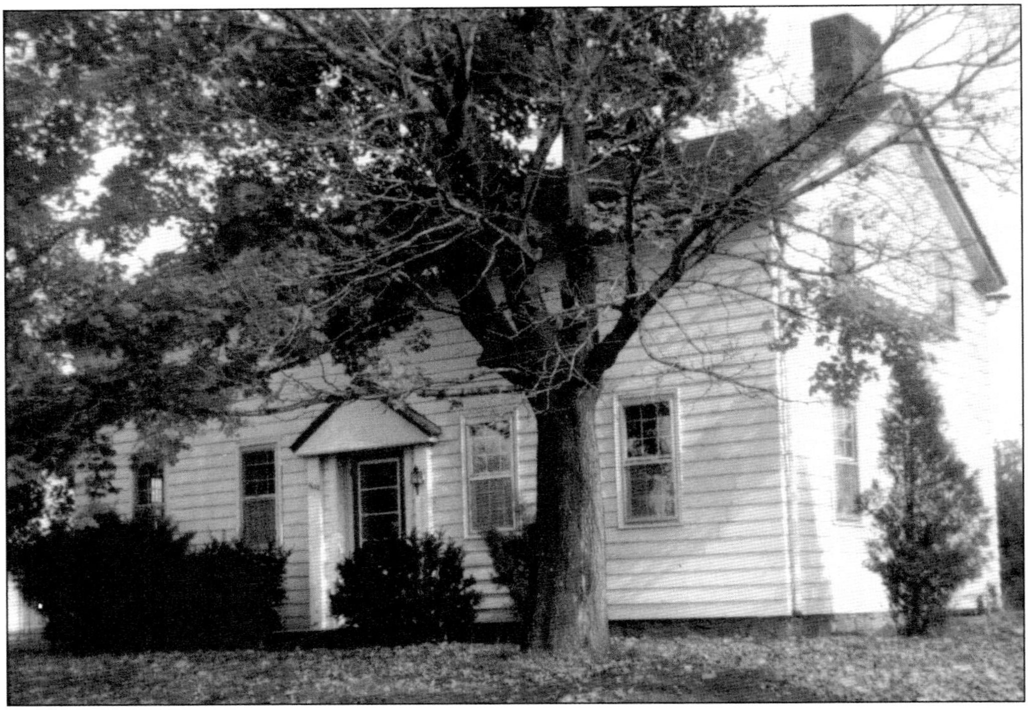

The house at 1620 Qualtrough Road in West Penfield was built in 1832 for Lawrence Johnson, an early settler and farmer in Penfield. This house, built of mud and straw, was called an adobe house. Lawrence Johnson died in 1865. His obituary in the March 9, 1865, issue of the *Penfield Extra* read, "In Penfield, Feb. 21st, Lawrence Johnson, an old resident of this town, known as 'old uncle law.' He was buried on Saturday." In the 1930s, the house was sided over. The Lawrence Johnson house became a Penfield landmark in 1975.

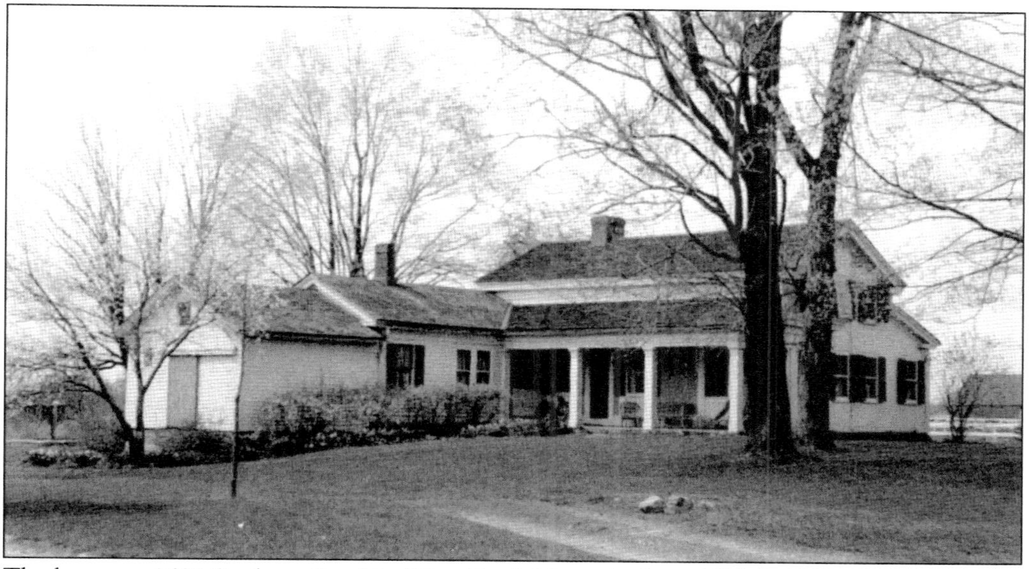

The house at 1689 Scribner Road in West Penfield was built in 1835 for Silas Higbie, an early settler and farmer in Penfield. The February 26, 1866, issue of the *Penfield Extra* reported an auction at the Higbie Estate: "AUCTION, Silas Higbie, having leased his farm, will sell . . . his entire stock, and farming utensils, such as horses, cows, hogs, wagons, sleighs, &c., &c. J. W. Conklin, Auctioneer." The Silas Higbie house became a Penfield landmark in 1974.

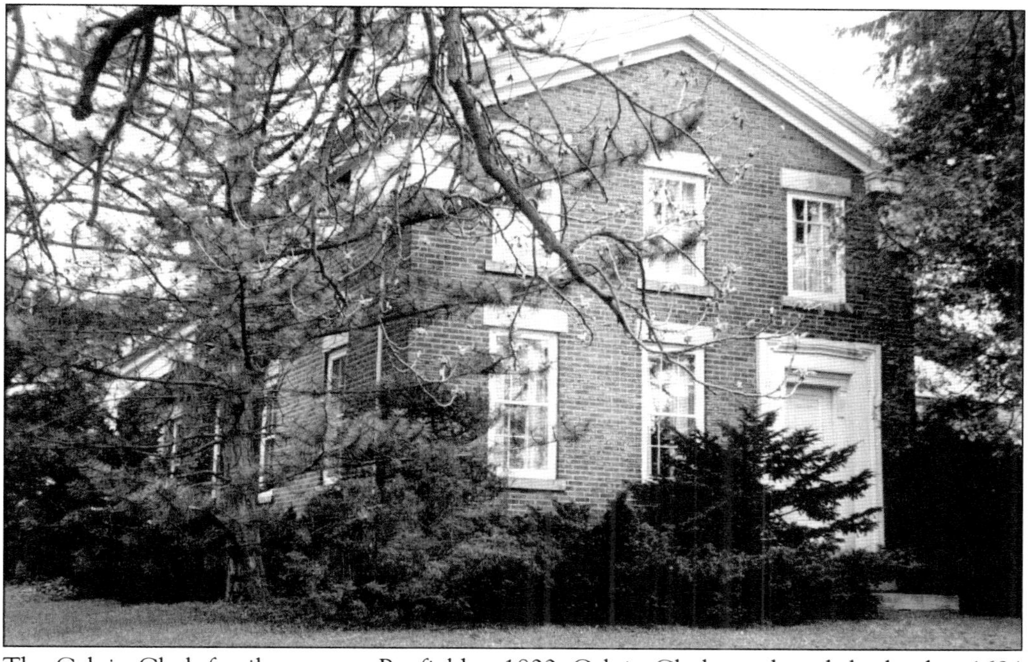

The Calvin Clark family came to Penfield c. 1800. Calvin Clark purchased the land at 1684 Scribner Road from Daniel Penfield and built an early structure. Clark was believed to have been killed in the War of 1812. In 1852, the Clark family built this Greek Revival home. In 1855, Luther Clark, Calvin's son, took over the ownership of the house. The Luther Clark house became a Penfield landmark in 1975.

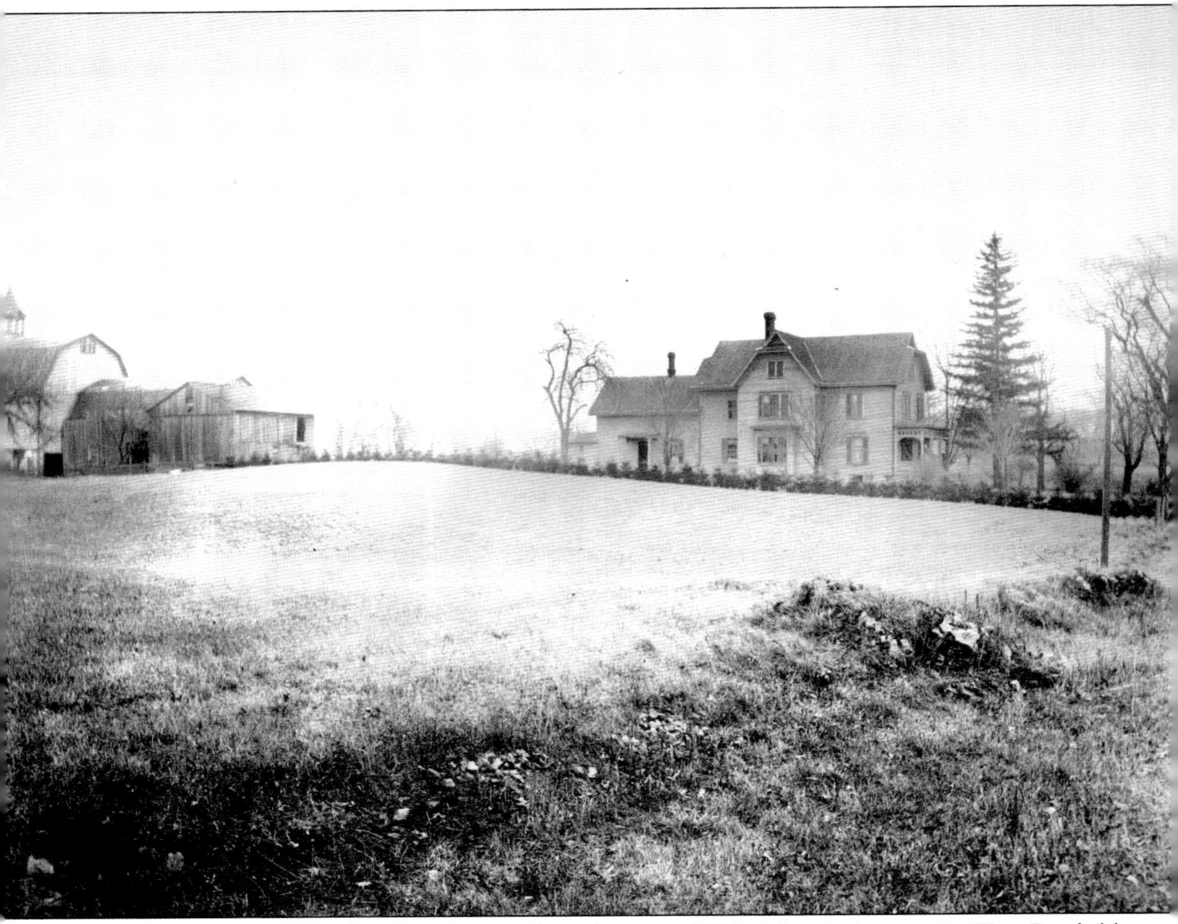

In 1907, Ora Welcher lived in this very large house at 2730 Atlantic Avenue in West Penfield. Welcher also owned 81 acres at Penfield Center and Webster-Fairport Roads. Surrounding the house was 79 acres of land. Many years later, most of the 79 acres was sold off to the town of Penfield for the Scribner Road Elementary School and the Bay Trail Middle School.

Eight

Pioneers and Early Settlers

Town meetings in those days were occasions of the greatest importance. Everybody came. There was exchange of news, gossip and some quarrels, much drinking and carousing. Quite often a fight and if the weather was suitable, a ball game.

—A. F. Church, March 1919

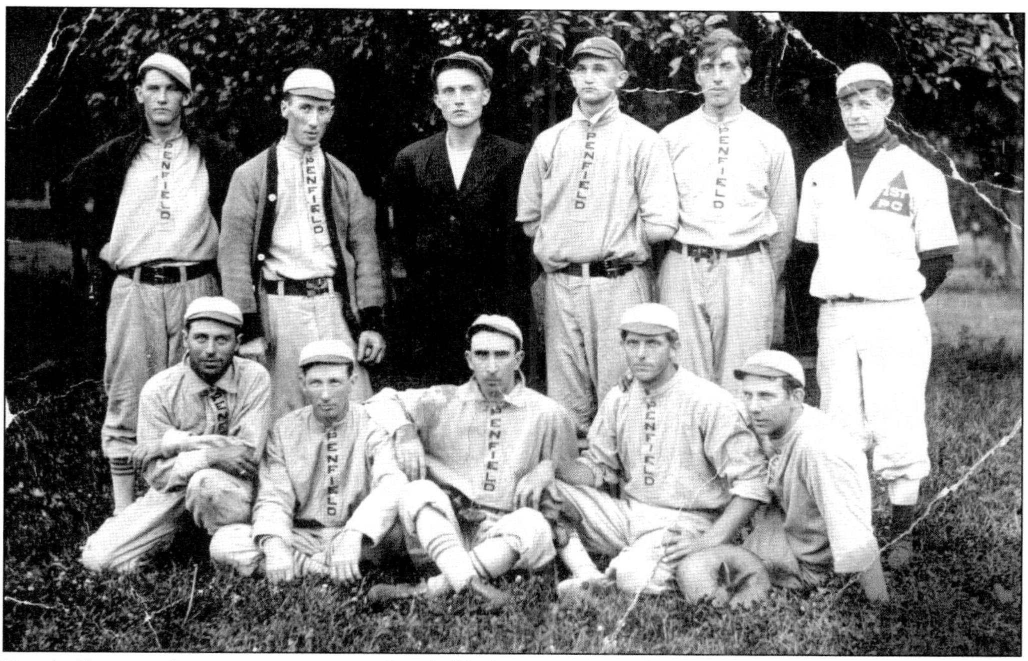

Baseball was a favorite pastime in Penfield. It was quite often played right at Penfield's Four Corners intersection.

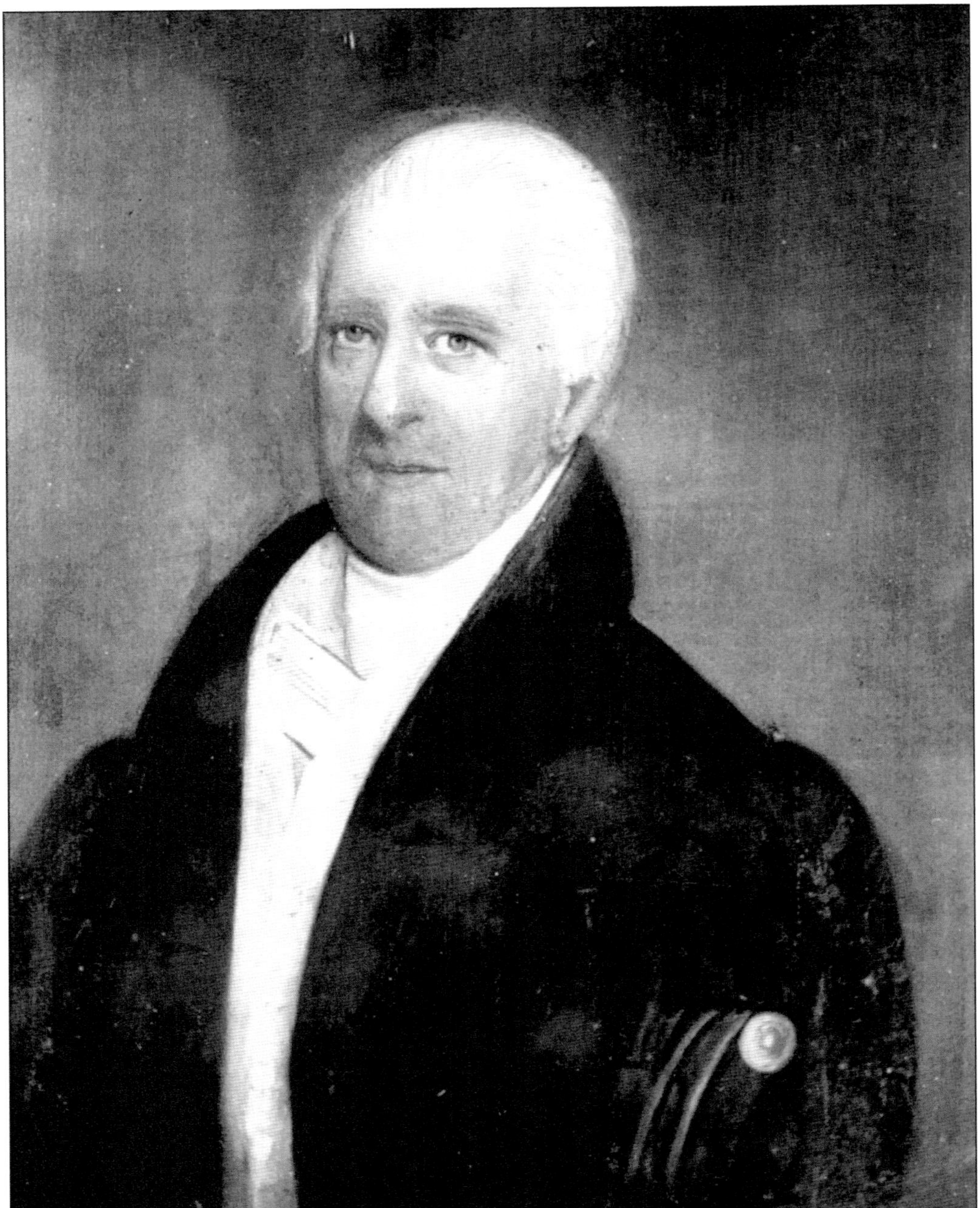

Daniel Penfield was born on April 25, 1759, in Guilford, Connecticut, son of Isaac and Esther Penfield. He served in the Revolutionary War under Oliver Phelps. In 1795, Penfield purchased Township 13, Range 4, which was to become the town of Penfield. In 1810–1811, he moved his family to Penfield. He owned much of the town, especially all water rights to the Irondequoit Creek in Penfield. In lieu of mortgage payments, he would graciously accept wheat and other farm products for his mill from the early settlers as they were becoming established in the town. Penfield died in 1840 and is buried next to his wife in Oakwood Cemetery.

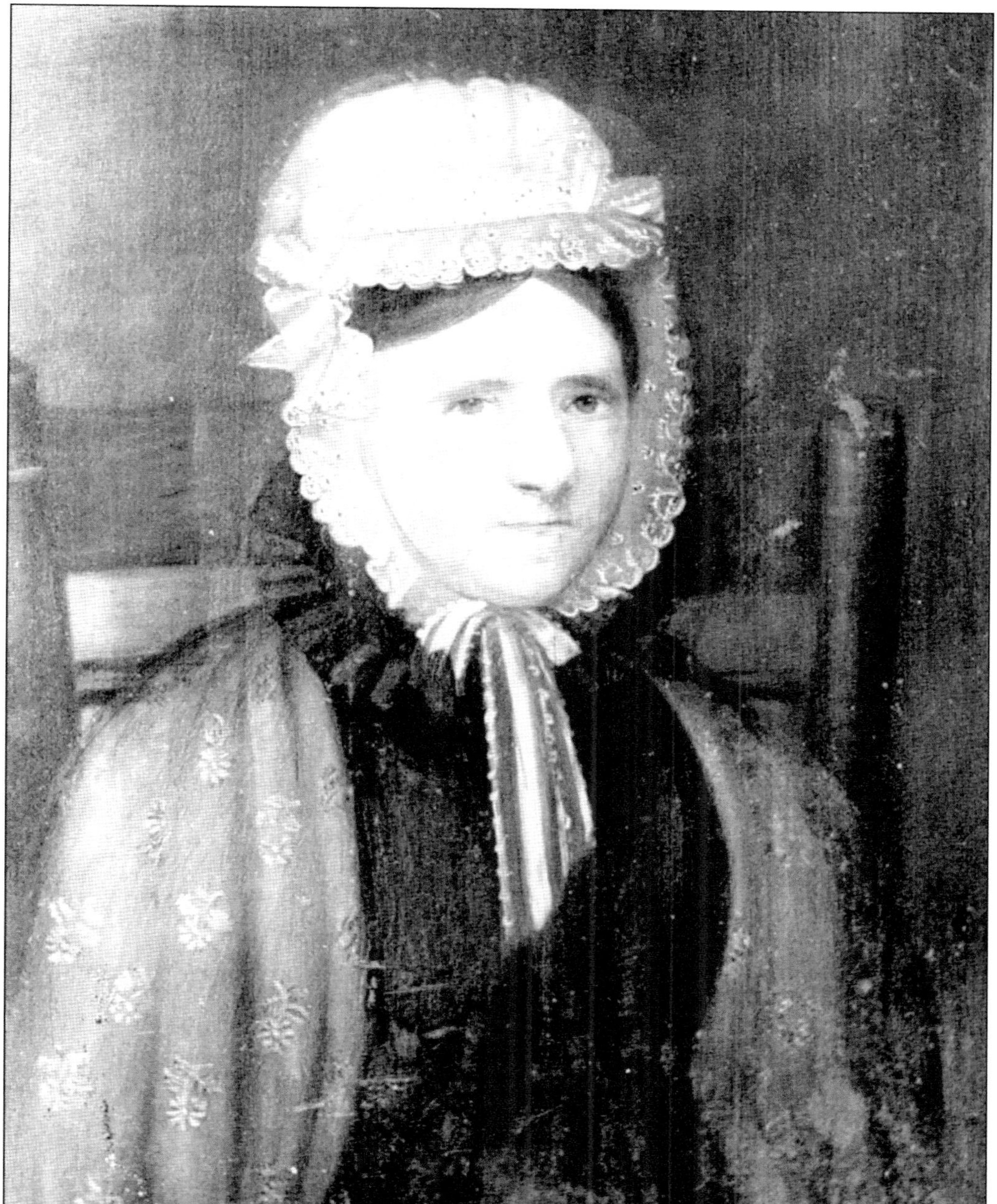

Mary Fellows Penfield was born on September 10, 1762, in Sheffield, Connecticut. She was the daughter of Gen. John Fellows and Mary Ashley. John Fellows was an aide-de-camp to George Washington during the Revolutionary War. Mary Fellows married Daniel Penfield c. 1784. They had five children before moving to Penfield. Mary's brother, Henry Fellows, moved to Penfield in 1813 from Canandaigua. Mary Penfield died in 1828 in Penfield.

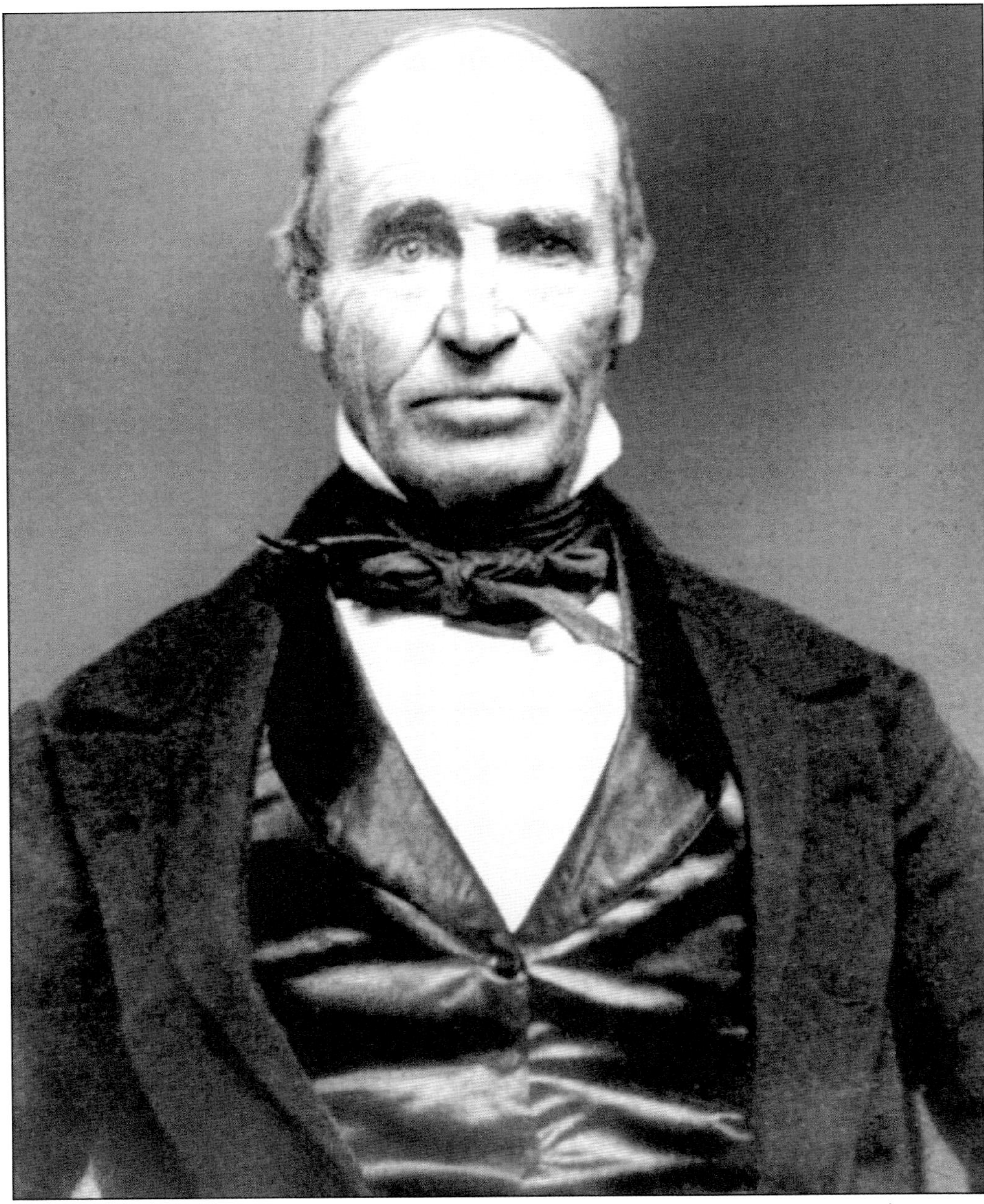

Samuel Rich, son of John Rich and Mercy Chipman, was born in 1785 on Cape Cod. In 1799, at the age of 14, he traveled from Massachusetts on foot to visit his sisters in the area. During his stay, he visited the falls of the Irondequoit Creek and was very impressed. Years later, in 1809, with his father's financial help, he came back to Penfield, again on foot, and built a sawmill on the creek. He married Mary Case. In 1821, he and Andrew Lincoln built a gristmill on the west side of the creek just over the Penfield line in Perinton, since Daniel Penfield owned all the water rights in Penfield. After his first wife died in 1842, Rich married Mary Hill, moved downstream, and built a sawmill in 1846 and a gristmill 1848. He died in Penfield in 1875.

Elias Beach, son of Labias Beach, was born in 1793 in Connecticut. A veteran of the War of 1812, Elias came to Penfield with his family in 1835 after living in Rochester for a number of years. He became a carpenter and was a member of the board of supervisors in 1852. The family moved to Albion in 1854, where their daughter, Cora, had been attending seminary school. Elias lived out his days in Albion. He died in 1875 and is buried in Mount Albion Cemetery. (Image courtesy of Tom Taber.)

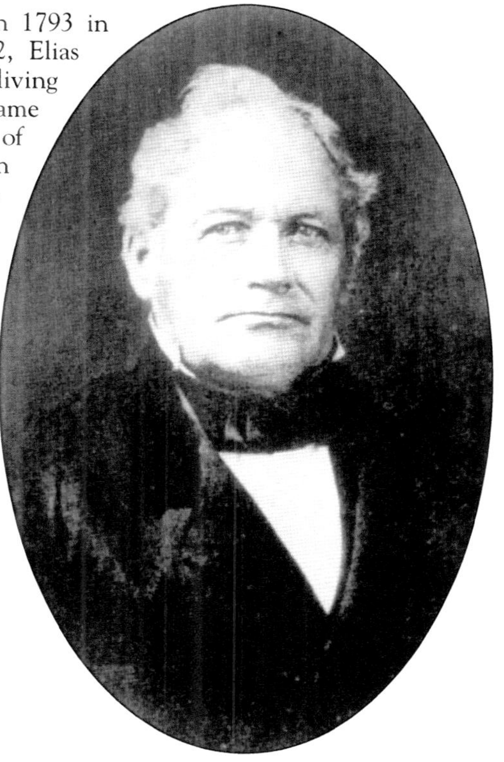

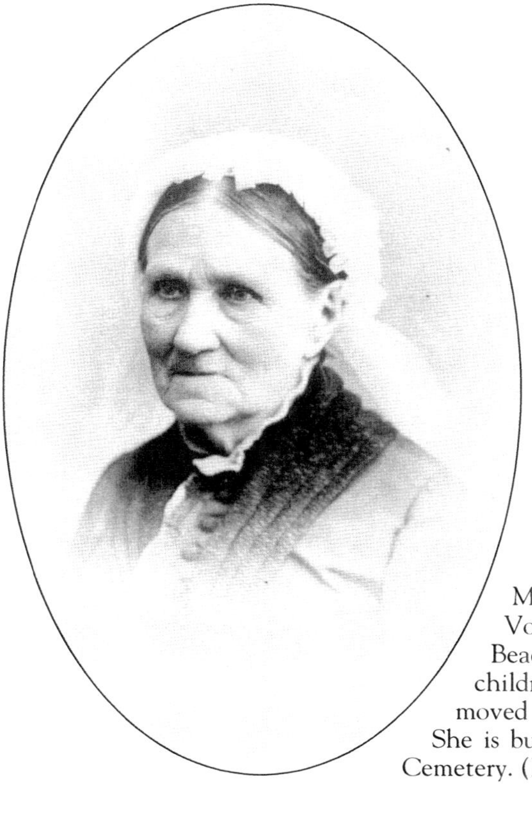

Maria Vosburgh Beach, daughter of Jacob Vosburgh, was born in 1802. She married Elias Beach in 1820 in Rochester. They had nine children. After her husband's death in 1875, she moved back to Rochester and died there in 1892. She is buried next to her husband in Mount Albion Cemetery. (Image courtesy of Tom Taber.)

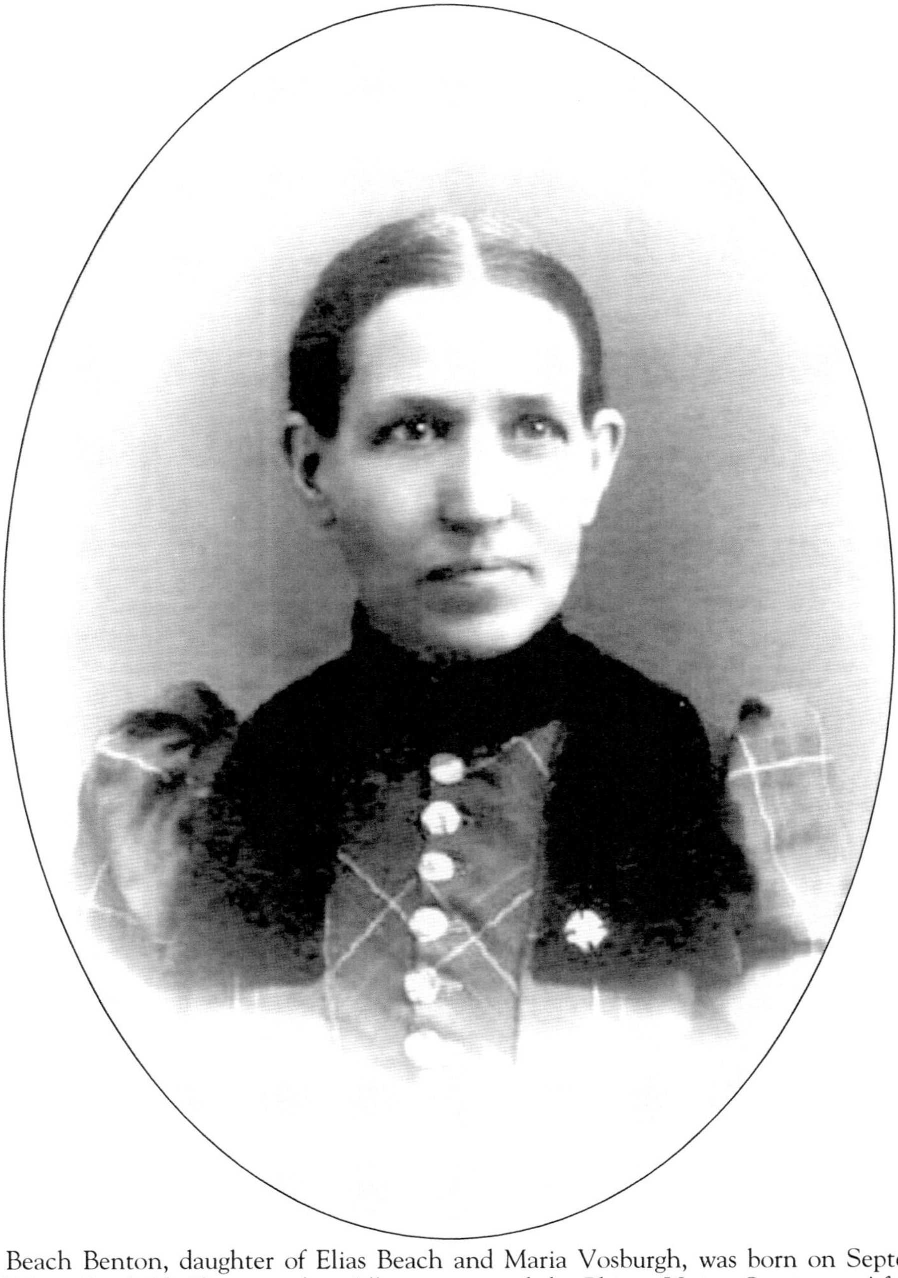

Cora Beach Benton, daughter of Elias Beach and Maria Vosburgh, was born on September 11, 1838, in Penfield. She moved to Albion to attend the Phipps Union Seminary. After her graduation in 1854, her parents and three siblings joined her in Albion. In 1857, she married Oliver "Charlie" Benton. In August 1862, her husband enlisted in the Artillery Division of the 17th New York. During the Civil War, Cora wrote 160 letters to her husband. These letters became famous. She wrote of her loneliness, anguish, and of the civilian life of wives, while her husband fought in the war. Benton made it safely through the war, and they lived out the rest of their lives happily married. She died in Gaines in 1902, and he died in 1907. They are both buried in Mount Albion Cemetery. (Image courtesy of Tom Taber.)

Calvin W. Owen, son of William Owen and Lucy Kellog, was born on July 12, 1798, in Sheffield, Connecticut. He came to Penfield on June 11, 1815, at age 17. He was a carpenter's apprentice to his Uncle Matthews. Owen became the deacon for the Methodist Episcopal church and was involved with the blueprints for the Penfield Seminary. He married Clarrisa Beebe in 1829. About the time he arrived in Penfield, he started keeping diaries. He kept them until his death in 1883. He is buried in Oakwood Cemetery alongside his wife.

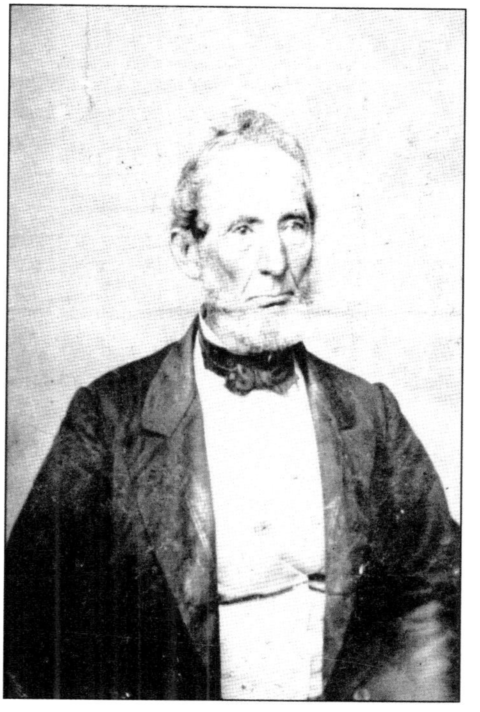

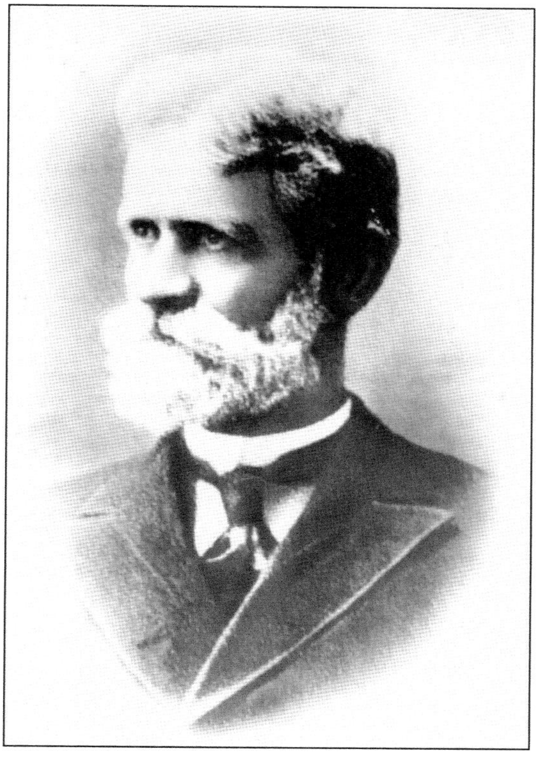

Almon Strowger was born on October 19, 1839, in Penfield to Samuel Strowger and Jane Clarke. In 1861, he enlisted in Company A, 8th New York Cavalry Division. In late 1864, he returned to Penfield and became a schoolteacher and, later, the principal of Penfield High School. In 1883, Strowger moved to Kansas and then to Kansas City, Missouri, in 1887. In 1889, he designed and patented the first dial telephone switch. In 1891, Strowger moved to Chicago and created the Strowger automatic telephone exchange. He then repatented a better design for the dial telephone, and on November 3, 1892, the first automatic telephone exchange took place. The first installation of this system was in Albion. Strowger died in 1902 in St. Petersburg, Florida. Some 47 years later, he was finally memorialized for his achievement in telephony with a ceremony and a plaque on his grave.

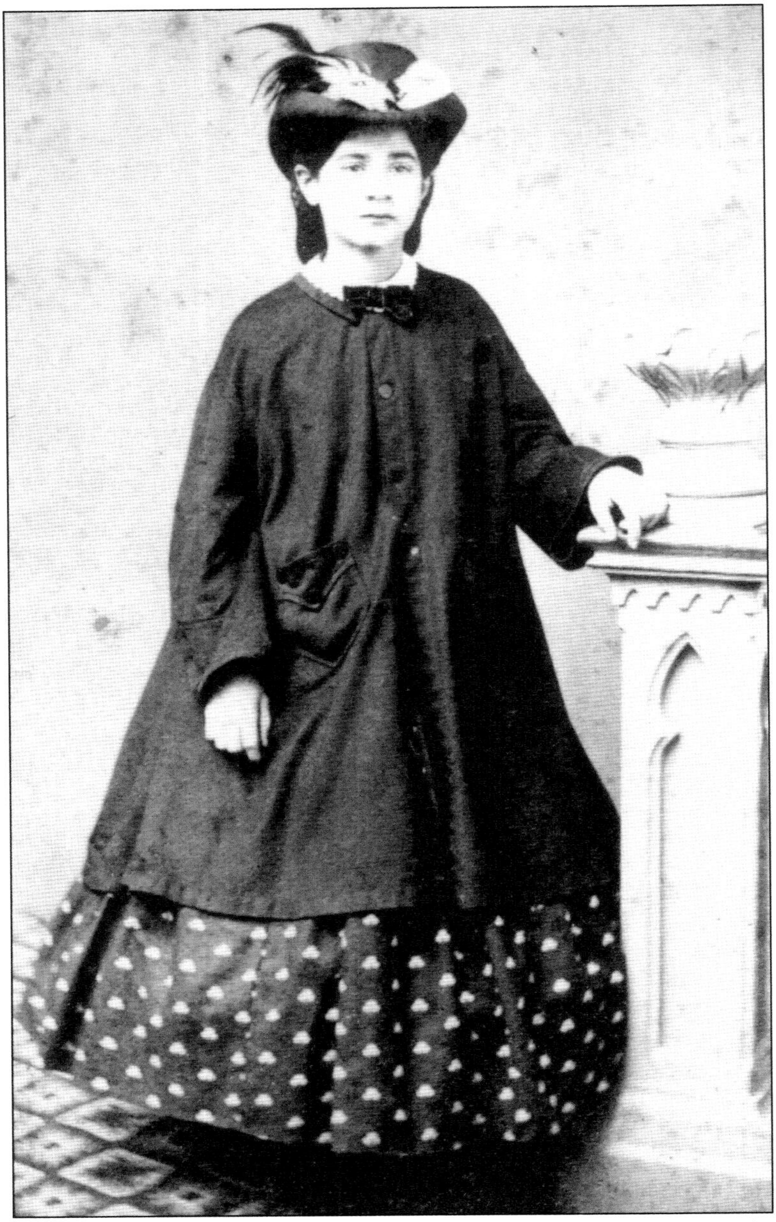

Ellen Theresa Williams was born in Penfield in 1849. In the 1850s, her father, Leroy K. Williams, won a printing press in a card game, and his son Leroy Jr. began using the press to produce advertisements. When the Civil War broke out, Leroy Jr. enlisted. Having learned how to set the type, 12-year-old Ellen Theresa decided to publish a newspaper for Penfield. She took on the name "Little Nellie" and, in December 1861, started publishing the *Penfield Extra* every Thursday. People from all over the country subscribed to the paper. Sadly, Leroy Jr. was killed in the war. Little Nellie continued publishing until April 1866. On her 19th birthday, she married Henry Braden. In 1875, she died at the age of 26. It is thought that her husband and two children removed to Salamanca, where his family resided and perhaps where Little Nellie is buried.

EXTRA OFFICE CALENDAR FOR 1864.

Sunday,	Monday,	Tuesday,	Wednesday,	Thursday,	Friday,	Saturday,
—	—	—	—	—	1	2
3	4	5	6	7	8	9
0	11	12	13	14	15	16
7	18	19	20	21	22	23
4	25	26	27	28	29	30
1	—	—	—	—	—	—
—	1	2	3	4	5	6
7	8	9	10	11	12	13
4	15	16	17	18	19	20
1	22	23	24	25	26	27
8	29	—	—	—	—	—
—	—	1	2	3	4	5
6	7	8	9	10	11	12
3	14	15	16	17	18	19
0	21	22	23	24	25	26
7	28	29	30	31	—	—
—	—	—	—	—	1	2
3	4	5	6	7	8	9
0	11	12	13	14	15	16
7	18	19	20	21	22	23
4	25	26	27	28	29	30
—	—	—	—	—	—	—
1	2	3	4	5	6	7
8	9	10	11	12	13	14
5	16	17	18	19	20	21
2	23	24	25	26	27	28
9	30	31	—	—	—	—
—	—	—	1	2	3	4
5	6	7	8	9	10	11
2	13	14	15	16	17	18
9	20	21	22	23	24	25
6	27	28	29	30		

PROSPECTUS
OF THE
PENFIELD EXTRA,
PUBLISHED BY
NELLIE WILLIAMS.
A Little lass of Fourteen Summers,
WHO IS THE SOLE
EDITRESS AND COMPOSITOR,
And probably the youngest Publisher and Proprietor
Of a weekly Newspaper in the world.
Terms only Fifty Cents a year,
INVARIABLY IN ADVANCE.
WEEKLY CIRCULATION FOURTEEN HUNDRED COPIES.

TERMS OF ADVERTISING.
For the space of twelve lines of this size type, being one inch, between rules, down the column, we invariably charge the following rates:

1w	2w	3w	1m	2m	3m	6m	1y'r
40	50	60	70	120	200	300	500

A larger or smaller space in the same proportion.
There will be no deviation in the above prices, and those sending us cards for insertion can state the space they wish them to occupy. No additional charge for resetting and altering cards from time to time.
No additional charge for an occasional editorial, occupying the same space of advertisers card. Our rates are very low, considering our circulation.
The Extra is an excellent medium for advertising cards which need a far and wide circulation, as its subscribers and Exchanges reach from New Brunswick, to numerous places in California, upper, and lower Canada, and is probably read weekly, by ten thousand people, from preface to finis.

	Sunday,	Monday,	Tuesday	Wednesday,	Thursday,	Friday,
July,	—	—	—	—	—	1
	3	4	5	6	7	8
	10	11	12	13	14	15
	17	18	19	20	21	22
	24	25	26	27	28	29
	31	—	—	—	—	—
Aug,	—	1	2	3	4	5
	7	8	9	10	11	12
	14	15	16	17	18	19
	21	22	23	24	25	26
	28	29	30	31	—	—
Sept,	—	—	—	—	1	2
	4	5	6	7	8	9
	11	12	13	14	15	16
	18	19	20	21	22	23
	25	26	27	28	29	30
Oct,	—	—	—	—	—	—
	2	3	4	5	6	7
	9	10	11	12	13	14
	16	17	18	19	20	21
	23	24	25	26	27	28
	30	31	—	—	—	—
Nov,	—	—	1	2	3	4
	6	7	8	9	10	11
	13	14	15	16	17	18
	20	21	22	23	24	25
	27	28	29	30	—	—
Dec,	—	—	—	—	1	2
	4	5	6	7	8	9
	11	12	13	14	15	16
	18	19	20	21	22	23
	25	26	27	28	29	30

On Christmas Eve, the *Penfield Extra* would print a new calendar for its readers. This 1864 calendar is from the December 24, 1863, issue. The *Penfield Extra* of June 20, 1863, includes a reader's observations on Little Nellie: "We have known her for quite a number of years, and have never seen anything but modesty and good manners attend her. She is beloved by all that know her in her native town, may long life, happiness and many such pleasant journeys attend her in this life is the wish of a lady of Penfield."

RESOURCES

Brahler, Verna K. *I Remember When . . . Penfield*. Penfield, New York: Town of Penfield, 1961.
Church, Aristides F. "Reminiscences of Mr. Church." Penfield, New York: Penfield Local History Room, 1935.*
Church, Aristides F. "Reminiscences of Boyhood of A. F. Church." Penfield, New York: Penfield Local History Room, 1919.*
Church, William P. "A Couple Not to Be Forgotten." Penfield, New York: Penfield Local History Room, 1935.*
Covey, Dora and Lulu. "Covey Family Notes." Penfield, New York: Penfield Local History Room.*
Frank, Maude E. *Images of Early Penfield*. Rochester, New York: Jostens Printing and Publishing, 1985, 1994.
Knebel, Al. *Over Home!* Penfield, New York: Town of Penfield, 2003.
Mallory, Marion. "The Mills on the Irondquoit" (drawing). Penfield, New York: Penfield Local History Room, 1985.*
Owen, Calvin, "Diaries & Manuscripts." Penfield, New York: Penfield Local History Room, 1850–1880.*
Raymond, Grace. "The Irondequoit As I Have Known It." Penfield, New York: Penfield Local History Room, 1940.*
Shedd, James and Dorothy. "Lovett's Corners." Penfield, New York: Penfield Local History Room, 1953.*
Taber, Thomas R. *Hard Breathing Days: The Civil War Letter of Cora Beach Benton*. Albion, New York: Almeron Press, 2003.
Thompson, Katherine W. *Penfield's Past*. Rochester, New York: Christopher Press, 1960, 1990.
Williams, Ellen Theresa, ed. *Penfield Extra*. Penfield, New York: Town of Penfield, 1861–1866.
Eldridge, W. G. and A. M., eds. *Penfield Press*. Penfield, New York: Town of Penfield, April 15, 1893.

*Denotes an unpublished body of work.